# Questions
# &
# Answers
# in the Practice of
# Family Therapy

## Volume 2

Edited by

## *Alan S. Gurman, Ph.D.*

*Professor,*
*Department of Psychiatry,*
*University of Wisconsin Medical School*

Brunner/Mazel, Publishers ● New York

# Questions
# &
# Answers
# in the Practice of
# Family Therapy
# Volume 2

**Library of Congress Cataloging in Publication Data**
Main entry under title:

Questions & answers in the practice of family
  therapy.

  Includes bibliographical references and index.
  1. Family psychotherapy. 2. Marital pscho-
therapy. I. Gurman, Alan S. II. Title: Questions
and answers in the practice of family therapy.

[DNLM: 1. Family therapy—Examination questions.
WM 18 P895]
RC488.5.Q47          616.89′156          80-22460
ISBN 0-87630-308-4

MANUFACTURED IN THE UNITED STATES OF AMERICA

# PREFACE

In the Preface to the first volume of *Questions and Answers in the Practice of Family Therapy*, I wrote that the basic rationale for the volume was twofold. First, it was clear that the professional literature on the practice of marital and family therapy had no shortage of ambitious and stimulating discussions of the theories and principles of treating families. Far less frequently, the literature presented, in everyday conversational language as would be used in informal collegial discussion, down-to-earth discussion of the handling of common clinical issues, problems, and decisions. The second, and related, rationale was that the accumulated practical wisdom of experienced family therapists, born of years of clinical work, had a great deal to offer both beginning and advanced clinicians, but that a good deal of this wisdom had, at least in public contexts, remained unarticulated. Thus, the strategy for the first volume was to bring to bear explicit statements of how seasoned family therapists actually *think* and what they actually *do* in common clinical situations.

Judging by readers' reactions to the first *Q and A*, as it has come to be called, the goals of that volume were achieved. For example, James Framo described his experience of reading the first *Q and A* as "opening the door to the treatment rooms of . . . family therapists whose theoretical persuasions cut across the entire spectrum of schools. . . . It's as if one were eavesdropping on experienced clinicians' unguarded remarks."

This second volume of *Q and A* continues the aim of offering clear, straight-talking translations of clinical theory about family process and changing families into clinical practice. Several dozen family therapists of various orientations set forth their action-oriented views on a wide variety of issues and problems encountered in actually doing family therapy. Some of the questions raised involve garden-variety matters that are faced regularly by practitioners, and it is instructive to read the creative and varied ways in which these issues are both thought about and dealt with. Other contributions address clinical decisions and populations with which most family therapists have had little, if any, experience (e.g., families with handicapped members, families with survivors of the holocaust, families with adopted children); it is hoped that the informed experience of the authors of these contributions may provide a useful orientation to such clinical situations when they arise in the reader's clinical practice.

Whether one is reading here about the common or the uncommon event, dilemma, or need in family therapy, the collective clinical mileage of these several dozen contributors offers therapists new options for helping families, and a vicarious vehicle with which they may examine their own assumptions, ruts, and impasses. Just as families get "stuck" in their own process, family therapists, like all psychotherapists, also often limit their own possibilities, either by unquestioned adherence to single views of the therapeutic world or by mere insufficient exposure to the ideas and experiences of colleagues in the field. As family therapists, we are concerned with the business of change, yet it is we ourselves who must change and allow in new information if we are to continue to meet the demands of our chosen task. Hopefully, this second volume of *Q and A* will continue to expand the reader's options in helping to promote such change.

**Alan S. Gurman**
*Madison, Wisconsin*
*January, 1982*

# ABOUT THE EDITOR

Alan S. Gurman, Ph.D., is a Professor of Psychiatry at the University of Wisconsin Medical School in Madison, Wisconsin. He is also the Director of the Psychiatric Outpatient Clinic and Co-Director of the Couples/Family Clinic.

He is the editor (with D. Kniskern) of the *Handbook of Family Therapy* and the author of over 70 professional publications. In 1978, he was co-recipient (with D. Kniskern) of the award for "Outstanding Research Contribution in Marital and Family Therapy" presented by the American Association for Marriage and Family Therapy, and in 1981 he received an award from the American Family Therapy Association for "Distinguished Achievement in Family Therapy Research."

A Fellow of the American Association for Marriage and Family Therapy, Dr. Gurman is also a member of the Commission on Accreditation for Marriage and Family Therapy Education, a member of the Board of Directors of the American Family Therapy Association, President of the Society for Psychotherapy Research, Editor of the *Journal of Marital and Family Therapy*, and an advisory editor for several other professional journals in family therapy and psychology. He also maintains an active private practice of psychotherapy.

# CONTENTS

## SECTION III
## Treatment of Severe Disorders

## SECTION IV
## Special Areas and Issues

## SECTION V
### The Growth of
### the Family Therapist

# SECTION I

# Engagement and Resistance

# 1. Resistance: Family- or Therapist-Generated?

**Question:**

I am a graduate student just beginning to learn family therapy. I look forward to doing couple and family work, but I am concerned about the role I may have to play to be effective with difficult cases. My impression from early course work, reading, and supervision is that the best known approaches are typically coercive, manipulative, or moralistic, and intervention techniques frequently appear either to invalidate the participants' experiences of what is going on, or to be authoritarian and accusatory in tone. The key issue here seems to be "resistance" and how to deal with it. What concerns me is how couples and families have come to be viewed so widely as out to defeat the therapist. Can you comment on this and suggest a way to work with resistance which does not pit families and therapists as adversaries and does not rely so heavily on the uses of authority?

**Discussion:**

It is not difficult to get the idea, from reading the marital and family therapy literature, that people who come in for therapy really do not want to change. Partners and families are regularly portrayed as dedicated to maintaining the status quo and undermining the therapy undertaken to assist them. The basic problem is that patients, whether conceptualized as individuals or as social systems, are presumed to be getting something important out of their symptoms or problems and therefore resist change. Why else would they keep it up? As Apfelbaum (1980, 1981) points out, relationships can be so consistently frustrating and painful that it is hard to believe that they have no purpose in being that way. This presumption explains what keeps the process going and what makes the participants resist when someone tries to do "therapy."

There is another view, however (in particular, see Wile, 1981), that troubled relationships are just as depriving as they look, and that

3

nobody gets anything valuable out of keeping things that way. Whatever those involved are "getting" out of the symptom or problem is a pathetic caricature of what they could get if they knew how or if they felt more entitled to have it. Rather than viewing the behavior of persons in families as directed by unconscious wishes, covert patterns of reinforcement, power plays, or system imperatives, this contrasting view sees symptomatic behavior as evidence of deprivation and an inability to achieve enough influence in some important relationship to meet the minimum needs for satisfaction and security required to allow that relationship to be viable. In other words, symptoms have no primary functions and therefore are by no means necessary.

Viewed from this perspective, what is depicted in the predominant family therapy literature as the result (*function*) of a covert design, symptomatic behavior, is now seen as just the opposite: a sign that the relationships in question are tumbling out of control and that, for the time being, the family is incapable of performing one of its central tasks, that is, having a beneficial effect on its members.

Where does this gratification/status quo-maintaining model of personal and family behavior come from? It is far too content-biased and unidimensional to be derived from general systems theory or "ecosystemic epistemology." It is beginning to grow clear that the structural, strategic, and systemic approaches to family therapy have unwittingly inherited the principle of unconscious purposiveness from classic psychoanalytic depth psychology. This ideological holdover greatly influences how family therapists think about both individuals and family systems. In turn, it affects the style and posture family therapists take toward patients, carrying over an adversarial tone and generating much of the "resistance" that is the subject of so much discussion and that is the target or "enemy" of so much therapist behavior, in what seems like an escalating arms race between therapists and families.

One of the great ironies now being explored is that the family system is family therapy's stand-in for the Freudian unconscious. It seems that, in spite of years of corrective commentary, the conventional view of the family as a system governed by homeostasis-maintaining principles is little more than the Freudian equilibrium model in disguise, applied at the level of "family" instead of "personality" organization (see Ransom, 1980). The individual patient has been rescued at the cost of making the family the patient, but the basic structure of thinking about such matters seems little changed.

Depth psychoanalysis has taught us to be suspicious of what patients do and say, and to look for particular types of unconscious purposes that contradict conscious intentions. Long ago, Perry (1926) recognized the early Freudian perspective "as the view that the real motives of conduct are those which we are ashamed to admit either to ourselves or to others." Thus, the woman who appears to feel guilty and depressed about not responding sexually really does not want to enjoy sex. And couples in conflict who act as if they are desperate to solve their problems have no real intention of giving up their punitive or exploitative ways.

The underlying view which generates such suspiciousness about what patients say and do rules out collaboration (despite talk of the need to establish a "working alliance"). According to Apfelbaum (1981),

> The analyst cannot help treating the patient as an adversary, as someone possessed by an unconscious "will" that never sleeps, ever ready to take advantage of the slightest misstep to undermine and thwart the aims of the analysis (p. 134).

The opportunities for analyst and patient to work shoulder-to-shoulder against a common foe are severely limited by this underlying belief.

This principle of unconscious purposiveness has proved to be the most enduring element in the legacy of psychoanalytic thinking, appealing even to those therapists who reject all other elements of that model (Apfelbaum, 1981). It has gone underground and reemerged in many forms in many therapies. In my view, it has had a devastating effect on family therapy, taking form in the myth of family homeostasis and the myth of power as the juggernaut in family relations. It has led to the same adversarial posture toward patients as orthodox psychoanalysis—ironically, the approach family therapy was originally intended to replace.

The underlying assumption which leads to the view that collaboration in family therapy is naive or only for those lacking in therapeutic mettle, or who need to be liked by their patients, is that individuals or families in treatment *need* a symptom or patient; or, at the very least, they want or need to keep doing what they are doing. This is an assumption which, in addition to its depth analytic heritage, stems also from a corruption and erroneous application of the idea of circular causality.

It is fundamental in family therapy to think in terms of "circular causal loops." Each person's behavior is viewed as a reaction or accommodation to the others. Every significant behavior (communication) can be thought of as a stimulus, a response, or a reinforcement, depending upon where the observer chooses to "punctuate" the interaction. The most frequently cited example in the literature is perhaps that of the husband who withdraws because his wife nags, and whose wife nags because he withdraws. This behavior proceeds in escalating spirals until some limit in the implicit rules of the relationship is pushed. At this point there are two possible outcomes: the relationship goes into a "runaway" of positive feedback loops resulting in its ending or turning into something quite different; or a triggering mechanism activates negative feedback loops which eventually restore the system to an earlier state, thereby setting the stage for the whole process to repeat itself over and over again (the infamous "game without end").

As a description, this phrasing is formal and elegant, and obeys the canons of "recursive epistemology." A problem arises, however, because therapists must always go one step beyond description—and that one step is *always* out of a "recursive epistemology" into a "dualistic" one, out of "circular" into "lineal" causality. At issue is the realization that the *theory of circular causality is not a theory of causality*; it is an abstract description of a sequence of unbroken occurrences which can be analyzed into "events" for pragmatic purposes. Since a therapist always has a purpose, and that purpose is generally something on the order of trying to assist in bringing about change, he or she must inevitably break into the sequence somewhere in order to introduce something new which might lead to something different. This interruption embodies and, therefore, necessarily proposes a theory of cause and effect, as an act of conscious purpose always does.

To avoid dualism, we must avoid being therapists. Doing family therapy requires a shift to conscious purpose and thus a shift to thinking in terms of causes and effects with their inevitable "pollution" (latent and/or unanticipated consequences of therapeutic intervention resulting because we can take into account only a fraction of the total of ecosystemic relationships surrounding the "part" we are seeking to change). Thus, as therapists take the extra step and attempt to account for what is going on in terms that will suggest an intervention, attributions of purpose either to the individual (system) or to the family (system) occur. Unfortunately, at this juncture the depth analytic vision of unconscious motivation enters again and family members become described as "double-binding," "colluding," or having "hidden agendas"—and above all, as "being controlling," or "attempting to control" one another. What is significant about these personifications is not that they are made but that they are one-dimensional and predominantly derogatory and reproachful.

A complementary axiom is the entrancing statement that "the family strives to maintain homeostasis," as if the family or the family system, whichever is intended, had a "need" or "intention" or "investment" in maintaining the status quo. When the family system is reified, especially when it is turned into an object to be "changed" by an imaginary "outside" [the therapist(s)], and when "homeostasis" is construed as a goal rather than a methodological construct, these operations lead inexorably to the view that the family system is trying to keep things as they are. This is an anthropomorphic attribution of motives or intentions to a pattern of organized social behavior which does not have the capacity for such processes. This way of using the concept of "system" is another disguised stand-in for earlier invalid analogies in the human sciences. Wilden (1980) calls our attention to two such "system analogies" that are particularly revealing: that which abstracts the family from its material basis and makes it into one gigantic "mind" (e.g., an enthusiastic extension of Bateson's perspective); and that which, as if by equal and opposite action, takes the organism analogy to the point of making the family equivalent to the "body" which is missing from the "mind" in the first analogy (e.g., the modernized equivalent of the social organicism of the 1920s and 30s as embodied in Pearse and Crocker's [1943] *The Peckham Experiment*).

If the implications of these observations are pursued, it is not surprising to discover that patients "resist" and are seen as attempting to outwit or defeat their therapists. Such behavior is reasonable when understood in its context. What they are resisting, for the most part, is not each other, but instead the attitude and the approach taken by the therapist. For the student new to family therapy, one proposition to consider is that, in the balance, patients resist their therapists' behavior more than they resist giving up their symptom or getting over their problem; or, to put it another way, the major portion of what in the literature is called "resistance" is therapist- and therapy-generated rather than patient- or family-generated.

Two observations below summarize the discussion thus far and elaborate the proposition of therapy-generated resistance. The implications to be drawn begin to make a case for the desirability of a collaborative model of family therapy.

First, when the therapist's behavior is guided by an underlying idea that an unconscious purposivism or covert design is at work, *and* when that purposivism or design is believed to be governed by principles that direct behavior toward seeking gratification and/or maintaining the status quo, a suspicious, accusatory tone inevitably informs and pervades the therapy process. Family members will react defensively to the suggestion or implication that they are getting something out of the problem, that they have hidden agendas, or that they do not really want to change. Efforts to force or trick them into changing will, for obvious reasons, also be met with resistance. Participants will very likely feel misunderstood, invalidated, or manipulated. The most likely (and I would add "healthy") response will be to resist such approaches.

Second, when the family system is reified and bestowed with the qualities of an unconscious or id having *predetermined* purposes, the therapist creates a mythical adversary of extraordinary proportions, larger than life—a force so potent that grounds are easily constructed to rationalize and justify even more potent therapeutic "weapons." Institutionalized license is thereby granted to perform violence on the family, for the family's own good. In the most comprehensive and sophisticated account of family therapy to date, Hoffman (1981) paints a heroic picture of the family therapist struggling against great odds, trying to keep out of the clutches of the family's "game," and having the strength to withstand the hostility and negative responses from members of the family that commonly result when they react to the dramatic, coercive, and manipulative measures that are believed to be needed to help them.

By now we should all know from the "Milgram Experiments" and from Zimbardo's "Stanford Prison Study," as well as from examples from history such as the Inquisition and the Vietnam War, that whenever mechanisms are invented to depersonalize or decontextualize one of the co-respondents in a relationship by the other, the likelihood of the former becoming the object of dehumanized treatment by the latter is greatly enhanced. Assuming that the basic orientation of any "therapeutic" approach is revealed with considerable fidelity by the representative metaphors used to describe the nodal relationships involved (Wilden, 1980), Hoffman's (1981) new book provides a disturbing series of examples. The text is replete with military metaphors and references to contests and games. Extolling the virtues of the "systemic approach" of the Milan Associates (e.g., Selvini Palazzoli et al., 1978), Hoffman states that "the enemy the clinician must attack is not any family member or even the malfunctioning family itself, but what they call the family 'game' " (p. 183).

This recent development strikes me as an example of Newspeak and mystification in the discussion of psychotherapy. By suggesting that they are not treating the family or even family members, four members of a treatment team define themselves as not acting upon persons, but upon an abstract enemy, the "family game"; thereby they create a platform from which to attack thinking, feeling persons with weapons designed to leave them unable to resist either the therapy team or their own homeostatic imperative. This phrasing is reminiscent of earlier conceptualizations such as, "We are not killing people, but the

Devil in them," or, "We are not fighting the Vietnamese people, we are fighting communism." This kind of construction seems so obviously provocative, and the violent nature of so many family intervention methods seems so apparent, that I find it hard to believe that such formulations are being accepted with so little critical debate. It now seems necessary to ask, with Coyne (1981), "Does the family system have members?", and to consider what difference this makes. One conclusion is that family members in treatment are debating the issue by resisting adversarial approaches to their problems.

The uncritical acceptance of these methods and their underlying ideas appears to be based upon the belief that they are somehow necessary and unavoidable. (See Poster, 1978, for tools to resist accepting the idea that *any* social reality is natural or necessary.) A new student of family therapy is often taught that the general adversarial orientation criticized here is the only possible way to do successful therapy. This may prove to be a faulty assumption, however, if we pursue the proposition that *it is the therapist's posture and method rather than the family's proclivities that create the major "problem" of resistance*. Further, if we assume that non-therapy-induced resistance (e.g., reticence, caution, fear) is rooted in the likes of pessimism, inhibition, deprivation, mistaken belief in one's own approach, and other varieties of human "fallibility" (see also Rabkin, 1968) rather than gratification or the drive to control others, such behavior then takes on new meaning. It is no longer seen as a problem, and the potential to form effective collaborative relationships in therapy is created.

In closing, some nontechnical suggestions for beginning family therapists who want to pursue a collaborative approach are the following:

1) *Resist ends-justify-the-means rationalizations.* Reject comparisons of family therapy with warfare or surgery. The cold, unempathic surgeon with skilled hands has no equivalent counterpart in psychotherapy.

2) *Avoid double standards.* For example, if invalidation and transactional disqualification are viewed as pathological among family members, don't be deceived into thinking they can be therapeutic when they occur between therapist and patient. Therapeutic double binds are neither (see Sluzki and Ransom, 1976).

3) *Continuously reexamine your underlying assumptions about human nature and human relationships.* Whatever your avowed approach to family therapy or whatever techniques you employ, all will be informed by these underlying assumptions.

4) *Stretch your therapeutic skill and direct your forcefulness toward*

*working with and through family members rather than against and around them.*

## References

Apfelbaum, B. Ego analysis versus depth analysis. In B. Apfelbaum, M. H. Williams, S. E. Greene and C. Apfelbaum, (Eds.), *Expanding the Boundaries of Sex Therapy.* Revised edition. 2614 Telegraph Ave., Berkeley, CA, 1980.

Apfelbaum, B. Foreword. In D. Wile, *Couples Therapy: A Nontraditional Approach.* New York: John Wiley & Sons, 1981.

Coyne, J. Does the family system have members? Unpublished manuscript, University of California, Berkeley, 1981.

Hoffman, L. *Foundations of Family Therapy: A Conceptual Framework for Systems Change.* New York: Basic Books, 1981.

Pearse, I. and Crocker, L. *The Peckham Experiment: A Study in the Living Structure of Society.* London: Allen and Unwin, 1943.

Perry, R. *General Theory of Value.* New York: Norton, 1926.

Poster, M. *Critical Theory of the Family.* New York: Seabury Press, 1978.

Rabkin, R. Is the unconscious necessary? *American Journal of Psychiatry*, 1968, *125*, 424-428.

Ransom, D. Love, love problems, and family therapy. In K. Pope, (Ed.), *On Love and Loving: Psychological Perspectives on the Nature and Experience of Romantic Love.* San Francisco: Jossey-Bass, 1980.

Selvini Palazzoli, M., Boscolo, L., Cecchin, G., and Prata, G. *Paradox and Counterparadox.* New York: Jason Aronson, 1978.

Sluzki, C. and Ransom, D. (Eds.) *Double Bind: The Foundation of the Communicational Approach to the Family.* New York: Grune & Stratton, 1976.

Wilden, A. *System and Structure: Essays in Communication and Exchange.* Second Edition. London: Tavistock, 1980.

Wile, D. *Couples Therapy: A Nontraditional Approach.* New York: John Wiley & Sons, 1981.

**DONALD C. RANSOM, Ph.D.**
*Associate Professor*
*Family and Community Medicine*
*University of California*
*San Francisco, CA*

## 2. The Interface of Family and Therapist Values in "Resistance"

**Question:**

There are times in meeting new families when I find it difficult to establish a therapeutic alliance; there are other times when, believing that the therapeutic alliance is well-established, therapy gets "stuck" in sessions which seem unproductive, often accompanied by underlying anger. I believe that I have made a reasonably good systemic diagnosis and assessment but something is still missing. I am uncertain about where to look for further clarification. What other factors might be contributing to the difficulties?

**Discussion:**

Traditionally, we have viewed the inability to establish a good therapeutic alliance with a new family or the abrupt termination of ongoing treatment as "resistance" on the part of the family. Such a view of "resistance" as residing in the family members is static and linear, a disservice to the families we see, and consequently unproductive to our work as therapists. We find it more helpful to view "resistance" in its transactional context, to regard it as a "bad fit" between therapist and family, often involving fundamental differences in purpose, goals, values, and/or style. We propose to define "resistant behavior" as comprising those transactions which occur between therapist and family, and ultimately result in impasses in therapy or in the abrupt termination of therapy. To understand most comprehensively these interactive patterns, we believe it is important not only to look at family dynamics and therapist techniques and strategies, but also to examine the cultural, socioeconomic, and occupational values which undergird all behavior. We believe that value differences, implicit and explicit, between therapist and family contribute to difficulties or stalemates in therapeutic progress and to abrupt and angry terminations.

11

Values and beliefs underlie all human behavior—the behavior of the therapist, the behavior of the family. Based on its value system, the family brings to therapy its conceptions of the "right" way to do things, the "right" way to be a parent, the "right" way to be a wife/husband, the "right" way to be a patient in treatment. The therapist also brings implicit or explicit conceptions of the "right" way to do things, based not only on his or her personal life experience but also on the values learned in psychotherapy training. For example, a family may come to therapy expecting an openly authoritative therapist who gives advice and solutions to problems. However, they may meet with a therapist who expects the family members to examine their behavior, offering guidance in that exploration but assuming that the family will find its own solutions. The family members may present themselves as compliant, "good" patients, willingly answering the therapist's questions, awaiting the therapist's advice, and hoping for something specific: a task, an assignment, an answer. The therapist, struck by the family's compliance and passivity, may become frustrated with the family's inability to carry forward the exploration that has begun. If the family members feel that they cannot do what is expected of them, they may feel confused, inadequate (again), and frustrated. They may then view themselves as failures, and feel even angrier or hopeless. The cycle of despair is further amplified, to the point that they may leave therapy or bypass an important issue thinking (correctly) that they were not understood or helped. The therapist, also frustrated, may label the family's behavior as "pathology" and place the focus of explanation on "resistance" which resides "within" the family system. In this example, neither therapist nor family was "correct" or "incorrect" with regard to expectations. Yet the therapy quickly reached an impasse because fundamental purpose and style differences were not understood and, therefore, not addressed.

Consider the following case illustration. A couple comes for therapy. They have been separated for some time following the husband's affair. The couple cannot move toward a divorce nor can they begin to move back toward a reconciliation and continuation of the marriage. They are immediately resistant to any interventions which push them in either direction. The husband is guilt-ridden and considers his affair a sin, a sign of how bad he is. The wife feels wronged, blames the husband, and also regards the affair as a sin.

It is not necessary for the therapist to change his or her beliefs and to agree that the affair is a sin or that the husband is to blame; but it is essential that the therapist accept the husband's point of view as valid before introducing any differences of his/her own. Since the husband is guilt-ridden and feels he is *bad* and deserves to be punished, the therapy will not move until this is acknowledged and validated as true *from his point of view*. It will be futile to try to equalize the guilt between the wife and husband and to view the wife's behavior as provocative or try to help her share the responsibility until the husband's sense of sin has been accepted and dealt with.

One way to approach this is to frame the therapy as some type of penance (not necessarily explicitly, but possibly so). It may also be helpful to explore the issue of punishment with the husband and to help him define how much punishment and penance are necessary before *he* can feel forgiven, if indeed he can ever forgive himself or feel forgiven. In assessing the dynamics of the family system and planning interventions, the therapist has many alternatives. In the case illustration just described, the therapist may view the affair as "one of those things" and seek to diminish its significance, and then refocus the therapy on other issues. The therapist may explore the past history and backgrounds of husband and wife, looking for similar situations, and explain the current situations as a replication of past events. The therapist may explore the immediate past history and frame the affair as the inevitable outcome of a chain of events involving both husband and wife in reciprocal interactions, or may give the affair a positive connotation.

If the therapist does not find a way to view behavior in terms of guilt and sin, *and* cannot accept the couple's world view, he or she will (understandably) meet with resistance from the couple. The therapist needs to find a bridge between his or her own frame of reference and the family's; this will enable the therapist to join with the family in creating a working therapeutic alliance. When value/belief differences between family and therapist are not acknowledged, the experience of both parties may be one of antagonism, hurt, or misunderstanding.

In our view, for therapy to be successful the therapist's style and interventions must be congruent with the value/belief system of the family—especially at the beginning phase of therapy. It is the therapist's responsibility to understand the family's underlying value/belief system as well as his or her own. In so doing, s/he may discover different expectations for therapy between the family and him/herself. From our experience, many failures in therapy are influenced by unacknowledged differences in perspective between family and therapist. Based on this greater awareness, the therapist can choose more accurately the therapeutic approaches or strategies which will be most effective and, therefore, helpful to the continuing work with the family.

**DORIS S. HEYMAN, Ph.D.**
*Faculty Ackerman Institute for Family Therapy*
*New York, NY*

*and*

**VICKI ABRAMS, M.S.W., A.C.S.W.**
*Private Practice*
*Livingston, NJ*

# 3. Creating a Therapeutic Alliance in Marital Therapy

**Question:**

I've had a good deal of experience doing individual psychotherapy, but have only recently gotten involved in doing marital therapy. At this point, I'm still feeling somewhat confused about handling the opening moves of couples therapy, especially in terms of establishing a working therapeutic alliance. Since marital therapy is usually rather brief, it seems that the alliance has to get cemented very fast. How can this be done as quickly as seems to be needed, especially since so many couples enter therapy with different agendas and goals?

**Discussion:**

The marital therapist almost always faces the problem of being caught between a technical Scylla and Charybdis early in therapy. Since most marital therapy is indeed quite brief, averaging about 15 sessions (Gurman, 1981), the process of bringing about change cannot be delayed for very long, yet a working therapist-patient alliance must be developed for change to begin. Almost every major "school" of marital therapy acknowledges the need for such an alliance (e.g., Jacobson, 1981; Nadelson, 1978; Stanton, 1981).

Whatever one's theoretical allegiances, it is essential in the opening phases of marital therapy, as at every other phase, that the therapist have a clearly articulated theory or set of premises which guide his or her interventions. I myself find that a broad-based object relations view of marriage readily allows a coherent integration of specific interventions from a number of therapeutic "schools," such as behavioral and strategic (Gurman, 1980, 1981). It is from this conceptual vantage point that I offer some guidelines for creating a therapeutic alliance in marital therapy.

Obviously, a therapist does not "stage" treatment in terms of first developing an alliance, and then intervening to produce change. To the contrary, early interventions must be aimed at both establishing an alliance *and* producing meaningful change. Thus, all early interventions directed toward producing change within the marriage must also facilitate the patient-therapist alliance. Moreover, as Jacobson (1981) emphasizes so convincingly, the first phase of treatment must also be geared toward increasing collaboration between the spouses. Given the high level of resistance to change common to most couples in therapy (Gurman, 1981), accomplishing the latter goal of husband-wife collaboration is itself a major undertaking, and the simultaneous achievement of a working patient-therapist alliance often seems to be an insurmountable task. Here, I will briefly discuss the three major targets of early alliance-building in conjoint therapy from an integrative perspective (Gurman, 1981). All three dimensions must be attended to simultaneously, and concern with all three dimensions is consistent with a model of therapy which holds that both individual and dyadic change must occur in successful couples therapy.

The first alliance that must be established is between the *therapist and each marital partner*. Usually, this alliance must be established in the very first session. The best practical criterion of these alliances having been realized is phenomenological: Each spouse must feel that something of personal value has been gained in the first contact. The method(s) by which such felt satisfaction is obtained will vary from individual to individual. Some patients experience an alliance with the therapist as the result of no more dramatic therapist intervention than the offering of empathy and warmth. Others require more structured responding in terms of interactional insight (e.g., identification of repetitive interaction sequences) or genetic insight, and still others require at least minimal direction for behavior change outside the treatment context. Moreover, a husband and wife of the same couple may require different experiences in the first session with the therapist to feel a sense of a developing working alliance. While therapeutic attention must be given to each spouse, it need not be routinely given in equal amounts. For example, in the common situation in which conjoint therapy is begun in the context of one spouse's symptomatic, presentation (e.g., depression, phobia) rather than with "the relationship" mutually presented as problematic, the non-symptomatic spouse may need either a good deal more *or* a good deal less alliance-building attention than the symptomatic spouse, and the therapist must be able to discern this difference almost at once.

The second alliance that needs to be fostered early in treatment is between the *therapist and the couple qua couple*. While the couple does not, of course, have a palpable, organismic existence as a psychological entity apart from the separate existence of each partner, they do share a behavioral and dynamic relatedness which must be considered functionally in its own right. Thus, the therapist must identify early the unspoken language, implicit agreements, and unconscious contracts (Sager, 1981) which simultaneously bond the partners together and create the medium for the emergence of the current continuing conflict. The therapist must learn to speak to both spouses at the same time, even when overtly addressing only one of them. While this connectedness between therapist and couple must obtain throughout the longer middle phase of therapy as well, the groundwork for its therapeutic use must be laid early in the treatment process, usually within the first three sessions.

This alliance is most rapidly established by speaking to the mutually contingent manner in which the spouses collude to keep aspects of themselves and of the other spouse out of awareness. In contrast to the middle phase of therapy, when interpretation of the collusive process may be appropriately aimed at eliciting rather high levels of anxiety in each partner (Gurman, 1981), the interpretive aim here is to give tentative public acknowledgment of the main ways in which the partners' overt struggles reflect the growth-oriented purposiveness of their initial attraction and commitment to one another.

Interpretation oriented toward this dyadic process simultaneously serves to strengthen what may be called the "therapeutic marital alliance." This therapeutic marital alliance is not meant to refer to an increased feeling of commitment to the marriage per se, e.g., to its indefinite continuation by each partner, but simply to a felt sense of getting down to work in the treatment. In order to foster this alliance with the couple *qua* couple, the therapist must, of course, have obtained sufficient understanding of each spouse's individual relationship history, and of the couple's joint history, to be able to place the current marital struggle in developmental perspective.

Such interpretations quite early in therapy usually address issues that have rarely, if ever, been overtly spoken about by the couple and, therefore, require an empathic therapeutic context. Nonetheless, despite the concerns of many marital therapists that to engage in such interpretive probing would be premature, the offering of such a tentative cognitive "map" is infrequently rejected by either spouse, and rarely rejected by both spouses. While the underlying dynamic struggles in the marriage may have been repressed for years, the mere emergence and current presence of either overt relationship conflict or relationally relevant individual symptomatology signifies that the hidden agendas and conflicts are, in the couple's phenomenology, already closer to conscious expression. Thus, such early empathic interpretation is usually not as jarring as might be expected.

The third alliance dimension, that of the *husband-wife pair*, is strengthened by the therapist's focus on the therapist-couple alliance, but requires additional intervention aimed toward acknowledgment of differences in personality style and equalization of fundamental relationship strivings. Couples in crisis, of course, can be predicted with confidence to detail, and even exaggerate, the differences in their overt "styles" of relating to one another, how they each respond to conflict in life in general, etc. While many of these differences are often not only quite real, but also easily perceptible in early contacts with the couple, they must not obstruct the therapist's vision so that he/she fails to recognize the spouses' similarities, if not commonalities, regarding their most basic unspoken relationship fears and needs. Numerous writers have emphasized that people tend to choose partners who have had similar developmental failures, yet who adopt different patterns of defensive organization (Gurman, 1978).

The therapist's concrete goal here is to confront the couple with the fact that while they behave quite differently with each other in conflict situations, they are fundamentally each struggling with similar individual conflicts, and each seeking similar relationship ends. While taking this position may seem to some therapists to be a mere "tactic" to foster marital collaboration in the therapy, its efficacy, and possibly its psychological accuracy, is attested to by the sense of relieved acceptance it so often receives when offered to couples.

As noted earlier, the therapist must be working simultaneously in the early phase of therapy not only to establish the three sides of the therapeutic alliance, but also to produce some behavior change that is consistent with the couple's stated purpose(s) for seeking treatment. In working toward the latter, of course, the therapist further strengthens the alliance between him/herself and the couple and each individual spouse. In the majority of cases, the most appropriate position to take is to work toward producing rapidly at least some perceptible improvement in each spouse's overt behavior. Often, this requires focusing on the most coercive, destructive and distance-generating behavior patterns. In general, the alliance-building phase of marital therapy is not the proper time for using paradoxical intervention (Gurman, 1981). More direct interventions are called for, e.g., behavioral tasks, boundary regulating instructions, and conflict management and containment techniques.

## References

Gurman, A. S. Contemporary marital therapies: A critique and comparative analysis of psychoanalytic, behavioral and systems theory approaches. In T. Paolino and B. McCrady (Eds.), *Marriage and Marital Therapy*. New York: Brunner/Mazel, 1978.

Gurman, A. S. Behavioral marriage therapy in the 1980's: The challenge of integration. *American Journal of Family Therapy*, 1980, *8*, 86-96.

Gurman, A. S. Integrative marital therapy: Toward the development of an interpersonal approach. In S. Budman (Ed.), *Forms of Brief Psychotherapy*. New York: Guilford, 1981.

Jacobson, N. S. Behavioral marital therapy. In A. S. Gurman and D. P. Kniskern, (Eds.), *Handbook of Family Therapy*. New York: Brunner/Mazel, 1981.

Nadelson, C. C. Marital therapy from a psychoanalytic perspective. In T. Paolino and B. McCrady (Eds.), *Marriage and Marital Therapy*. New York: Brunner/Mazel, 1978.

Sager, C. J. Couples therapy and marriage contracts. In A. S. Gurman and D. P. Kniskern (Eds.), *Handbook of Family Therapy*. New York: Brunner/Mazel, 1981.

Stanton, M. D. Marital therapy from a structural/strategic viewpoint. In G. P. Sholevar (Ed.), *Handbook of Marriage and Marital Therapy*. New York: Spectrum, 1981.

**ALAN S. GURMAN, Ph.D.**
*Professor*
*Department of Psychiatry*
*University of Wisconsin*
*Medical School*
*Madison, WI*

# 4. Focusing on and Defocusing from the Presenting Problem in Family Therapy

**Question:**

> As a beginning family therapist, one of the first things I learned was that it is necessary to shift the family's focus from the identified patient (I.P.) or "spread the problem" among the family members and onto the family relationships. Thus, any further scapegoating or distortion of the perception of one family member by the others is prevented. However, in observing family therapists at work, I am confused by the fact that sometimes they seem to approach a family by focusing and emphasizing the presenting problem, while in other cases they deemphasize or defocus from the presenting problem. What motivates these choices? What are they based on? Can you offer some guidelines for when to use one or the other approach?

**Discussion:**

First, let me give you a general and rather categorical answer. All family therapy involves, by definition, a reframing of the presenting symptom in one person to a problem in the nature of family interactions. However, this redefinition can be explicitly shared with the family, or it can be a more or less covert way in which the therapist thinks about a problem or conflict situation without attempting to change the family's view about who or what is the problem. Both approaches are legitimate ways of organizing the therapeutic process. Both are roads that can lead to family change.

To answer the part of your question that refers to scapegoating, focusing on the presenting problem as stated by the family need not necessarily result in further distortion or scapegoating of one member. It is possible to remain focused on the identified patient and simultaneously introduce new family interactional patterns through such strategies as enlisting everybody's cooperation in changing the problem, altering the family's ways of handling the problem, or interrupting unproductive solutions. Considerable marital change can take place, for example, through stimulating new alternatives in the way the parents interact around a child's problem. These interventions can all be done without ever educating the family members to think in systems terms, or without their having to accept the proposition that other family problems or marital issues should be dealt with before the presenting problem can be solved. It is important to keep in mind that the proposed therapeutic solution should involve at least two or three people and require an interactional change; otherwise the focus will indeed remain on one person rather than the family system.

The question of when to remain focused or when to "spread the problem" is difficult to answer with clearcut guidelines that can be applied to all families. Nevertheless, I can attempt to be more specific by introducing some parameters that may help in organizing your clinical decisions. These will be discussed under three categories: 1) the therapist's conceptual orientation; 2) issues of timing and purpose during the therapeutic process; and 3) certain family characteristics (severity of presenting problem; number, nature, and degree of clarity of problems).

## Conceptual Orientation

As you are probably aware, family therapists do not operate from a unified conceptual framework. There are varied conceptions about what has led to the dysfunction or the meaning of the problematic behavior, how to produce therapeutic change, and what are appropriate therapeutic goals. Some of the differences in approach you have observed can probably be traced to differences in conceptual framework that require different emphasis on focusing and defocusing as treatment strategies. (For a comprehensive exposition of various conceptual approaches, see Gurman and Kniskern, 1981.) Here, I can only comment briefly on this matter. Although most therapists would like to see the presenting problem solved, they vary on the extent to which family issues other than the presenting problem become the subject of therapeutic change. The psychodynamic, intergenerational and the experiential approaches, for example, tend to emphasize the need to resolve several past or present issues that are assumed to be underlying or connected to the presenting problem before any meaningful change can take place. Defocusing from the presenting symptom or the I.P. serves these therapeutic goals much more readily than concentrating on the resolution of the presenting problem. The latter approach is used most clearly by the strategic and the behavioral approaches, in spite of differences in their conception of what constitutes the problem or how to solve it. Strategic family therapists focus on the family's presenting complaint because it provides the most strategic and most relevant base for altering the interactional patterns that maintain the symptom (Haley, 1973; Madanes, 1981; Sluzki, 1981; Weakland et al., 1974). Behavior therapists also focus on specific problem behaviors and their characteristic dyadic responses and attempt to produce behavior modification only in those areas desired by the clients.

Other models seem to focus on the specific problem/s presented by the family initially but they also defocus in the sense that they add to the therapeutic contract those problems identified either during an extensive and comprehensive assessment state (Epstein and Bishop, 1981) or as the family structure unfolds (Minuchin, 1974).

While it is possible to think about focusing and defocusing as anchored on conceptual and technical variations, it is equally possible to think about them as necessary, and not mutually exclusive, parts or intermediate steps of any assessment and intervention process. Even within the same conceptual orientation, therapists will use both, or one or the other operation, depending on the clinical situation, as it will be discussed in the next two sections.

*The Process of Therapy*

The question of when to focus on and when to defocus from the presenting problem depends to some extent on issues of timing or stages during the therapy process. In the initial stage of therapy, focusing facilitates the formation of a therapeutic alliance insofar as the family's version of reality is accepted rather than challenged. Often, therapists observe resistance on the parents' part to shift the focus from a child to their marriage, or resistance from couples to shift the focus from one of them as the identified patient. When emphasizing the presenting problem these reactions are avoided and each family member can be asked to cooperate in overcoming the difficulty without provoking mutual blame or arousing personal defensiveness about creating the present situation. Through focusing, valuable relational information around the problem can be gained. Focusing also contains a meta-message of hope and confidence that the problem is solvable, in contrast with a meta-message about numerous difficulties that need to be solved in connection with the presenting problem. The first message is particularly important for families that may already be burdened by many social stresses and look for tangible solutions to their problems.

Other families come to therapy entertaining many expectations for positive change after having defeated many professionals and appearing to have every intent to continue to do so. A therapist should be wary of focusing on a problem and conveying a message of confidence and optimism that the problem is solvable. Defocusing to obtain an initial long list of unresolved problems and failed solutions can be utilized to convey a sense of pessimism about the possibility of obtaining rapid change. This puts the resistant clients in a paradoxical situation where they have to convince the therapist that the problems are not so extreme or that improvement is possible (Watzlawick, Weakland and Fisch, 1974).

Defocusing during the initial stages can also be a helpful strategy with families where there has been a lot of rigid concentration on negative aspects of a person's behavior for so long and with such frustrating results that shifting the focus onto others, either more positive aspects or "worse alternatives" (Haley, 1973), may provide much needed relief. Initial defocusing may also be necessary to join those families that are inclined to search for various past events and present family dynamics as plausible causes, since they may become somewhat distrustful of a therapist who focuses too quickly, without attempting to thoroughly understand the roots of a problem.

Once a therapeutic alliance has been formed and some preliminary assessments made, the extent, the length of time and the purpose for which focusing and defocusing strategies are used depend on the particular therapeutic task at hand and on each therapist's view of how family change comes about. For example, focusing can be used to escalate a conflict and induce a therapeutic crisis (Minuchin, Rosman, and Baker, 1978); to paradoxically "prescribe a symptom" (Hare-Mustin, 1975); or to rectify an incongruous hierarchy (Madanes, 1981). Defocusing can be used, for example, to deal with structural problems in the family (Minuchin, 1974); to address issues involving the families of origin (Bowen, 1971); or to encourage honest communication and expression of feelings in various interpersonal areas (Duhl, Kantor and Duhl, 1973; Satir, 1972).

During the termination phase, the family may present the therapist with new problems and difficulties to solve. It is generally better to remain focused on the gains obtained in relation to the original goals and avoid searching for areas where the therapeutic work may appear to be incomplete. Since families always confront developmental transitions of different kinds, once therapist and family have been involved in a therapeutic relationship, they run the risk of creating self-fulfilling prophecies by labeling problems of everyday life as pathological

(Sluzki, 1981). However, if concentration on the new symptoms or con-flicts appears to be a necessary undertaking, a new therapeutic contract may be developed. Another way to handle the family's offers of new problems to solve at this stage is to defocus onto larger and mostly mysterious "life issues." The therapist can philosophically comment on the impossibility of ever winning completely, the need to continue the struggle, the eternal misunderstandings between the generations, and other curious aspects of life. At the ending phase, focusing is also helpful to give the family credit for positive outcome in concrete areas (Stanton, 1981). Improvement can occur very rapidly in some families and occasionally the therapist may wonder if resistance to change will appear later. In those situations the therapist can focus back on the presenting problem and "encourage a relapse" (Haley, 1973) to the original situation, whereby the client is put in the paradoxical position of having to demonstrate to the therapist that the improvement is indeed a solid one.

## Family Characteristics

Another way of looking at the appropriateness of focusing and de-focusing is to examine these operations in the light of some family characteristics that seem to "fit" better with one or the other approach: These are: 1) severity of the presenting problem; and 2) number and nature of avenues of entry.

Family problems come in a range of severity or seriousness. Although family therapists seldom classify families along this dimension, in ac-tual practice accommodations are probably made to better solve prob-lems of varying severity. At the most severe end of the spectrum are life-threatening problems such as suicide attempts, severe anorexia, asthma, or drug addiction, and crisis situations such as death of a family member, serious accidents, relocation, or family violence. At the milder end are problems such as small disobediences, school pho-bias, temper tantrums, underachievement, and mood swings.

The urgent nature of life-threatening problems or acute situational stresses demand the immediate action that can most often ensue from focusing on the problem. Some therapists may feel, however, that de-focusing from the presenting problem can help decrease the emotional reactivity and make some crisis situations more manageable.

On the other hand, a number of the least severe problems appear on occasion to be too small to warrant even the search for professional consultation, until one regards them in the light of other family issues. For example, a family brought a 14-year-old girl to therapy with the complaint that she sometimes disobeyed her parents by coming home one hour after the prescribed evening time. Other family issues present were the recent suicide of a close relative, incest, and the terminal cancer of the oldest daughter. In situations like this one, focusing for a long time on the presenting problem would curtail a meaningful discussion of the family's life predicament. Such a discussion could only take place by shifting the focus away from the identified patient.

Families also vary on the number of avenues of entry to their system that they offer to the therapist—some families offer many avenues while others offer very few. Most families seem to offer several entries, either through perceiving more than one problem, or through offering several "theories" as explanations for the presenting problem. Sometimes those families that offer many avenues may overwhelm the therapist with too many problems to handle. In those cases a sort of "one-thing-at-a-time" approach, focusing on the most pressing or most important problem, serves to organize the therapeutic process constructively for family and therapist alike.

Those families that have a narrow, clear definition of a problem will probably respond more cooperatively if that problem is always referred to, one way or another. However, if carefully handled, the introduction of alternative contextual ways of looking at a problem situation need not necessarily lead to developing new lists of difficulties to be solved therapeutically. Rather, defocusing may be a strategy for encouraging new ways of perceiving and responding to difficulties.

The nature of the presenting issue will also determine to some extent which one of the two operations seems appropriate. Families that present one pointed and circumscribed behavioral difficulty, such as enuresis in a child, can usually be more readily treated with a narrow focus than the family undergoing a divorce, or a newly reconstituted family unit going through multiple adaptational struggles.

Individual symptoms that arise from interactions between family members and other social systems may require "spreading the problem" as a necessary therapeutic step until a new focus for therapeutic work is developed. For involuntary clients, such as families referred by the court for suspected incest, focusing the discussion on the issue of incest may be preceived as accusatory interrogation and underline the family's view of the therapist as an ally of the court system. Defocusing to other family issues may be the correct strategy in these types of situations. Direct work on the problem may also be contraindicated in child abuse cases where parents deny that the abuse has taken place.

In sum, the severity, the nature and the number of problems presented by the family, the particular stage in the process of therapy, and the therapist's conceptual orientation will play a part in the decision of when, how, and for what purpose focusing and defocusing operations are used.

Finally, a word should be said about the reciprocal interaction between family and therapist. Although ideally the therapist should make conscious decisions about focusing or defocusing, depending on the evaluation of what is appropriate to the situation, it seems possible that at times the therapist can be inducted by the family to adopt one or the other approach. In doing so, the therapist may unwittingly select, by focusing or by defocusing, to discuss only that which the family feels comfortable in discussing, and in the process dampen a degree of stress necessary for change.

## References

Bowen, M. The use of family therapy in clinical practice. In J. Haley (Ed.) *Changing Families*. New York: Grune & Stratton, 1971.

Duhl, F., Kantor, D. and Duhl, B. Learning, space and action in family therapy: A primer of sculpture. In D. Bloch (Ed.) *Techniques of Family Therapy: A Primer*. New York: Grune & Stratton, 1973.

Epstein, N. and Bishop, D. Problem centered systems therapy of the family. *Journal of Marital & Family Therapy*, 1981, 7, 23-31.

Gurman, A. and Kniskern, D. (Eds.) *Handbook of Family Therapy*. New York: Brunner/Mazel, 1981.

Haley, J. *Uncommon Therapy: The Psychiatric Techniques of Milton Erickson, M.D.* New York: Ballantine Books, 1973.

Hare-Mustin, R. T. Treatment of temper tantrums by a paradoxical intervention. *Family Process*, 1975, *14*, 481-485.

Madanes, C. *Strategic Family Therapy*. San Francisco: Jossey-Bass, 1981.

Minuchin, S. *Families and Family Therapy*. Cambridge, MA: Harvard University Press, 1974.

Minuchin, S., Rosman, B., and Baker, L. *Psychosomatic Families*. Cambridge, MA: Harvard University Press, 1978.

Satir, V. *Peoplemaking*. Palo Alto, CA: Science & Behavior Books, 1972.

Sluzki, C. E. Process of symptom production and patterns of symptom maintenance. *Journal of Marital and Family Therapy*, 1981, 7, 273-280.

Stanton, M. D. Who should get credit for change which occurs in therapy? In A. S. Gurman (Ed.), *Questions and Answers in the Practice of Family Therapy*. New York: Brunner/Mazel, 1981.

Watzlawick, P., Weakland, J. and Fisch, R. *Change: Principles of Problem Formation & Problem Resolution*. New York: Norton, 1974.

Weakland, J., Fisch, R., Watzlawick, P., and Bodin, A. Brief therapy: Focused problem resolution. *Family Process*, 1974, *13*, 141-168.

**CELIA J. FALICOV, Ph.D.**
*San Diego Family Institute*
*San Diego, CA*

# 5. What's in a Name?
## Redefining Family Therapy

**Question:**

As a family therapist I sometimes encounter families who are resistant to engaging in family therapy. Some of these families will say they don't need family therapy. With other families, only certain members will attend therapy sessions, even though additional family members have been invited. I feel in such a bind. Is there something peculiar about these families' dynamics which makes them resist family therapy or am I becoming ineffective as a family therapist? What can I do to engage resistant families and proceed with helping them?

**Discussion:**

In the past two years our conceptualizations of family dynamics have been greatly influenced by the brilliantly creative work of the Milan (Italy) Family Therapy team (Selvini Palazzoli et al., 1978)—particularly by Dr. Gianfranco Cecchin and Dr. Luigi Boscolo. Utilizing their focus on context, multiple systems levels, and paradox, we noted that engagement problems are rarely isolated within either the family system or the therapist system. Rather, we became cognizant that, in the process of these two separate systems attempting to *merge* within the context of family therapy, engagement problems sometimes *emerge*.

Studying the puzzle of engagement at the higher level of the therapist-family system expanded our intervention alternatives. We will now describe one intervention which we call "redefining family therapy" or "the context by another name sometimes smells sweeter!"

We have found that with many engagement problems which arise at the therapist-family level, the family poses a paradox to the therapist. The family gives the message, "We need help from you, a family therapist," then quickly follows with, "We don't need family therapy." If therapists respond to this paradox by firmly standing their "family therapy" ground, this rigidity provokes a variety show of resistance from the family. Thus, a vicious cycle escalates and the control/power issue raises its head, consuming the energies of both parties.

27

We would propose that family therapists meet the paradox of the family with a counterparadox made possible by relabeling the therapy being offered. We have found that when the two separate systems of therapist and family are unable to converge within the context labeled "family therapy," a different label on that context can make a difference.

Engagement problems dissolve when the family therapist responds to the family's paradox, "We need help from you, a family therapist. We don't need family therapy," with the counterparadox of: "I am a family therapist. I won't offer you 'family therapy.' I'll offer you 'developmental therapy,' 'sibling therapy,' 'supportive family meetings,' 'assessment,' or 'follow-up'." We have experienced these new names for "family therapy" to be enhancing to the formation and consequent functioning of the therapist-family system.

In a situation where one very important family member was not engaged in the therapy process, redefinition of "family therapy" produced "engaging" results. The scenario follows: The senior author supervised an experienced family therapist who felt that the phenomena of suction had occurred in her work with a blended family. The blended family consisted of mother, father, three children from father's previous marriage, and one child from the present marital union. The identified patient was the father's second (middle) child from his first marriage. This 10-year-old boy (I.P.) was presently in a residential treatment program for children where the family therapist was employed.

The therapist offered the information that the number and structure of therapy sessions had been: 14 individual sessions with the I.P.; 10 individual sessions with the father (mother had been invited); three sessions with father and 4 children (mother had been invited); and one session with the "whole" family system. The therapist was very concerned about mother's nonparticipation in therapy.

During the supervised session (at which mother was absent), it became apparent that one of the core issues of this family was its developmental struggle to become a "new" family. Following some extensive intersession discussion between the supervisor (senior author) and the family therapist, it was decided that the therapist would use the intervention of "redefinition of therapy."

Upon returning to the awaiting family, the therapist shared with the family the observation-hypothesis which had been made regarding the normal developmental struggle the family was presently experiencing in its quest to become a "new whole family." The family members were then told that due to this present struggle, it would be more appropriate for the family therapist to offer "developmental therapy" rather than "family therapy" (since they weren't a "family" yet).

The therapist contacted the session-absent mother and arranged to share in person the opinion from the supervised session. The mother responded most favorably and has regularly attended the "developmental therapy" sessions since that time.

A variation on this theme of "family therapy" = disengagement, "developmental therapy" = engagement was successfully employed during a supervised session where the whole family was absent. This family's pattern was to vary the attendance of family members to therapy sessions in exact opposition to those members requested by the therapist. This day, on which none of the family came to therapy, a letter was mailed to the family, part of which follows:

> Since you were unable to attend the 3:00 P.M. consultation time with Dr. Wright today, we took the opportunity to utilize that time to discuss your family. Through this consultation discussion, we can to a clearer understanding of one of the core problems in your family. This is the problem of your family struggling to decide whether or not you want to be a whole family. Therefore, it has been a mistake for us to invite you to come here as a family because we don't know on which days you feel like a family and on which days you don't.
>
> In our experience in working with families, we have found it to be a common occurrence that when a new husband/father joins a family, it takes some time to feel like a "whole" family. So we have the impression with your family that you are struggling with this normal and very common developmental problem.
>
> As a result, instead of family therapy, we would like to offer you developmental therapy. So for the next appointment, if it is a day when you are feeling more like a family, the whole family may wish to come. However, if it is a day when you are feeling less like a family, then part of the family or one member of the family may wish to come. Since you have the knowledge about which days you feel more like a family and which days you feel less like a family, we would like you to decide who will come to the next appointment on Monday.

This intervention freed the therapists from the continual symmetrical relationship they had entered into with the family. The therapists had previously demanded that the entire family come to therapy. This was ineffective since the family was presently struggling with the issue of: "Who belongs in our family?" The therapists' sanctioning of the family's previous efforts to vary family attendance to sessions and thus control the therapy process freed the family to put its energy into working in therapy.

Redefining "family therapy" as "follow-up" has also proven to be a powerful technique. With one family who wanted to terminate prematurely, we positively connoted the desire to terminate but offered a "follow-up" session. Six "follow-up" sessions were attended, in which the family never again mentioned their desire to terminate.

So, "What's in a name?" Would you relish a "lump of fish eggs" as much as you would a "feast of caviar"? It's doubtful. We, then, need to be sensitive to "resistant" families and speak *their* language, giving "family therapy" the name that will promote engagement and allow change to begin.

## Reference

Selvini Palazzoli, M., Cecchin, G., Boscolo, L. and Prata, G. *Paradox and Counterparadox*. New York: Jason Aronson, 1978.

**LORRAINE M. WRIGHT, R.N., Ph.D.**
*Associate Professor*
*Faculty of Nursing*
*University of Calgary*
*Calgary, Alberta*
*Canada*

*and*

**WENDY L. WATSON, R.N., M.S.**
*Assistant Professor*
*Faculty of Nursing*
*University of Calgary*
*Calgary, Alberta*
*Canada*

# PART A

## *General Assessment Issues*

# SECTION II

# Assessment and Treatment Planning

# 6. A Simple Marital Assessment Test

**Question:**

When you first see a new couple in therapy, are there any tests which are predictive of success or failure in resolving marital problems?

**Discussion:**

Because life is full of surprises, predictions of other people's decisions are risky at best, but there are some strong hints which can be used to assess the odds. One imagination exercise which I use in my initial interview sequence is easy to do and can open up a discussion of many issues, while providing a rule of thumb for rough prediction.

After gaining some foreground perspective on a couple's marital problems, some developmental history for each, and an account of the personalities and marriages of each set of their parents, this exercise can be introduced as something for them to imagine—something which is completely impossible in actuality. I ask them each to imagine in detail the marriages of her mother to his father and his mother to her father as if they had really taken place, instead of the actual marriages; and to keep in mind the influences that people who are married have on each other's development. Then I ask them, starting with what they know of each parent's temperament, style, and values at the time of marriage, to develop as full a picture as they can of what this other marriage would have been like—its strengths and weaknesses as a marriage and as a parenting union, its style of expressing affection, its means of handling differences.

With couples who are especially contentious, or when one dominates the discussion, it is useful to have them work on this task separately and to compare results before trying to reach agreement. The exercise engages their imaginations and is generally pleasurable. Usually, one of the imagined pairings would work quite well, perhaps better than the actual marriages of the parents and sometimes better, in their own view, than the marriage of the couple themselves. The other pairing usually contains most of the problems and may be seen as impossible, leading to inevitable divorce or lifelong strife. This pairing, which points to the problematic identifications in a dramatic manner, enables the therapist to offer a bridging explanation of the marital impact of identification with a parent. The therapist is able to clarify, for instance, that in the patient's own marriage, his father's style in him may be fighting with her mother's style in her. This quickly opens up these identifications for examination, and the work of differentiation can begin. Generally, this approach leads to rapid acceptance of the effects of identification.

In some instances, both partners agree that both of the imagined pairings would be impossible and can provide substantiating detail. I discount those which extrapolate from a single sociological variable (educational, social class, age, religious, or racial differences), because these matter so much less now than they did a generation ago. What remains is a group of people who will probably have great difficulty working out their marital problems and who will face a high risk of divorce. Even though people are, of course, more than their identifications, it is surprising how often this works.

Another useful task for assessing a marital relationship is to evaluate a couple's feelings for each other in terms of the following dimensions of love, drawn from Harlow and Mears' (1979) observations. After acknowledging that it is often hard for people to agree on what love is and how much they love each other, I explain that the task is easier if people can consider the various elements which combine, in varying proportions, in love.

One component is the love of a mother for a child, which can be called nurturance. Another is the love of a father for a child, which has strong elements of protectiveness and of sharing knowledge about the world. To this is added the love a child feels for a parent, dependent love. Feelings of friendship and comradeship, which grow out of childhood peer relationships with siblings and others, are also part of love. And sexual love, the sexual attraction and desire of a man and woman for each other, is another important dimension. A final characteristic (a special form of peer friendship) is how well the two function as partners in running the practical business of living, including the degree of congruence of their goals and lifestyles.

I sometimes ask couples to rate the intensity of their feelings for each other, on a scale of 1 to 10, for each of these six dimensions and to guess how their spouse will answer. They write their answers silently and then compare notes. This allows me to draw a quick focus on the degree to which their feelings are complementary. A discrepancy between a self-rating and a spouse's rating is a measure of a couple's lack of communication in that specific area, and often leads to fruitful discussions.

Pointers to major trouble are low scores on sexual attraction and low scores on friendship and partnership, which leaves only the parent-child dimensions to hold the relationship together. Low scores on only one of these three variables suggest more readily resolvable problems. If the spouses are not at all complementary in their parental and child components—one feels little dependency and the other feels a strong parental love, or one feels great dependency and the other feels little parental love—this is another indicator of serious difficulty. Comments based on their responses encounter little resistance and provide a smooth transition into the next phase of therapy.

### Reference

Harlow, H. F., and Mears, C. *The Human Model: Primate Perspectives.* Washington, D.C.: Winston & Sons, 1979.

**LEONARD J. FRIEDMAN, M.D.**
*Assistant Clinical Professor of Psychiatry*
*Harvard Medical School;*
*Private Practice*
*6 Garrison Road*
*Wellesley, MA*

# 7. Focusing on Concrete Issues
## in Marital Therapy:
## The Smooth-Rough Scale

**Question:**

Many of my clients seem to have a hard time focusing on concrete conflict situations. They are preoccupied with whatever they experience as their major relationship problem, and this preoccupation pervades their daily living and their perception of one another. In therapy, they continue to analyze this "big problem" or to fight about it. Other couples do report continuous fights and conflicts about every aspect of their lives, but, as both clients and therapist become overwhelmed by this flood of problems, nobody seems able to distinguish among the various conflict areas and get a systematic handle on the issues. How does one get couples to discuss the concrete issues and conflicts of everyday living in a systematic and productive way?

**Discussion:**

It is obviously important in marital therapy to be able to deal effectively with daily relationship events. The perceived "major" problem may be too complex and too abstract to manage directly. Attempts to rationalize and analyze this global relationship problem can be a way of avoiding concrete problem-solving. Continuous fights and conflicts, on the other hand, may obscure the real issues. As the saying goes: "If one wants to eat an elephant, one had better chop him into little, more manageable pieces."

One way of dealing with these problems is to give the couple a homework assignment, consisting of a daily paper-and-pencil exercise called the "smooth-rough scale." I will describe this exercise in detail and also indicate how the general principles of the scale can be used for other clinical problems.

*Designing the Scales*

The first assignment is for each partner of the couple to calibrate the endpoints of this subjective, bipolar scale. The instructions are as follows:

> I would like for each one of you to review your relationship from the time you first became involved with one another to the present, and to determine the moment that the relationship felt most valuable and "smooth" to you. Describe that moment or situation briefly and indicate how your partner *behaved* to make this the best of all times. By definition any other time together has been less "smooth," so the second part of this exercise is to determine the most distressed, unsatisfactory, "rough" moment. Again, describe briefly what happened, focusing on your partner's *behavior*. These two events, the smoothest one and the roughest one, mark the boundaries for feeling good or bad in your relationship. Each one of you can now draw a vertical line and construct a scale about your relationship. The lower end of the line is where you put the roughest moment and you give that event a score of 0. The upper end has the smoothest moment and you give it a score of 10. All other events and moments in your relationship fall somewhere between these two points and could subjectively be rated with a number between 0 and 10. I will teach you some ways in which you can use your scale later on, but for now I am only going to ask you to think about your smooth-rough scale, focusing on the following important points:

a) The scale describes the range of possibilities for smoothness and roughness in your relationship. It is quite likely that your future experiences will continue to be somewhere between these two extremes. If you are very lucky you may have a few super smooth experiences, an 11 or maybe a 12. If you are unlucky you may get a $-1$ or $-2$. But, basically, this is it!

b) The absolute ideal image of relationship smoothness lies far above point 10, just as the absolute image of roughness is far below point 0. The scale encompasses the realistic range of possibilities, not the range of your deepest fears and dreams.

c) Consequently, it does not pay off to continuously aspire for an everlasting 10 or an almost ideal 15. A more realistic goal is to work toward higher average scores.

exercise is to sharpen your awareness of the range of possibilities

d) The words "smooth" and "rough" are chosen because they are relatively vague and general. People interpret these words according to their personal value system. For some people, smooth is in the first place feeling close; for others it is having a good time together; and for still others it is a sense of companionship. Roughness means, for some people, loneliness; for others, conflict. That is why the endpoints in your scale may be different from those of your partner. You may want to discuss this with one another.

*Daily Rating*

For the next homework assignment, the following instructions are given:

It can be useful to you to make daily smooth-rough ratings. Pick a specific time of the day during which you can most easily take about 15 minutes off together. Although each of you is to make his or her own ratings on his or her own scale, it is good to be in each other's presence, as you may want to share the information. The exercise goes as follows: Take every day a new sheet of paper, draw a vertical line, mark the ends with the number 0 for roughness and 10 for smoothness, and reflect for a while about the moments you were together in the past 24 hours. Determine the smoothest moment, write down in a few words what happened, and rate this moment subjectively on your 0 to 10 scale. In your description please emphasize your partner's *behavior* during this interaction. It does not help a lot to state that the smoothest moment of the day was breakfast when your partner was very "friendly." Try to see what being "friendly" means very concretely. For instance, you could observe that breakfast was smooth and that your partner kissed you good morning and prepared your favorite dish.

Once you have found and rated the smoothest moment, it follows that all other moments were more rough. Determine and rate the roughest time and describe the partner's behavior during the event. Some people find it very difficult in the beginning to make a rough rating. Others have an easy time finding rough moments but cannot come up with the least rough—or smooth—point. Always start with the one you find easiest to determine. This exercise is designed to help you to become more aware of the range of smoothness and roughness in your relationship. You will gradually, after a few days, pay more attention to how you feel in the relationship during the day, and it will become easier to rate both extremes. The goal of this exercise is to sharpen your awareness of the range of possibilities in the daily relationship, and to help you to acquire a clearer perception of your partner's behavior.

One additional piece of advice is to switch roles in reminding the other that it is time to do your exercises. Otherwise, the person who always initiates the exercise will feel more and more responsible and committed to doing this work, while the other will become gradually less invested.

The daily smooth-rough exercise is often quite useful to the partners individually: Rigid perceptual distortions and unrealistic expectations may begin to change and each partner acquires a more pragmatic orientation towards relationship change. Persons who tend to be overly rational and out of touch with their feelings learn to become more aware of positive and negative emotional states and to link them to specific events.

The benefits of the exercise can be substantially increased if the partners can share their individual smooth-rough scores with one another. It should be a balanced way of getting positive and negative feedback on how one's behavior is perceived by the partner—thus often inducing behavior change—and it can be a vehicle for restoring communication and problem-solving about personal issues. However, therapist and clients have to make a decision as to how direct and how detailed the process of information-sharing should be. For instance, couples who tend to get into unproductive fights and arguments whenever they discuss a personal issue can be instructed initially only to exchange the sheets of paper on which they did the rating, and to avoid talking about the content. A next step can be to read the scores and events out loud, but to prohibit any discussion. Other couples may benefit from a structured information-sharing process in which each spouse paraphrases the information given by the partner. At any rate, the therapist needs to emphasize that the goal is to share information and to gain a good understanding of the partner's *perceptions*, and *not* to discover the absolute truth or to justify why certain behaviors occurred. Finally, couples with more advanced communication skills can use the information to solve problems and to plan for change.

*Analysis by the Therapist*

The couple should be requested to bring all the daily scales to the therapy session. Clinically, the therapist can focus on the content or on the individual client's perceptual style and/or capacity for self-disclosure. For instance, a narrow range of scores, centering around the mean, may reveal a problem of being unaware of feelings, a problem in linking emotional states to concrete events, or a problem in self-disclosure. Scores which are skewed high or low often indicate that the client tends to be selectively sensitive to smooth or rough events and to repress the opposite side. Extreme scores may indicate a tendency to overreact.

With regard to the content, the therapist can pay attention to common characteristics in the reported negative events and in the positively appreciated events. This may lead to inferences about personal values, core conflicts, and core cognitive constructs applied to the partner and the relationship.

The principle of a 10-point bipolar scale, with daily "forced" high and low ratings, can be used as a tool for cognitive restructuring in a variety of other clinical situations in marital therapy. As has been extensively documented, spouses tend to attribute their partner's behavior to stable dispositions, and these attributed "personality traits" distort further perception and become self-fulfilling prophecies. For instance, a husband is perceived by his spouse as domineering, while he perceives her as dependent. The therapist can instruct the wife to rate each day the most dominant behavior of the husband. Once this has been determined, all other behaviors are, by definition, less dominant and she can rate his most submissive behavior during a given day on a 10-point dominance-submissive scale. The husband rates his wife's most independent and dependent behavior. Thus, they can learn to see a "personality trait" as a "range of possibilities" between extremes, rather than as an extreme, generalized stable characteristic. Another application is, for instance, the daily rating of the partner's most trust-inspiring versus jealousy-inspiring behavior. In sex therapy (low sexual desire problems), the client can learn to be more aware of the sexual aspects of the relationship by describing and rating the most sexually stimulating moment of the day versus the most aversive one.

Though this type of homework assignment is certainly not a panacea for all possible problems in marital therapy, it has an extended range of applicability and can be quite a useful and helpful element in the overall therapeutic strategy. The homework task itself is relatively short, time-efficient and directly rewarding, which is important since people often find paper and pencil assignments rather tedious and tend to avoid them.

**JOHAN VERHULST, M.D.**
*Associate Professor*
*Department of Psychiatry and*
*Behavioral Sciences*
*University of Washington*
*School of Medicine, Seattle, WA*

# 8. Complementary and Symmetrical Couples

## Question:

I find working with couples particularly difficult—more so than with families. What conceptual guidelines might I follow specific to the system of the couple?

## Discussion:

I want to suggest a way of thinking about couples which can help both the therapist and the couple clarify the direction of their work. Couples can be described as fitting into one of two categories: complementary or symmetrical. "Complementary" will be used to indicate a coupling in which the partners are different in their styles—a fast thinker and a deliberate one, an early riser and a night owl, a country person and a city person. These are couplings in which two people act to balance each other, each filling in for underdeveloped areas in the other. "Symmetrical coupling" will refer to a coupling of partners with similar styles—for example, both gregarious or both reserved. Each type of coupling has its assets and limitations. While it must be said that there are no pure types, thinking in this way is useful in helping couples mine their resources and evaluate their limitations.

Two areas of strength typify complementary couplings. First, they are good at functioning in the world around them because between the two quite differently organized people are held a great many of the skills needed in managing daily affairs. Second, the couple provides an excellent context for the development of self-sufficiency in each of the partners, as each has firsthand in his/her partner a teacher of elements not yet developed in him/herself. The different attributes of the partners are frequently points of dispute, and it is important to help couples see their differences for the major developmental assets that they are.

There are two areas of strength which characterize symmetrical couplings. First, since the partners are similarly organized, the potential for harmony and ease of communication is great, and a sense of being soul mates is often present. Second, as the couple share many of the same underdeveloped areas, they have the potential for providing for each other a highly empathic learning context, in which they understand intuitively the nature of each other's struggles as each works toward his/her own resolutions.

The primary communication modality of complementary couplings is verbal. Partners organized differently experience the world differently and must rely on an increasingly refined use of words to accurately communicate about their experience. The primary modality of symmetrical couplings is nonverbal. Since the partners' ways of experiencing are similar, mutual understanding is to a great extent implicit, characterized by the common expression, "on the same wave length."

Perhaps related to their verbal orientation, complementary couplings have a lower level of internal intensity, with greater energy available for dealing with the outer world. Symmetrical couples, with much of their experience immediately shared, tend to be more internally intense, with less energy available to outer world activities.

The sexual activity of the two types is quite different. Sexual expression is usually problematic in complementary relationships, due to the partners' different styles, while it tends to flow easily in symmetrical relationships in which nonverbal communication is the natural modality.

Each type of coupling has its own difficulties to contend with. Complementary partners tend to suffer from internal friction as they struggle with the differences between them. It is important to help people turn blaming into appreciation for the important contribution the differences make to the relationship.

Symmetrical partners struggle with their shared short suits. They may have trouble coping with some element of the outer world, such as their economics; or they may have internal difficulty due, for example, to a shared inability to express anger or to plan revitalizing activities.

A major source of difficulty for both types of couplings is fusion between the partners, which occurs while partners are as yet incapable of being free-standing adults and are dependent on each other for a sense of survival. Fusion in complementary couplings takes the form of a calcification of the complementary roles each partner plays for the other, locking each partner into increasingly caricatured stances. Fusion in symmetrical couplings overwhelms partners with a loss of sense of self. For example, in their similarity and nonverbal free exchange, their boundaries become difficult to discern. One of the assets of this type of couple is their ability to merge; but if they fuse, they cannot get free again and must break the relationship to reestablish a sense of self. Thus, there are relationships between people who cannot live together and cannot live apart, characterized by a series of breaks and reunions.

There is a kind of developmental logic to understanding the relationship of these two types of couplings to each other, resulting from a comprehension of their inherent difficulties. Most simply, in terms of the maturation of an individual, his/her early coupling will most often be complementary, while later coupling (if it occurs) will tend to be symmetrical. Before achieving a sense of self-sufficiency in the world, people are generally drawn to and can be more successful in complementary pairings. They have at hand a partner to take over where they are weak, and a teacher to help with their development.

Once people have achieved a sense of self-sufficiency, they are capable of maintaining a symmetrical relationship and will be drawn in that direction. They will have acquired a capacity to control the intensity—the surrender and reconstitution of personal boundaries—and their shared short suits will be developed sufficiently in an individual manner, so as to form a viable couple.

People are frequently dissatisfied because their expectations of coupling are stereotyped and do not fit the type of couple of which they are a part. Typically, complementary partners seek the sort of sexual exchange which belongs to a symmetrical relationship, and symmetrical couples wish for more varied and stimulating verbal exchange. To be part of one type and expect the fruits of the other is destructive to the valuation of the partners and of their coupling. In working with couples, therefore, it is tremendously helpful to be able to clarify with them what they can and cannot expect from each other and their coupling, so that they can arrive at the greatest possible appreciation of each other and their relationship.

**PHOEBE PROSKY, M.S.W.**
*Faculty*
*Ackerman Institute for Family Therapy*
*New York, NY*

# 9. Assessment Tools and Procedures in Integrative Psychotherapy

## Question:

I understand that your model of integrative psychotherapy is multidimensional, i.e., it focuses not only on the interpersonal, (marital and family), but also on the intrapersonal and transpersonal or spiritual dimensions of relationship systems. What are the goals of integrative therapy? What assessment instruments do you use to assess the different dimensions of integrative therapy, and what strategy do you use to administer the assessment battery? How frequently do you administer your self-assessment questionnaires?

## Discussion:

The goals of integrative psychotherapy (Friedman, 1980a, 1980b, 1981, 1982) are to increase intrapersonal, interpersonal (mainly marital and family) and, often, transpersonal or spiritual harmony or well-being. In order to assess these dimensions during marital/divorce/separation and family therapy, I have found a series of multidimensional assessment instruments to be extremely useful. The general strategy I use is to administer a battery of self-assessment questionnaires to my clients during or before the first therapy session (taking 15-30 minutes) and between the first and second therapy sessions. Wherever possible, clients are taught to self-score the questionnaires, and the scores are immediately recorded. The scores are fed back to clients and briefly interpreted to them in the first or second session. They serve to focus the treatment sessions by concentrating on achieving concrete, easily assessable goals—for example, enhanced self-esteem and well-being, reduced stress, enhanced marital adjustment, and increased positive child behavior. Clients seem to take pleasure in hearing positive reports of their gains as measured by self-report questionnaires with numerical scores that change over time in a positive direction.

The questionnaires that I routinely give in the first session are:

1) a stress-symptom inventory known as the Hopkins Symptom Checklist (SCL-90);
2) a brief self-esteem questionnaire (10 items); and
3) a brief well-being questionnaire (14 items).

The stress symptom checklist has nine subscales with separate measures of anxiety, depression, anger and somatic complaints. Norms and percentile scores are available for a general population, clinical population, etc. The well-being and self-esteem questionnaires can be scored along a 0-100 continuum with low scores representing low self-esteem and well-being, and high scores representing high self-esteem and well-being. In my experience, clients usually come into therapy with high stress scores, low well-being, and low-to-moderate self-esteem scores.

After the first session some questionnaires are given every therapy session, e.g., four of the subscales of the SCL-90 (41 items), a brief relationship satisfaction subscale and the parent or child behavior checklist (if appropriate). Some questionnaires are given every other session (well-being and intergenerational relationship) or every fourth session (self-esteem, wellness and meaning, and wellness and transcendence). Other questionnaires are administered every four or eight weeks, e.g., the relationship adjustment (Locke-Wallace and Spanier) measures or the divorce adjustment (Fisher) measures. When the scores change in a positive direction over the course of therapy, I am supportive and complimentary to my clients, i.e., I provide very positive feedback. Usually significant positive shifts take place during integrative psychotherapy from the second to fourth sessions. When scores on the stress symptom checklist go below 20, for example, intrapersonal harmony has almost always been achieved.

When couples come for marital therapy or families for family therapy, I also administer a relationship adjustment questionnaire during the first session which takes about 10-15 minutes to complete. This questionnaire is a composite of the Locke-Wallace Marital Adjustment Test, the Spanier Dyadic-Adjustment scale and a five-item negativity subscale. This composite relationship adjustment questionnaire can be scored so that there are three overall marital or relationship adjustment scores and six subscale scores. Four subscales come from the dyadic adjustment test, i.e., cohesion, consensus, satisfaction, and affection. The two remaining subscales give separate scores for positive and negative satisfaction or well-being in the relationship, which generally have low or zero correlations with each other. The dyadic adjustment scale can also be used for non-married couples living together.

Norms are available on these questionnaires for happily married couples and clinically troubled and divorced couples. It takes about five minutes to score the entire questionnaire. If the therapist desires, he can feed this information back to the client in the first or second therapy interview.

Frequently, I have found it valuable to give Stuart's marital pre-counseling questionnaire to a couple during the first therapy session. The couple is then asked to complete it during the week. This comprehensive questionnaire includes a number of interesting and worthwhile scales measuring marital happiness, decision-making, coping, communication, and sexual relations. It also provides clients with a positively focused frame of reference for marital therapy.

If an individual enters therapy for problems relating to separation or divorce, each is given (in addition to the stress symptom, self-esteem and well-being questionnaires), the Fisher Divorce-Adjustment questionnaire to fill out between the first and second session. This 100-item questionnaire assesses a person's adjustment to the process of separation or divorce along six dimensions (emotionally disentangled from the former love partner, dissolution of anger toward the former love partner, self-esteem, social self-worth, openness to social intimacy and the completion of grief work). A total score and six subscale scores can be converted into percentiles (0-100) and the results compared to normative tables provided by Fisher of adjustment to separation or divorce. Again the results can be fed back to the clients, usually in the second or third session.

The relationship adjustment and divorce adjustment measures assess the horizontal axis of interpersonal family relationships. In order to assess a client's perception of the vertical axis, i.e., parent-child or parent-grandparent relationships, I have been utilizing a 25-item child and a 25-item parent behavior checklist, and a 20-item intergenerational-relationship questionnaire (parent-grandparent). All three questionnaires can be scored on a scale ranging from 0 to 100, with low scores indicating perceived intergenerational disharmony and high scores indicating perceived intergenerational harmony. Changes from low to high scores over time indicate the client perceives that a more positive relationship is occurring between him/herself and his/her respective parent or child.

Recently I have been experimenting with two new questionnaires in order to see if I can assess the transpersonal dimension of integrative psychotherapy. I have been giving clients the Ryan and Travis wellness and transcendence questionnaire (25 items) and the Ryan and Travis wellness and meaning questionnaire (12 items). These self-assessment questionnaires hold out the possibility of tapping certain aspects of the spiritual and existential dimensions of relationship systems. The data are still too incomplete to draw any definite conclusions at this time, but appear to be very promising.

Whenever possible a battery of questionnaires is sent to clients (following a phone call) in order to conduct follow-up, self-report assessments at intervals ranging from three months to one year. This provides the therapist with the opportunity to see if an individual's gains are maintained over time. During the course of treatment (usually after 8-10 sessions), graphs are drawn demonstrating the changes that have taken place. By this time substantial changes have usually occurred during treatment on these measures. (If not, the therapist should use this information to reassess and modify his/her strategy, tactics, and interventions). The graphs are shown to clients at this time and every few sessions thereafter. Most clients find it extremely rewarding to see the progress they have made.

Keeping systematic but easily kept records and graphing the data also permit the therapist to track the client's positive changes over time. This becomes very rewarding to the therapist. In my experience between two and 24 therapy sessions (with an average of about 13 sessions) occurring between a one-month and twelve-month period (average, five months) are sufficient to get positive results in most of the cases treated with integrative psychotherapy. Consequently, this is a very cost-effective approach. Follow-up data accumulated so far seem to indicate that the changes that do occur are almost always maintained or enhanced during the ensuing year. I have found that I am able to administer these assessment questionnaires to both my clinic and private practice clients.

## References

Friedman, P. Integrative psychotherapy. In R. Herink (Ed.), *Psychotherapy Handbook*. New York: New American Library, 1980(a).

Friedman, P. An integrative approach to the creation and alleviation of dis-ease within the family. *Family Therapy*, 1980(b), *2*, 179-185.

Friedman, P. Integrative family therapy. *Family Therapy*, 1981, 3:3.

Friedman, P. Multiple roles of the integrative marital psychotherapist. *Family Therapy*, 1982, 9:2.

**PHILIP H. FRIEDMAN, Ph.D.**
*Coordinator of Training in*
*Marital and Family Therapy*
*C.A.T.C.H. CMHC*

# 10. Deciding Whom to Include in Family Interviews

## Question:

How many members of the family should I see in order to do family therapy? I don't know if I should start with the person who is referred to me or ask to see the family right away. If a couple comes in with a marital problem, should I see the children? Should I see the parents alone in a family that presents with a problem in a child?

## Discussion:

You will probably receive many different answers to this question because there are a variety of practices among family therapists. Many would say that family therapy has very little to do with the number of people in the room. It is not perceived simply as another treatment modality; rather, family therapy is seen as a conceptual framework that informs the therapist's practice at all times. It is a way of thinking about people and their problems. Thus the therapist could be involved in family therapy with one person (Carter and Orfanidis, 1976), a couple, a nuclear family, an extended family, or a social network. The common thread underlying all of these practices is the goal: to effect change in the family relationship system.

I believe that we should have a flexible concept of who constitutes the family for the purpose of engaging in family therapy. I like to see as many family members as possible, at least in due course; however, I am comfortable in seeing only one person if circumstances bring this about. With all families I find it useful to build into the contract (mutual understanding) that it may be helpful, as we go on, to see different members of the family alone or in various combinations, i.e., spouse-spouse, father-son, mother-daughter, or sibling group. By bringing up this possibility very early on in the contact, I find that it permits me greater latitude in determining who should be seen at different stages in treatment. Then, too, the idea of varying the sets of persons seen is not suddenly thrust upon the family totally unprepared. As part of the beginning contract, I explain to the family that I will always try to make clear to them why I recommend interviews with different combinations of family members.

If a couple comes to me with a marital problem, very early in the contact I ask to see them with their children. This helps to give me (and them) a sense of their functioning in the role of parents as well as spouses. In the preoccupation with their marital conflict they may lose sight of the role as parents that they share.

In families where the child is the presenting problem, it is useful that other siblings be present in family interviews. Though some family therapists do not like to include very small children, I believe their presence yields valuable information about the family relationship system. It is, of course, helpful to listen to the content of the communication between all family members as well as to observe the nonverbal process that goes on, such as seating arrangements and body movements. Interviews with the parents alone are a valuable part of the procedure, not only to gain further understanding of their relationship, but to underscore their importance as the responsible adult members of the family. Both sets of interviews, those with children present and without them, help to clarify the function that the presenting child's behavior serves for the entire family system.

Irrespective of how many family members I see, I usually construct a genogram and an ecomap (Hartman, 1978) at the outset of treatment. Thus, I bring up very early in the contact the subject of family of origin and the possibility of including members of the extended family in future interviews. I try to convey the importance of these relationships. In my practice I have found it very helpful to bring into interviews grandparents, not only as a vital part of the support system for the family in crisis, but also because so many problems in spouse and parent-child relationships are related to unresolved problems in the family of origin (Framo, 1976).

I draw an ecomap together with the family in order to learn about their interface with outside eco systems. I attempt to find out what the natural and formal support systems are in the life of the family—which ones need to be strengthened and which systems should be part of the interventive effort. The way is always left open to bring significant others into interviews if necessary.

## References

Carter, E. A. and Orfanidis, M. Family therapy with the one person and the family therapist's own family. In P. Guerin (Ed.), *Family Therapy*. New York: Gardner, 1976.

Framo, J. L. Family of origin as a therapeutic resource for adults in marital and family therapy: You can and should go home again. *Family Process*, 1976, *15*, 193-210.
Hartman, A. Diagrammatic assessment of family relationships. *Social Casework*, 1978, *59*, 125–132.

**MILDRED FLASHMAN, M.S.W.**
*Associate Professor*
*Boston University*
*School of Social Work*
*Boston, MA*

# 11. Families' Concerns About Physical Symptoms and Diseases

**Question:**

Frequently family members discuss each others' physical symptoms, pain, and diseases. These are often an indirect reason for seeking treatment. How should a family therapist handle issues, concerns, and questions about physical symptoms and illness in the treatment? How are physical symptoms and disease allowed to become problems within the family that have a negative effect on medical treatment and physical health?

**Discussion:**

There is a special status accorded to discussions about physical symptoms and diseases in families, and this results in special problems in family therapy. To a family therapist, a family member's symptom or disease is just like other types of symptom—drinking, acting-out, depression—something that needs to be explored in terms of its role in the entire family system. However, families typically have a very different way of seeing and using physical illness, and their way is quite often supported by their primary physician and other health professionals. Therefore, when physical illness crops up in families in therapy, it presents special problems to the therapist.

To the family, physical problems are an entirely different species from emotional difficulties. Yet, as psychosomatic theory and recent stress research notes, many emotional experiences and types of experience can be transformed into physical symptoms and ailments. Thus, a woman who is angry at her husband and feels helpless to confront him can develop headaches several hours after her feeling. The headaches allow her to express her feeling, and also allow her to get what she wants from her husband. The family therapist would not get far by asserting that the headache was an expression of her anger. Rather, he or she would have to create an experience for the couple so that they could see the pairing between anger/frustration/helplessness and headaches, and secondly, between expressing these feelings and the absence of headaches.

When a family brings up physical symptoms within family therapy, this can have several functions. It can be a way to mention its distress. It can be a legitimate way for one member to express concern and act protectively toward another. It can be used to devalue psychotherapy, and allude to treatment with a "real" doctor for a "real" ailment. Often, when a family is in psychotherapy and also a member is in medical treatment for a symptom that is triggered by stress or emotional contact, the medical treatment can inadvertently undermine the family therapy. It is important for the physician and therapist to be in contact, and for the therapist to explain what he/she is doing and why. Also, some families have a physical crisis or retreat toward physical crises rather than face an emotional issue. The medical crisis may lead them to avoid facing difficult psychological issues.

Minuchin et al.'s (1978) book, *Psychosomatic Families*, is almost the only theoretical model of the role that physical illness plays in the family. My own book, *Healing From Within*, presents a psychosomatic perspective on physical illness, which offers details on how families can work to help themselves when one member has a physical crisis. Both these books suggest that the body is used in a special way by other family members. People express their concern, especially when physical health seems endangered, by increasing their vigilance and concern over the body of the ill family member. For example, in working with couples where the husband had heart disease but did not adhere to treatment recommendations, especially about changes in diet and exercise, a particular constellation was observed. The wife tried to be helpful in doing things for the husband, and by pressuring him in a parental way. The husband, in response to the wife's attempts to help and her genuine concern, became angry, withdrew, experienced stress, and therefore ate more and resisted her suggestions. The key to treatment adherence was to separate the couple. The wife was asked to focus on her own needs and physical health, and the husband was given as much responsibility for his own diet and exercise as could be arranged. Each family member learns to help himself, and the intrusive/rebellious interaction is muted.

Two other constellations have been observed with physical symptoms. In one, commonly with a child, the physical symptom is a pathway for a parent or spouse to dedicate her (usually) life to taking care of the other. The issue is that the helper's need to have a meaning in life seems somehow to maintain the illness. The related pattern, reported above, is where the person with the pain or illness uses the symptom indirectly to control others and to express anger.

It is my observation that a large number of chronic and serious physical symptoms are aggravated by the interactional use to which the symptom is put. Primary physicians, since they do not interview the family or are not familiar with family dynamics, often miss this dimension of illness. Yet, when a symptom or illness is necessary to family functioning, it can remain, despite treatment that should bring it under control or cause a remission. Therefore, in my work, I have found that the use of family interviewing and brief family and/or individual therapy can be of use in medical clinics.

The format for a family health exploration is a series of interviews with the person having the physical illness, and his or her spouse, or parents. The exploration is to look systematically at the role of the symptom or disease within the family, and what aspects of family life might have influenced the development of the illness, and what dynamics might make it difficult to recover. Most families or couples can uncover several ways that the symptom helps the family, e.g., sources of secondary gain which inhibit treatment. The family members can then agree to use other means to get what they obtain from the symptom. They can express their feelings more directly, ask for what they want, or advise each other rather than coerce them.

Another important component of the family health exploration is teaching family self-care. Family health is significantly influenced by the way the family seeks health care, eats, exercises, and does things. For example, family members can utilize techniques of psychophysiological self-regulation to reduce stress and pain, and to overcome serious physical symptoms (as an adjunct to medical treatment). The ways that family members support each others' health, and do not reward each other for being ill is an important part of the self-care component of the family health exploration.

Physical illness is an important area for the family therapist to explore with a family. Also, physical illness is itself an area that suggests the need for some short-term family counseling. Many physical symptoms do not lie within the individual, but are products of the family system as a whole.

*References*

Jaffe, D. T. *Healing From Within*. New York: Knopf, 1980.
Minuchin, S., Rosman, B., and Baker, L. *Psychosomatic Families*. Cambridge, MA: Harvard University Press, 1978.

**DENNIS T. JAFFE, Ph.D.**
*Visiting Lecturer in Psychiatry*
*UCLA School of Medicine, Los Angeles, CA;*
*Co-director, Health Studies*
*Saybrook Institute, San Francisco, CA*

# 12. Therapist-Initiated Termination from Family Therapy

**Question:**

Even though a lot of family therapy is short-term, some families or couples continue for a long time, in some cases perhaps too long. If a particular course of therapy has been relatively smooth and productive, but the couple or family is making no moves to end the therapy, when is it advisable that the therapist initiate a termination?

**Discussion:**

At this point the therapist may wonder why the family isn't expressing any negative feelings. If there are no feelings of discomfort or restiveness expressed by members of the family, then it is likely that they aren't saying anything. We all know that the therapy relationship in many ways represents a mirror image of the outside world. In the course of day-to-day events, all kinds of experiences occur: The car breaks down, a child graduates, the stock market goes up, a close relative becomes ill. The family members should be able to perceive analogues of all these events in their relationship with the therapist, as well as in their relationships with each other. No therapist is perfect and no family is perfect either.

Consequently, if the therapy is going properly, the family should feel some desire to quit throughout the whole course of the work. If they do not verbalize these feelings, their failure to do so should be investigated. By asking a question rather than suggesting an end, the therapist will serve as a model of noncompulsive investigatory behavior. He or she will appear interested and considerate.

To the question, "How come no one ever talks about quitting?" the family is likely to respond in a variety of ways. For example, family members may say: "We didn't want to hurt your feelings"; or one member may say, "I've been thinking about stopping but it seemed that everybody else was enjoying it and I didn't want to bring this up and spoil things"; or they may relate that there really are some problems, but they didn't want to bring them up because if they could convince everyone that things are going better, then they would be able to stop.

All of these answers suggest that further work is indicated. The principals, however, may decide that they wish to terminate the therapy and no further work may be contracted for. Therefore, the question of when one should begin to think about termination all boils down to what one's goals are for the treatment. If the therapist perceives that the goal which had been set has now been reached, he/she may relate that it is his/her impression that the goals of therapy have been reached and ask if they wish to discontinue their work together. If the family members are positively suggestible, they will probably agree to terminate; if not, they may opt to stay. It may also be the case that in the course of the family work they have discovered some additional problems which they wish to explore. The therapist will then decide if he/she wants to work further with this family, refer them, or terminate them with a suggestion that they work on their own with the proviso that they can contact him/her should the need arise.

My opinion is that therapy with a family should be terminated when the members are age-appropriately mature and fully functioning. One way to assess this is by studying the dreams that the family members bring in. The dreams should depict a situation in which three or more people are presented with a problem and successfully deal with it. At this point, therapy can be terminated by mutual agreement.

**MICHAEL BECK, Ph.D.**
*Private Practice*
*Babylon, NY*

# PART B

# *Assessment and Treatment Planning with Various Types of Families*

# 13. Indications and Choice of Treatment Modality with Disturbed Adolescents and Families

**Question:**

When a symptomatic, seriously disturbed adolescent patient presents for evaluation and/or treatment to a clinic, inpatient service, or private practitioner, questions often arise as to the ideal choice of treatment modality. Should the individual be treated or the family? Often therapists of various theoretical persuasions will argue vehemently for one approach or another. How do we understand and conceptualize the problem and the treatment in order to make an informed recommendation?

**Discussion:**

In this discussion I will attempt to somewhat systematically conceptualize various modalities of treatment and try to elucidate some general principles or guidelines for thinking about the complex problem of indications and choice of treatment modality. We know that change in the intrapsychic life of any family member affects the dynamics of the family and, reciprocally, that dynamic change in the family affects the intrapsychic life of the individual. Certainly, then, the clinician needs to be familiar with the individual psychology of the adolescent and adult, as well as the psychodynamics of the family as a small group and the marital couple, in order to be effective in treating the symptomatic adolescent. Frequently the issue is raised as to whether intrapsychic and intrafamilial psychopathology are mutually exclusive or complementary frames of reference. I would argue for a both/and position rather than an either/or position when it comes to considering individual and family psychopathology. Within a psychodynamic framework, they are far more complementary and additive in perspective than they are competitive or mutually exclusive frames of reference.

The question is not when would we recommend family treatment as opposed to individual treatment, or couples treatment as opposed to individual treatment, but when and under what circumstances individual treatment makes sense, and when and under what circumstances couples or family treatment makes sense, and when and under what circumstances various combinations of those treatments make sense. I think that, if we can have some generally agreed-upon principles about what each one of those treatment's specific functions and goals are, then, while we will not always be able to answer the difficult questions, at least we can help to tailor a treatment to the specific situation based on general guidelines. In this way, we may approach having a more rational prescription of therapy or therapies.

We are all quite familiar with individual psychotherapy. We think about individual therapy as a modality of treatment that addresses the internalized or structuralized inner difficulties of the individual. These internal difficulties involve intrapsychic conflicts—for example, low self-esteem based on internal fantasies in the healthier patient, and varying degrees of anxiety over abandonment in the less healthy patient. However, even here, these concerns about abandonment are conceptualized or presented as an internal problem. (Obviously the cases that I am describing as optimal for individual psychotherapy are more often the exception than the rule these days.) But I am not implying that a therapist would just merely treat this patient with individual therapy, but that those are the kinds of issues, the internal ones, that are likely to be addressed in individual therapy.

In the other therapies, we are more likely to focus on or have as our major interest the externalization or interpersonal effects and influences of the individual's inner psychopathology in interaction with significant others. Marital or couples therapy, distinguished from "counseling" by its interpretive nature (Titchener, 1966), would be therapy for marital strife where each of the partners is externalizing his or her difficulties into the marriage in an interlocking and mutually collusive way. Here, it is usually impossible for the individuals to attend to their inner conflicts and inner turmoil because they have located, or at least because they experience, the difficulties as residing outside of themselves in the marital relationship. Actually, quite often a useful outcome of this kind of work can be the reinternalization of projection and the owning of inner difficulty which then may lead each of the partners to pursue in more depth his or her individual problems in individual therapy.

In his classic paper on "Indications and Contraindications for Exploratory Family Therapy," Lyman Wynne (1963) suggested that family therapy was useful for the clarification and resolution of any patterned intrafamilial "relationship difficulty," i.e., problems in reciprocal interaction to which each person is contributing, collusively or openly, or relationship problems in which all of the participant family members have a vital and continuing stake, on either a conscious or an unconscious level. In other words, we are interested here in the interplay between the individual and the couple or family, and in the extent that external factors, external interferences, or "external resistances" (Shapiro, 1978) reinforce, fuel, and perpetuate the difficulties of and the internal resistances to treatment of the individual identified patient.

For example, because he/she is part of a system, the adolescent's delicately balanced internal forces are in constant interaction with external forces of the family. The external counterpart to the adolescent's regressive dependent strivings is the family's prohibition, however unconscious and covertly conveyed, against separation. The family's prohibition against separation often contributes significantly to the failure of growth in the adolescent and to the internal resistances of the adolescent to treatment. Just to be in treatment for the adolescent often represents a loyalty conflict for him (Boszormenyi-Nagy, 1972; Stierlin, 1977). As I have indicated elsewhere (Berkowitz, 1981), whatever the actual details of the treatment program, one principle cannot be overemphasized: Individual psychotherapy for the severely disturbed adolescent patient alone, without providing some form of treatment for the parents, is often doomed to failure.

Finally, I would like to underline the differentiation or distinction between the use of the various treatment modalities for evaluation purposes and their use for treatment purposes. Inclusion of the family for diagnostic or assessment purposes is crucial as part of a total evaluation, particularly with the more severe psychopathologies. Then, an assessment can be made as to what extent the individual pathology is fixed in place because of parental defensive requirements or collusive family needs.

## References

Berkowitz, D. The borderline adolescent and the family. In M. Lansky (Ed.) *Family Therapy and Major Psychopathology.* New York: Grune and Stratton, 1981.

Boszormenyi-Nagy, I. Loyalty implications of the transference model in psychotherapy. *Archives of General Psychiatry,* 1972, *27,* 374-380.

Shapiro, R. The patient, the therapist, and the family: The management of external resistances to psychoanalytic therapy of adolescents. *Journal of Adolescence,* 1978, *1,* 3-10.

Stierlin, H. *Psychoanalysis and Family Therapy.* New York: Jason Aronson, 1977.

Titchener, J. The problem of interpretation in marital therapy. *Comprehensive Psychiatry,* 1966, *7,* 321-337.

Wynne, L. Indications and contraindications for exploratory family therapy. In I. Boszormenyi-Nagy and J. Framo (Eds.) *Intensive Family Therapy: Theoretical and Practical Aspects.* New York: Hoeber, 1963.

**DAVID A. BERKOWITZ, M.D.**
*Associate Clinical Professor*
*Department of Psychiatry*
*Tufts University School of Medicine*
*Boston, MA*

# 14. Young Children in Family Therapy

## Question:

I have been learning about and doing family therapy over the past two years of my training as a mental health professional. I am now entering private practice and will continue to do family therapy. Do I have to do anything special in planning my office? My real question is, what about the children in these families who will come to my new office, especially the little ones? What will they do during the family sessions? What will I do about the mess they make?

## Discussion:

Let's discuss the "real" question first! Children, especially younger ones, are a problem to some family therapists who do not welcome their presence. Some family therapists tolerate children's activities and others even enjoy them.

What is the problem? The problem is not singular but many-faceted. One important aspect is that young children, in particular, do not act, in family sessions and out, like adults. They do not easily sit in one place, talking quietly through family therapy sessions. Rather, they move around, play, and investigate by action, rather than words. Many adults are not comfortable with play in their office. Therapy is "serious work" and play is what you do when you relax and take a break. So the "real" problem is the attitude of the therapist toward play—his or her knowledge of and experience with play. Most adults do not regard play as child's work. And therapists who have been trained primarily to treat adults may easily recognize the theoretical importance of childhood but not when put into action, particularly by younger children.

There is another aspect of including young children that is important to recognize. Young children often make adults uncomfortable. As we become adults, we banish from our consciousness some important elements of childhood. When children are present, their play and fantasies exert a strong regressive pull. Unless we are willing, this regression

65

may not feel pleasant. We may be required to notice some "childish" reactions in ourselves, or, in order to avoid such recognition, we may want to banish the children. The primitive nature of children may make us uncomfortable, but at the same time children in family sessions provide access to deep levels of family life. So, the partial answer to the first question, the real one, is that we must determine whether we can accept the stimulation of the child within us that including young children in our sessions causes.

Now to the practical aspects. As we have just said, if you are going to include young children, then they are going to play in your office. My first suggestion about planning your new office is to keep it simple for children and adults. Children require paper, pencils, crayons, perhaps playdough and a few toys, some space in which to play, and some safety from causing trouble when they move around. It is not necessary to have toys for children of all ages or complicated toys for all kinds of play. The toys are provided in order to allow the children to express themselves and also to remove themselves when the discussion gets hot.

I have just mentioned some freedom in moving around. It is not necessary to "childproof" an office in the same way that you do a house. But it is necessary to remove breakable or choice objects to some high level where they are not easily available for children. Some therapists provide a wet area in which children can paint, but this is not necessary. The most important part of the answer to this question really lies in the therapist's attitude and the provision of a few supplies.

Since your office will have paper and crayons, it is likely that the children will make drawings. Some therapists get scared when children draw. They immediately wonder, "What do I know about children's drawings?" or "What does that mean?" Again, it is the attitude which is most important. Therapists need to recognize children's play and drawings and include them in the therapeutic process in ways that will gradually become comfortable for the therapist and family members. It is not necessary to know all about the intricacies of the characteristics of the developmental level of children's drawings. However, it is necessary to recognize that a child has drawn something and to make a very simple comment about it. For example, a therapist might say, "May I see that?", after a child makes a drawing. If given permission, simple comments about the tree, the house, or whatever will suffice. Asking the child "why" is not recommended. Children cannot think in terms of "why" and such questions will not be useful for either the therapist, the child, or the family therapy process.

The family therapy literature is sparse on young children and play (see Ackerman, 1970; Bloch, 1976; Zilbach, Bergel and Gass, 1972). There are some notably playful family therapists, of whom Carl Whitaker is an excellent example. In his case descriptions there are examples and details of the way that he plays with young children. It is most important to remember, however, in reading such descriptions, that they may not fit your particular style. Carl Whitaker likes to "play-battle." Arm wrestling is a specialty of his but it may not be one of yours. Develop your own play. Use your own imagination and, above all, figure out what makes you uncomfortable if you are uncomfortable with children. Eventually, even if you don't enjoy playing, it may prove advantageous in your work with families.

One last comment about messes. Children do make messes, but therapists can say "No!" There is a confusion about the play of children which has to do with traditional verbal therapy. Play is not like free association. In talking therapies, the therapist is often in a position to encourage freedom of talk and to remove verbal inhibitions. With children, there are times when, rather than give encouragement, it is more likely that you will have to say "no" emphatically in words or in action. A child who is about to make a mess can be stopped by the therapist taking simple measures such as removing the toy or in other appropriate ways saying no. Adult-trained talking therapists rarely say no to a verbal production, but it is likely that they will have to say no when children are in the room. Children inevitably test the therapist's control of the family session. They are often little "terrors," because they lack mature control over their impulses. At other times, children enjoy the thrill of controlling an adult, and the therapist may fear his/her own retaliatory impulses, as well as what the child might do.

Limit-setting is crucial and involves the ability to tolerate the child's raw aggression and the therapist's own impulse to retaliate. As Winnicott has taught us, the normal child must strike out at the environment, while the adult/therapist must provide a holding environment in order to promote not only survival, but also development and progression. The presence of children, and sometimes their play itself, may provide valuable clues to the underlying feelings and issues in the family. Once they learn about family therapy, children are frequently more dedicated to the treatment process than their parents. I urge you to explore the slight modifications of your new office and the provision of simple play materials in order to facilitate the inclusion of young children in family therapy.

*References*

Ackerman, N. W. Child participation in family therapy. *Family Process*, 1970, *9*, 403-410.

Bloch, D. A. Including children in family therapy. In P. Guerin (Ed.), *Family Therapy: Theory and Practice*. New York: Gardner, 1976.
Zilbach, J., Bergel, E., and Gass, C. The role of the young child in family therapy. In C. Sager and H. Kaplan (Eds.), *Progress in Group and Family Therapy*. New York: Brunner/Mazel, 1972.

**JOAN J. ZILBACH, M.D.**
*Consultant in Family Therapy*
*Child Psychiatry*
*Massachusetts Mental Health Center*
*Associate Clinical Professor of Psychiatry*
*Tufts University Medical School*
*Boston, MA*

# 15. The Only-Child Family: A Unique Family System

**Question:**

The family with one child seems hardly like a family at all. I tend to conceptualize the family members as three separate but emotionally entwined individuals in the same unit, rather than two subunits of parents and children as in the larger family. Surveys reveal that 50% of patients seek psychotherapy due to marital problems. In only-child families the other half of the cases are most likely situations in which the child is the identified patient. When is conjoint family therapy indicated for these families? Why not treat the problems as presented by the family—the parent or parents when marital issues predominate, or the individual youngster with parents seen separately, as is traditional? Is it really useful to try to treat this type of family as a system?

**Discussion:**

It generally proves fruitless to push a method of working with which parents are uncomfortable. If the parents present themselves as the identified patients for help with marital problems or sexual dysfunction, careful attention and evaluation of the marital unit must come first. If the child is brought in as the identified patient, then he or she must receive the initial focus, both medically, as in the case of anorexia nervosa or other physical manifestations, and psychologically.

As part of the child or marital evaluation in these only-child families, I have found it imperative to include family sessions. As I have elucidated elsewhere (Feldman, 1981), these individuals make up a more indivisible unit which means a much greater likelihood that all three are participants in whatever type of psychopathology is extant. In one case where the couple complained of sexual problems, when the 10-year-old daughter joined us for a discussion of how the family operated, we learned that the parents would never insure privacy by locking the bedroom door. Bathroom doors were never locked either, as both mother and daughter feared being trapped in a fire. Even when the conjoint sessions are used primarily for the evaluation phase of marital problems and then discontinued, if parents decide to separate or divorce, it again becomes useful to see the family as a group for planning purposes.

The three following areas generally indicate the usefulness of conjoint sessions for only-child families: 1) child and adolescent behavior problems; 2) anorexia nervosa; and 3) a chronic patient.

Among the familiar situations in the first category is school phobia. We know how vital the mother's participation is in perpetuating the child's fears. In some of these families it is even useful to bring in the grandmother who usually lives nearby and reinforces the intergenerational style of clinging hostile-dependency (Whitaker, 1976). In the case of the male juvenile delinquent, the role of the passive reinforcing father demands attention, but so does the unconscious cooperation of the other two family members in this system.

Anorexia nervosa has become a timely, almost urgent educational topic for therapists. Involvement of the family is required in all of these cases. The patient's fears of sexuality, a distorted body image, and anxiety regarding the ability to cope with various life tasks all tend to grow in the fertile ground of the family's overly close and intrusive emotional climate. Whether the anorexic is the child or the mother (and the latter cases are beginning to surface more frequently now), the threesome family unit must be seen together at least as an adjunct to the treatment.

Any "chronic patient" situation, again whether it be the child or parent, by its very nature tells us that other approaches have not worked or maybe no approach can succeed in restoring the patient to a previous level of functioning or to some desired way of being. The other two family members must begin to work with the identified patient to plan for more realistic group goals. This is imperative because, if by some miracle the chronic patient begins to improve with individual work, the others may be at risk. In one case, after family sessions were discontinued and the son continued to improve, his mother committed suicide.

Family therapists have tended to differ with individually oriented or psychoanalytically trained therapists over the issue of technique. The former contend that family treatment must deal with the here and now rather than past history or developmental task completion. I would propose that both areas can and should be looked at in working with an only-child family. In these troubled families, using the oedipal triangle as a prototype, it is as though all three remain fixated in the oedipal conflict, rather than achieving the developmentally appropriate resolution of that period with its impetus toward independence and mutuality. I think parents and child truly benefit from investigating where and how each one is emotionally "stuck." They can then begin to alter the present pattern of the family system that prevents growth, but with greater understanding of the unconscious needs that developed the system in the first place. They are then free to move from anger or guilt and resentment to forgiveness and respect.

## References

Feldman, G. Three's company: Family therapy with only child families. *Journal of Marital and Family Therapy*, 1981, 7, 43-46.

Whitaker, C. A family is a four-dimensional relationship. In P. J. Guerin, (Ed.), *Family Therapy*. New York: Gardner Press, 1976.

**GAIL C. FELDMAN, Ph.D.**
*Clinical Assistant Professor of Psychiatry*
*University of New Mexico Medical School*
*Albuquerque, NM*

# 16. The Adopted Child in Family Therapy

**Question:**

I have been seeing a number of families lately with adopted children. In most of these families, the adopted child is the identified patient. What problems are specific to such families and how do you approach them? Please give clinical examples.

**Discussion:**

Problems and issues in family therapy related to adoption can be grouped under the heading of whether a child belongs to a particular family or not and the nature of that belonging. Interestingly, the word "belonging" also connotes ownership and this symbolizes one aspect of the difference between biological families and adoptive families. Purely biological families have become families through various processes including courtship, love, marriage, sexual intercourse, pregnancy, prenatal development, prenatal love, and birth. In the adoptive family, these processes have occurred in a different family from the one in which the child lives. In addition, there has been a bureaucratic and legal process, the result of which is the child's placement. Whitaker's (1976) idea that people are "fragments of families" brings to mind the question of from which family is an adopted child a fragment? To which family tree is the child attached? The biological family's, the adoptive family's, or both, or neither?

One process that is frequently occurring when an adoptive family seeks treatment is that of extrusion. This is manifested by either acting-out behavior or some form of developmental failure. The metaphor applies to biological families as well, since they themselves can be shown to have been acting out as families or to have experienced developmental arrests. The process of extrusion is both allowed and augmented by denial of one of two aspects of the adopted child's early life: his/her early maternal-infant experiences, and the reality of his/her adoption. My approach at this juncture is helping families integrate both aspects simultaneously.

The Moore family sought individual psychotherapy for their adopted son because of progressively increasing school failure. Family therapy was suggested during the initial telephone contact. Parental anxiety over the idea was so marked that both got on the phone to discuss its efficacy. The next step in the attempt at extrusion was the frequent mentioning during the early months of therapy of considering residential treatment. George's physical characteristics, differing considerably from his naturally born younger brother, and his approaching bar mitzvah also served to highlight his "not belonging."

The therapeutic approach to the problem of extrusion was twofold. The first consisted of making an attachment to the family and considering the family as the patient. A family history was developed, psychodynamics explored, interpretations offered, and thus a relationship with the family grew. Is this a form of adoption? The second consisted of challenging the family's denial of the reality of George's being adopted. Evidence that this was not being addressed included mother's comment that, when asked by a friend if she had breast-fed George or not, she was unable to remember. The details of George's adoption were carefully explored in order that some reality as to his actual attachment to this family be made conscious. It was suggested that the family develop rituals to acknowledge his adoption. For instance, they might celebrate it separately from his birthday. They could explain to him periodically, perhaps yearly and in conjunction with the aforementioned, how he came to be adopted into the family. A theoretical basis for this approach is the changing understanding of such things that is possible as Piagetian (1952) development proceeds. Perhaps there is an analogous process in a family's development as well. George's "belonging" in the family needed to be approached initially through a focus upon the nature of his belonging.

Another family in which extrusion was prominent sought therapy for their adopted son when his long history of acting-out reached proportions of legal significance. (Acting-out is probably the most common manifestation of the extrusion process.) Luke's behavior included stealing from neighbors, lying, running away, and taking the family automobile. His family also had been acting out. The Gormans had adopted Luke when he was 18 months of age. He was now 13 and they had contacted the adoption agency in order to explore returning him. The same initial approach to the extrusion problem is used: Facilitate a therapeutic attachment (adoption) to the family, and confront the relevant aspect of its denial. With the acting-out family, it is important to determine as early as possible which family dynamics are being expressed by the acting-out and for which relationships the adopted child has become a scapegoat. Otherwise, the family including the adopted child is likely to act out with respect to the therapy, end the treatment, and proceed with the extrusion.

It appeared that Luke's affect came from a combination of his mother's and father's marital struggle, their struggle as parents, and the family's unresolved grief over the death of his older sister. Three or four years before Luke was adopted, his parents' marriage had gone dead, allegedly over a slapping incident. Mother had objected to father's disciplining the kids, had slapped him, and he, impulsively, had slapped her back. He stated that he knew at that time that "it could never be the same," referring to their marriage. Mother remained indignant 15 years later for having been slapped, even though she had struck first. Their love had gone underground and at the time of therapy the marital difficulties were well known to all of the children. There had been much talk of divorce and several of the children recommended it as a way to reduce the constant and repetitious bickering.

The second and third conflicts come under the category of "parental." Mother was angry for father's taking the initiative in adopting Luke, and father was angry and felt left out by mother's decision to include "natural therapy" in their second oldest daughter's cancer treatment. The fourth issue was the family's unresolved grief over the death of the oldest daughter in an automobile accident 10 years earlier. Mother had responded by withdrawing. Father's guilt was exaggerated because of his occupation as a safety officer. Luke wondered if he had "lost all of his feelings" with her death. Early interpretation of these dynamics was important in helping the family see beyond Luke's behavior; reframing his "antisocial tendency" (Winnicott, 1958) as related more to his desire to be loved than the opposite also helped.

The Gormans, although clear about the reality of Luke's adoption, showed denial regarding his ever having been a cooing baby. I suggested they read *Before You Were Three* (Harris and Levy, 1977) together and to visualize Luke at each stage of development, even those stages prior to his having joined the family.

Facing the issue of the adopted child being a "real" member of the family or not is almost always relevant. Interestingly, this is the word ("real") that is most often used. There are no easy solutions to this question. An adopted daughter in a blended family recently told me that her adoptive father was her real father because he was the only one she had ever known. We got stuck over who the real father would be should her father proceed with adopting her stepbrothers and stepsisters.

The issue is important because coming from an adoption agency *is* a different experience for both the child and the family than being delivered by the friendly stork. Frequently, family members will describe their adopted member as "just like" anyone else in the family, using the comparison to imply a difference even though the content denies it. Of course, adopted children can be real members of their families, but denial of their reality, even though well-intentioned, inhibits this possibility. I suppose "real" means biological, whereas real without quotation marks implies connections to the family's past, committedness to each other, and permanence of relationship.

The desire of parents to see their adopted children as "real" was highlighted by Mrs. Moore's memory failure regarding her not having breast-fed George. Luke's mother at the first interview described her guilt over never having loved him in the same exact way that she loved her six naturally born children. One of the keys to working with the Moores was highlighting their delusion that he was not adopted. This of necessity included seeing my own wish to blur that distinction. Connected to the latter, and definitely preceded by a great deal of affective contact with and clarity about the family as the "real" patient, I agreed to see George individually to alternate with the family interviews. (This should only be done when extrusion is a dead issue.) In addition to mirroring the reality of George's different origins, it helped with age-appropriate separation-individuation. Suggesting to Mrs. Gorman that her love for Luke would naturally be different in some way from her love for her other children was helpful in allowing her to love him for himself rather than defensively and falsely out of guilt. She had felt guilty for most of his life about this and to some extent it had kept him from becoming a real member of the family.

Related to an adopted child's real membership in the family is the issue of replacement. Is his/her belongingness to the family predicated upon replacing a lost member or upon performing some predetermined function other than being a child? Like it or not, some adopted children are replacements. George was adopted subsequent to the death of the Moore's firstborn due to prematurity. Her name was Georgia, for which George is an obvious variation. One important approach to allowing George to be George was working directly with his parents over their much unresolved grief. This can be done including the entire family, just the couple, or, as in this case, with the help of another therapist. Concrete suggestions, analogous to bringing to consciousness the details of George's adoption, included coaching the family to find out more of the details of Georgia's death and burial, and visiting her grave site.

Luke's father openly acknowledged that his interest in adopting

Luke was to save his marriage. Luke came into the family, therefore, with the predetermined function of marital therapist. This also occurs, of course, in biological families. It may be a more important issue in some adoptive families, in which an inherent possibility of confusion over the child's identity already exists. The family therapist needs to apply for the job of marital therapist with these families.

A fourth consideration in regard to adoptive families in treatment is the issue of a "genetic mistake." Families occasionally externalize difficulties with their adopted child to the child's biological parentage. "You certainly don't take after your mother or me!" Failure to address this may have to do with the therapist's own anxiety, but to do so even subtly can often undermine this defense. Just commenting paradoxically, "It must be his genes," is often enough to point out this denial of responsibility and the resistance to belongingness.

The push for autonomy during adolescence is often an important one in adoptive families. Recently, I saw in the same day three families with adopted children all 13 years of age. The issue of which family an adopted child belongs to may be relevant here. An adopted child can feel caught between his/her loyalty to those who have raised him/her and his/her loyalty to those who procreated him/her. Sexual strivings at this age may be responsible for bringing this ambivalence to the forefront. It is important in therapy to acknowledge the potential for divided loyalty, to call attention to the possibility of finding the biological parents, and in terms of the autonomy issue to clarify from which family the adopted child is attempting to separate. Both the parents and the child may have thought about finding the biological parents, but never addressed it openly. If this issue can be depolarized through a cooperative effort by the parents and child, it can help the autonomy process proceed appropriately free of elements of extrusion, rejection, and lack of gratitude, as they relate to adoptedness.

To summarize, families with adopted children often have unresolved problems related to the belongingness of the adopted child and the nature of that belonging. Perhaps coming into therapy is a way of completing the attachment process impeded by the fact of adoption and its meaning to the family. The more the therapist can help the adopted child and his/her family "belong" to each other free of mythology, the more the adopted child can be whoever he/she is and the more the family can be whoever it is.

## References

Harris, R., and Levy, E. *Before You Were Three: How You Began to Walk, Talk, Explore and Have Feelings.* New York: Delacorte Press, 1977.

Piaget, J. *The Origins of Intelligence in Children*. New York: International Universities Press, 1952.

Whitaker, C. A. A family is a four-dimensional relationship. In P. J. Guerin, Jr. (Ed.), *Family Therapy: Theory and Practice*. New York: Gardner, 1976.

Winnicott, D. W. *Through Paediatrics to Psycho-Analysis*. New York: Basic Books, 1958.

**DOUGLAS A. KRAMER, M.D.**
*Atlanta Psychiatric Clinic
& Center for Personal Growth;
Clinical Assistant Professor of Psychiatry
Emory University School of Medicine
Atlanta, GA*

# 17. Therapy with Families of Cult Members

**Question:**

In what ways can the family therapist help families of young people caught up in nontraditional "religious" and quasi-therapeutic groups, many of which are called cults?

**Discussion:**

Let me set the stage for responding to this question by presenting three very brief scenarios involving families with members who have gotten involved in "cults."

*Case 1: Edwin and Amanda Blake.* Mrs. Blake called for an appointment in a state of distress. She and her husband received a call from their son, Robert (age 19) last night asking that they send his savings and car title to him at an address that was strange to them. He told them only that he was with some new friends working on useful community projects. The parents are afraid that he has become a "Moonie" and want advice on what to do next.

*Case 2: Claire Russell.* Mrs. Russell called, somewhat hysterical. Her daughter, Dana (age 18), left yesterday to attend summer classes in Denver and phoned this morning to say that she was joining a Hare Krishna group instead.

*Case 3: Nancy and Simon Gray.* Mr. Gray called, requesting counseling for the couple with respect to their son, Jon. The youth (age 20) is/was an honor student living at home, but has recently become involved with meditation and a related group (possibly the Divine Light Mission) to the exclusion of all other activities.

That these three initial entries, based on real cases, have similarities is obvious. They are also similar to millions of others that have occurred over the past 10-15 years. In each instance, a son or daughter has suddenly disappeared from his/her usual location or activities and has turned up within days or weeks as a member of what are regarded as cults. Often, the parents are unaware of the nature of the group and may even be pleased at first that their child has made new friends, in which case the call for a therapeutic appointment may not be made for several weeks.

Any therapist dealing with the families of cult members or the young person directly involved must set aside prejudgments regarding family conflicts or youthful psychopathology in favor of facts, both legal and psychological, regarding cults. To begin with, these groups are not all identical in practice or philosophy. They do tend to use many of the same recruiting strategies, however, often relying on deception in their initial approach and playing on guilt feelings and the desire for acceptance once they have "hooked" their prospect. Members of each cult are convinced that theirs is the only path to salvation and they practice active proselytization to spread their beliefs and acquire converts. The therapist must also be aware that the youth rarely seeks cult membership, but rather that the youth's vulnerability at a given point in time, if fortuitously met by an active cult recruiter, can result in at least an initial interaction with the group. A third point of which therapists must be aware is that cult membership is protected under the First Amendment for legal adults (age 18 in most jurisdictions) so that, legally, the parents have no right to interfere with their child's choice of beliefs.

Obviously, none of this information is going to console anxious and perhaps bewildered parents who are seeking your help. *They* seek to understand the apparently irrational behavior of their child; they seek to blame someone or something, perhaps each other, for the behavior; and they seek guidance in the present predicament and for their own future behavior. In what ways can you help the Blakes, Russells, Grays, and other distraught parents?

There is an immediate need to bolster the marriage relationship if it exists, or the self-esteem of the single parent. Reassurance that errors in parenting were not necessarily the major cause of the youth's vulnerability, nor were the father's or mother's range of activities, is urgent to avert disabling feelings of guilt or the breakdown of the marriage. Family dynamics can be explored after the effects of shock are reduced.

Urge the parent(s) to keep open all lines of communication with their child. They should assure the young adult of a warm welcome at home, whether for a brief visit or a full return. They should not badger the youth with "How could you do this (to us)?" or condemnations, for these actions will only confirm the group's preaching that parents neither love nor understand him or her, and would contrast badly with the warm acceptance the youth has found within the group.

Share your knowledge of the particular cult's ideology, structure, and life-style, and explain to the parents what members feel they gain from the group. Two of the primary benefits, according to ex-cult members, are the feeling of being accepted by peers and acquisition of a constructive goal to which youths can commit themselves wholeheartedly. A third source of gratification is freedom from the burden of decision-making. It is important that the parents know enough about the group so that they can discuss the goals and beliefs intelligently with their child if given the opportunity, and also ask him/her how these can be reconciled with goals and beliefs formerly held. Again, such a discussion should be nonthreatening if it is to be effective.

Inform the parents that kidnapping of a legal adult, even their own child, is illegal. Although no parents have yet been jailed for such attempts, they have had to experience being sued by their children when the kidnapping and/or deprogramming failed. They have been confronted with warrants for their arrest, trials, and unpleasant publicity. Put the parents in touch with a cult crisis center (available in several large cities), ex-cult members, or a parent support network. These resource agents can share their knowledge of the group and legal strategies for trying to recover the youth, and aid the parents through what may be years of hoping and waiting for a happy reunion.

If the parents continue to come for therapy, begin to explore the family dynamics and to plan for changes that will improve the family relationships when the youth returns. The literature suggests that one cause of vulnerability is a weak or nonexistent father-child relationship (Schwartz and Kaslow, 1979). If the youth has previously had only vague views to "fight" instead of clear values, he/she often welcomes the authority figure who leads the cult members in a definite direction. Another cause of vulnerability is a lack of self-direction, often derived from being over-directed and/or overprotected by parents. In some cases, the youth may be neurotic, addicted, or pre-psychotic, although these are less common states. Given one or more of these conditions, a precipitating event such as a major change in life pattern (entering college, traveling alone with little goal-orientation) or a depressing event (break-up of a romance, failing an exam), and the approach by an astute cult recruiter, almost any youth can be temporarily attracted by the promise of a positive change. A more lasting involvement follows sophisticated use of behavior modification techniques by cult members and leaders. As part of therapy, parents should come to understand these dynamics and to begin to alter their behaviors toward each other and their child.

Encourage the parents to use and share this information with any younger children they have. Attempts by cult members to recruit siblings is a frequent occurrence, and education is an important prevention strategy.

Help the parents to plan for any visit by the cult member. If possible, they should have present members of the extended family as well as the youth's friends in order to form a network of warmth, acceptance, and belonging that parallels the one in the cult. Alternative goal commitments to worthy causes, a common need in the idealism of late adolescence, should be explored beforehand so that they can be suggested at the time of the visit. An ex-member of the particular group, if available, might also be present. Tactful confrontation by such a veteran, who knows the cult's jargon, tactics, and ideology, may at least arouse questions in the youth's mind that will lead to eventual voluntary departure from the movement.

Also as part of therapy, many issues can be probed that constitute part of long-term planning. How can the parents help the youth overcome his/her guilt feelings? There will often be such feelings both in relation to the youth's treatment of parents while a cult member and in relation to leaving behind close friends within the cult. How much direction should the parents offer in terms of college or career-planning? Are there changes in the immediate or extended family (marriage, divorce, death) to which the youth will need to adapt—and how? The two major goals of the reentry-readjustment period are to restore or strengthen the youth's ability to think independently and to rehabilitate the youth socially (Singer, 1979). The more that these matters can be brought to the surface and dealt with, the smoother the youth's return to the family and community will be.

In summary, the role of the family therapist in these cases must be one of support first, and then of helping the parent(s) to prepare for the eventual return of their child. Guiding the family through a truly traumatic series of emotional responses—anger, guilt, shame, anxiety, and wistful hope—cannot and should not be done by a therapist who is uninformed about the cults, for the situation is not a typical clinical one. It is advisable for therapists in general to have some feeling for the complexities of cult involvement for one never knows when a Blake, a Russell, or a Gray will call.

## References

Cults and the family. *Marriage & Family Review*, 1982, *4* (3-4).
Schwartz, L. L., and Kaslow, F. W. Religious cults, the individual, and the family. *Journal of Marital and Family Therapy*, 1979, *5* (2), 15-26.
Singer, M. T. Coming out of the cults. *Psychology Today*, 1979, *12* (8), 72-82.

**LITA LINZER SCHWARTZ, Ph.D.**
*Professor of Educational Psychology*
*Pennsylvania State University—Ogontz Campus*
*Abington, PA*

# 18. Predictable Tasks in Therapy with Families of Handicapped Persons

## Question:

My work involves seeing families in which a family member has just been diagnosed as having a handicapping condition or disability. How can I be most useful to the family at this time? Are there predictable kinds of problems I should address and are there predictable forms of family dysfunction I should anticipate and seek to prevent?

## Discussion:

Families with a handicapped person face predictable problems in a number of areas. One set of problems involves making sense of the handicapping condition. While the presence of a handicapping condition in a family member suggests that other family members should not expect that the handicapped person act or develop "normally," it is difficult for family members to know what they *should* expect. Often, it is not possible to diagnose the handicapping condition or to know its etiology; the family is told that a handicapping condition exists and the degree to which it can be overcome cannot be specified. Or, in the more fortunate case when diagnosis is possible, knowledge as to prognosis is often scant. In addition, when statements about prognosis are possible, they are most often based upon data gathered from the study of institutionalized handicapped persons who did not receive what would currently be considered either sufficiently intensive or appropriate intervention (Hobbs, 1975). Or, they are optimistic projections based upon the presumed long-term effects of early intervention efforts even though there are no data related to the long-term results of such programs.

In addition to the problem of obtaining accurate information regarding prognosis for the handicapping condition, there are a number of problems involved in obtaining appropriate services (Gorham et al.,

1975). In many communities, a number of needed services are not available. Secondly, if they are available, the agency that makes the diagnosis may not be aware of them and thus will not inform family members of the need for them. Third, when they are available, they are likely to be available in a fragmented form, with services parceled out among a number of agencies, which have their own evaluation procedures, eligibility criteria, and preferred mode of service delivery. Thus, family members (almost always mothers) must become expert on how to deal with service systems and must devote large amounts of energy and time just to line up appropriate services. Even when found, these services must be paid for and may consume a large part of the family's income.

The difficulty in locating and obtaining appropriate services will be an ongoing reality problem for the family, since the needs of handicapped persons of different ages and stages of development require different services which are often provided by different agencies. So it is possible, for example, for a family to learn how to deal with the set of agencies that provide services for preschool-aged children, only to have to master the workings of an entirely new set of agencies when the handicapped child is of school age.

Another ongoing reality problem for the family will be how to use its resources so as to meet the needs of the handicapped child *and* of other family members. All too typically, the family organizes around the handicapped individual, as if his or her needs are the only needs that the family must respond to. It is all too common for the needs of siblings to be ignored unless they have problems in school or somehow come to a clinician's attention, and it is almost typical for the needs of spouses to be ignored or played out through concern for the handicapped child. Thus, for example, several studies have found that parents of handicapped children rarely go out without the handicapped child and almost never take vacations. Contributing to the likelihood of the family organizing around the handicapped person is the difficulty families encounter in obtaining baby-sitters or other forms of respite care. This difficulty has two unfortunate effects, keeping parents from having time of their own separate from the child, and maintaining the family's isolation from the world outside the household.

The reality problems encountered by families are exacerbated by the fact that handicapping conditions are stigmas. Families with a handicapped member live in a society in which it is better not to be handicapped. Family members, having grown up in this society, are likely to share the common view of the handicapping condition, thus becoming ashamed of the handicapped person and often, because stigmas are considered contaminating, of themselves. It is common for parents of a newly diagnosed handicapped child to cut off contact with their social network, becoming increasingly isolated (Berger and Fowlkes, 1980; Kearns, 1978). This isolation increases the family's focus on the handicapped child, making it more likely that the child will become what Bowen (1978) terms a "special" child, a target for parental anxiety and projection. Further, cutting-off from the social network of extended family, friends, and neighbors, sets up a feedback loop in which initial isolation leads to further isolation as the family finds it harder and harder to explain the handicapping condition to the network and to explain why the family has cut itself off from the network. In the extreme case, the family members may cease to deal with persons who are not connected with the handicapped child, limiting their contact to service providers and other parents of handicapped children.

As the above discussion should indicate, the issues confronting families with a handicapped child are extremely complex. The content of family intervention, therefore, will vary with the particular issues confronting the family at that time, e.g., whether the family needs to figure out what the handicapping condition is going to require in terms of services and family resources, or whether the family is dealing with an adult who will no longer be served by the school system but is, at present, unable to live independently. However, there are some predictable family issues to which attention must be paid.

The first task is to prevent the family from organizing itself around the fact of having a handicapped person in the family, to stop the family from freezing at the point in time when the handicap was labeled so that, as much as possible, family members can continue to grow and develop (Hollister, 1978). The danger is that the handicap will become the defining characteristic of the disabled person in his or her own eyes, and in the eyes of the family. Kearns (1978), for example, in a study of families with a retarded person who ranged in age from two years to over 40 years, noted that the parents spoke of the retarded person as if s/he was a young child and described the recognition of the child's retardation as the last major event in the family's life. Families will be more likely to freeze in time and to define the disabled person by his/her handicap if the family cuts itself off from its social network. So, one of the first tasks of family intervention is for the therapist to help family members maintain contact with the members of their social network. This may involve the use of network meetings in which the entire network is brought together to discuss the issues the family is facing (Berger and Fowlkes, 1980), or it may involve sending parents out to talk with their own parents or with other relatives about how members of the family dealt with similar traumatic incidents (Hollister, 1978). The aims of interventions directed at network members at this time are to prevent cutoffs, and to help the nuclear family view the handicap as one more problem similar to other problems which family members have overcome, rather than as a unique, catastrophic event which can only freeze the family in time.

The other major task facing the family therapist is to prevent the development or continuation of dysfunctional forms of family organization. With one additional nuance, families with handicapped members present all the usual forms of disorganization—cross-generational coalitions, hierarchical conflicts between parents and grandparents, disagreements between members of the executive subsystem, and so on (Foster and Berger, 1979). The nuance is that services for handicapped individuals, particularly handicapped children, are organized in such a way that the burden of obtaining services for the handicapped individual falls almost totally on mothers. Families with handicapped children, therefore, are prone to develop a type of organization in which mothers are extremely enmeshed with the handicapped child and central to him or her, while fathers are peripheral. The type of family organization I am describing is, of course, one of the typical forms of family organization encountered in child guidance settings (e.g., Minuchin, 1974), and the usual structural and strategic interventions can be used to help families change to more flexible and functional forms of organization (Foster and Berger, 1979; Foster, Berger and McLean, 1981). Network meetings may also be useful here to highlight the stress placed upon the mother and to arrive at other divisions of labor that do not reinforce the pattern of mother proximate to the handicapped child and father distant (Berger and Fowlkes, 1980).

I have noted above that the issues facing families with a handicapped member are many and are complexly interrelated. The task of the family therapist working with such families is complex, also, for the therapist is required to play a number of roles. Initially, family members may need patience, persistence, and support so that they can hear the information about the handicapping condition. The therapist may need to coach family members in how to translate this information so it can be understood by siblings; s/he may have to further the translation process by setting up enactments (Minuchin, 1974) in which the adults in the family talk with the children in the family about the handicapping condition or in which children talk with the handicapped person about the handicap. Similarly, the therapist may need to coach family members in talking with network members about the effects of the handicap on the family and, if network meetings are held, the therapist will direct them so that they serve as a ritual unfreezing of the family and as a means through which support is offered to family members in a way they can use.

The therapist has important liaison roles to play as well. S/he may serve as a convenor of the network of service people involved with the family so that services can be coordinated. Or, s/he may serve as an information clearinghouse for the family, gathering information from the different agencies and helping the family piece it together. Often, in order to gain acceptance from particular agencies, the therapist may consult with agency staff, helping them learn how they can help the family. Or, the therapist may approach other agencies such as churches currently uninvolved with the family in the hope of making them more receptive to the family's needs. At times, the therapist will serve as an advocate, training family members in how to deal with service systems—for example, how to ask questions until they are answered to the family's satisfaction, how to persist in requesting services family members think are needed. To support family competence, the therapist will make family members aware of the support available through groups of parents of the handicapped so that family members can use this support if they wish or may join such groups to engage in political action for the needs of handicapped persons.

Lastly, the therapist working with families of handicapped individuals has the predictable job of orchestrating his or her work with the family so that the crucial reality questions are dealt with while dysfunctional family structures are not supported.

## References

Berger, M., & Fowlkes, M. The family intervention project: A family network approach to early intervention. *Young Children*, 1980, *35*, 22-32.

Bowen, M. *Family Therapy in Clinical Practice*. New York: Aronson, 1978.

Foster, M., and Berger, M. Structural family therapy: Applications in programs for preschool handicapped children. *Journal of the Division of Early Childhood*, 1979, *1*, 52-58.

Foster, M., Berger, M. and McLean, M. Rethinking a good idea: Parent involvement in early intervention. *Topics in Early Childhood Special Education*, 1981, *1*, 3, 55-66.

Gorham, K., Des Jardins, C., Page, R., Pettis, E., and Scheiber, B. Effect on parents. In N. Hobbs (Ed.) *Issues in the Classification of Children*. Volume 2. San Francisco: Jossey-Bass, 1975.

Hobbs, N. (Ed.) *Issues in the Classification of Children*. Volumes 1 & 2. San Francisco: Jossey-Bass, 1975.

Hollister, M. Families who experience the loss of a child. In R. Sager (Ed.) *Georgetown Family Symposia*. Volume III (1975-1976). Washington: Georgetown Family Center, 1978.

Kearns, D. *Social networks of parents of the mentally retarded: Characteristics and influences on family functioning.* Master's thesis, Department of Psychology, Wichita State University, Kansas, 1978.

Minuchin, S. *Families and Family Therapy.* Cambridge: Harvard University Press, 1974.

**MICHAEL BERGER, Ph.D.**
*Deputy Director*
*Atlanta Institute for Family Studies;*
*Department of Psychology*
*Georgia State University*
*Atlanta, GA*

# 19. Brief Therapy with Nonfinishers

**Question:**

A number of young adults come into therapy because they are unable to complete academic work, especially term papers and . doctoral dissertations. This problem functions to impede these individuals from making age-appropriate changes in their lives, especially from adolescent in school to employed young adult, and concurrent changes in their relationships. What are some typical features of the family context of which these individuals are a part? How does this problem function in the family? What is an appropriate treatment approach for this problem?

**Discussion:**

In my experience, the family functioning of nonfinishers is basically similar. Often they are from academically achievement-oriented families. They are frequently put into the position of completing or replicating the career or unfulfilled career aspirations of a parent, e.g., "I never had the chance, but it's a great opportunity for you." At the same time, this symptom, like any other, functions to prevent a change in the individual life cycle and family system. By the inability to complete assignments, nonfinishers legitimate failure to act out career expectations and create a tactic in current marital conflict.

In my experience brief structural therapy is an effective technique, using relabeling and paradox to solve the problem without insight or massive change in family functioning. A simple strategy for change which I have found to be effective is to prescribe the symptom, e.g., "(purposefully) waste time" and at the same time alter the pattern of interaction minimally so that the symptom is less functional and there is some reduction in the conflict, perhaps getting the client and his or her spouse to cooperate in some interaction with the often over-involved parent of the nonfinisher. If there is a separation issue involved, I generally attempt to get the client to maintain the relationship but alter the contingencies, e.g., "Call your mother once a week for a chat." This can be seen in the following case summary.

John T. came into therapy because of his inability to complete his doctoral dissertation. He was the favorite child of his mother with whom he maintained a conflictual relationship. His father, a minister who traveled frequently during John's childhood, died when John was starting college. His mother constantly urged John to finish his degree, on which he had in his estimation only a few weeks' work and which he had been unable to complete for months. He had been married for eight years. The marital relationship was conflictual partly because of his wife's anger at giving up her graduate work so that John could get his degree. At the same time, he would not agree to have a baby because he did not have good job prospects without his degree. He was angry at her criticism of his work.

The problem was acted out in a similar fashion each day. John would go to the library in the morning, immediately become bored and then waste time, feel guilty about it, go home, and argue with his wife about how he had spent his day. Often this resulted in conflict and his leaving the house for a few hours to drink beer with friends at a local tavern, exacerbating the conflict on his return.

In the brief treatment of this problem, John was seen individually after meeting with the couple for two sessions for diagnostic purposes. A simple paradox was prescribed. John was asked to determine how much time he was capable of wasting each day. He said as much as was available, but we negotiated that he waste one hour a day. He was told that as soon as he arrived in the library he must go and read "trashy" magazines for an hour—and what he read must have absolutely nothing to do with his dissertation. After this he should go back to his study carrel, follow his usual routine, and leave at his regular time and no later. He was then to go home and tell his wife how much he had accomplished. Once a week he and his wife were told to call John's mother to "maintain contact." He was only able to maintain this prescription for three or four days and then began to work more steadily on his dissertation and completed the work.

In another case with the problem of an inability to complete an article for publication, an obsessive client who was extremely food-oriented was asked if he was willing to try a "cheap trick" to solve his problem. He agreed. The paradox was that he was to follow his usual routine, except that he had to waste the first hour and, if still not satisfied with his productivity, must then spend his lunch hour writing in detail how he had wasted the morning. He was also assigned the task of leaving at least one mistake in his final draft. He was also told to report progress to his wife and to mutually initiate contact with his parents.

These illustrations demonstrate that the not uncommon problem of academic "writer's block" can often be understood meaningfully in developmental terms and treated effectively with very cost-effective methods.

**JOHN SCHWARTZMAN, Ph.D.**
*Assistant Professor of Clinical Psychiatry*
*Center for Family Studies/*
*Family Institute of Chicago*
*Northwestern University Medical School*
*Chicago, IL*

# PART C

## *Treatment Planning and Family Boundaries*

# 20. Managing Secrets in Family and Marital Therapy

**Question:**

The introduction of secrets into family and marital treatment can raise a host of questions for the therapist. If one family member offers to share a secret "privately" with the therapist, should the therapist accept this offer? If it is revealed, what are the risks involved in the therapist's keeping or divulging the secret? Is it possible to continue treatment without revealing the secret? What if revealing it might drive the family or couple from treatment or precipitate a potentially dangerous crisis? Is it fair for the therapist to keep the secret? Is it fair to insist that it be revealed? If it is to be revealed, whose job is it—the one(s) who informed the therapist or the therapist him/herself?

**Discussion:**

In order to answer these questions, we need to define family secrets and to consider theoretical, ethical, and practical issues associated with them. Family secrets involve highly relevant information which is either withheld or differentially shared between or among people. Common examples of such secrets in treatment include: extramarital affairs, the true parentage of adopted children, and incest. In certain cases, a daughter's being sent away from the home to deliver and give up an illegitimate child or the existence in another town of one parent's children from a previous relationship might constitute a family secret.

The therapist must be able to recognize family secrets before s/he can manage them in treatment. While in many cases, the existence of a secret as such is perfectly clear to the secret-holder, this is not always the case. The confusion which surrounds secrets may sometimes make it difficult to recognize the secret as such, both for the therapist and the secret-holder. A typical remark might be, "Well, I always knew this was something I shouldn't talk about and I didn't really know whether my brother knew or not, but I never really thought of it as a secret before." With this type of situation in mind, the following rule of thumb is suggested, only partly facetiously, as an aid in identifying family secrets. The therapist should immediately consider the possible existence of secrets *anytime the word "know" needs to be used more than once in a sentence* (Karpel, 1980). For example, "I know but she doesn't know," or "I don't know whether he knows."

The therapist's readiness to recognize secrets does not mean, however, that what first appears to be a secret is necessarily just that. The most common categories of information which are often confused with secrets are *private* information and *trivial* information and, in both cases, the distinctions pivot on the phrase "highly relevant" in the definition given earlier.

The distinction between secrecy and mere privacy depends on the relevance of the information for the person who is unaware of it. The more relevant the information for the life of the unaware, the less justification there is for considering it simply a private matter for the secret-holder and the more the unaware is entitled to know it. A current secret extramarital affair, for example, is in most cases highly relevant to the other spouse since it involves issues of trust and deception. A traumatic episode in a parent's childhood, however, reasonably well resolved, with no apparent significant effects on his or her children, can more realistically be considered private. The parent may decide to share this material with the growing or grown child someday but is less likely to feel it is owed to the child by virtue of its implications for him/her.

This view derives from a recognition of the importance of fair give-and-take in relationships as essential for mutual trust (Boszormenyi-Nagy and Krasner, 1980). It is expressed in the previously unaware person's outrage when, belatedly informed of the secret, s/he insists, "I had a right to know. It was my life." This issue of relevance, of the unaware's entitlement to know information which may have a major bearing on his or her life, lies at the heart of all therapeutic considerations concerning secrets. Secrets are important precisely because they are so deeply connected with fairness, trust and, trustworthiness, first of all within the family or marriage and secondarily in the therapeutic relationship. If not for this, secrets would be merely an exotic communicational phenomena and something of a nuisance in treatment.

Secret-holders often counter the issue of relevance with that of protection—typically, "What he doesn't know won't hurt him." All that can be said here is that, in many cases of secrets, it is really more the secret-holder or some other person who is being protected and that this decision about what's best for the unaware is necessarily being made without his or her input.

In summary, we are not concerned here with information which is of a private nature; nor are we concerned with unshared but essentially trivial information. For example, "Mother told me that she's angry at sis for not doing her chores but told me not to tell sis." This information is, in a strict sense, secret but it is not highly relevant. Finally, we are not concerned with "shared" family secrets in which all members involved in treatment know the secret and only those outside the family do not.

The problems created by family secrets in treatment involve those cases in which: 1) one or more family members are unaware of the secret; 2) the information is relevant and nontrivial for the unaware; and 3) the therapist is informed of a secret but prevented from discussing it with the unaware. How the therapist chooses to manage these situations will depend in part on the anticipated consequences of allowing such secrets in treatment. These consequences generally mirror those which develop around the secret within the family and simply reflect the inclusion of the therapist into these already existing patterns. When the therapist is informed of a secret and agrees not to divulge it to the unaware, the following are possible consequences in treatment.

In terms of *information*, the therapist is given important information which, however, s/he is unable to use openly. Thus, s/he is involved in the web of deception and distortion and may find it difficult, if not impossible, to operate effectively in the interests of the family. *Emotionally*, the therapist becomes susceptible to many of the feelings that permeate the relationships around the secret. S/he may feel guilty for deceiving the unaware, resentful of the secret-holder for having revealed the secret, anxious about the complications developing in the case, and powerless to do anything about them. The catastrophic fears often associated with the thought of disclosing the secret (divorce, suicide, heart attack, etc.) are especially "contagious" to the therapist.

*Relationally*, the therapist inevitably enters into a secret alliance with the secret-holder by virtue of the secret they now share. S/he is thereby somewhat estranged from the unaware and the potential resources in their therapeutic relationship are thus diminished. In terms of *power dynamics*, the therapist is trapped into colluding in the "one-up" status of the secret-holder over the unaware. *Ethically*, by colluding with the secret-holder to deceive the unaware, the therapist endangers the unaware's ability to trust him or her. This runs a risk of undermining the enabling conditions of treatment. Finally, at a *practical* level, the therapist runs the risk of an unanticipated and destructive disclosure of the secret by the very person who has sworn the therapist to silence. This gives the secret-holder the power to undermine the unaware's trust in the therapist and, in some cases, to sabotage treatment altogether.

Faced with these risky complications, it is desirable for the therapist to avoid being placed or remaining in this position. This is sometimes difficult since the therapist's need for information which may have significant bearing on the case can easily conflict with his/her desire to avoid the risks of these disclosures. The optimal *therapeutic stance*, therefore, is one in which the therapist tries to balance the need to know against the risks of keeping secrets in a way that works for the best interests of all family members. When secrets are shared, s/he considers the relevance of the secret for the unaware, trying as much as possible to see this from his or her viewpoint. Finally, s/he helps the secret-holder consider the timing, circumstances, and consequences of disclosing the secret for all family members in an effort to minimize possibly destructive outcomes.

The therapist, in this way, acts as a *trustee* of the family's secrets and is mindful of his/her responsibility to all family members. The therapist's effort to embody this stance is, in the long run, more important than the particular decisions s/he makes concerning the secret in a particular case. It is also the best guarantee of the wisdom and effectiveness of those decisions.

The *application* of this stance depends, first of all, on whether or not the secret has already been shared with the therapist or simply alluded to without actual disclosure. The latter situation allows the therapist to employ a *preventive approach*; the former requires a *reparative approach*. A general preventive approach involves discussing the dangers and problems posed by special confidences in relational therapies and asking the individual, couple, or family members how they would like the therapist to handle this. It can be made clear, if they sanction such confidences, that this arrangement may prove unworkable at some point.

Once the therapist takes this position, any of the possible outcomes are virtually guaranteed to be more benign. It may prompt the person to agree to open disclosure; or, the therapist may find that the "secret" is really more in the realm of the private. If treatment cannot proceed without the secret being revealed, the therapist can say so. The members will have been forewarned of this and may be more able to tolerate discussion. If they are not and the therapy terminates, they have at least had the experience of a trustworthy relationship.

This approach works most smoothly when the first hints of the secret and the discussion which follows take place with all involved members present. However, a family member may allude to the secret in a private meeting with the therapist. If so, the therapist's approach can be essentially the same except that if the secret-holder opts for sanctioning secrecy, the therapist must insist that at least this be discussed with the unaware and agreed to by him/her before the therapist can proceed.

The only exception to this stance is one in which the therapist feels s/he cannot afford not to know the secret. An example might involve a case in which the therapist felt there was a high risk of suicide, with the secret possibly having a direct bearing on this. In these cases, the therapist may go along with the secret-holder temporarily or even press for the information to be revealed to the therapist. In this way, s/he stands a better chance of successfully managing a potentially lethal crisis and being able to address less urgent issues later in treatment.

If the secret-holder simply discloses the secret to the therapist without warning, the therapist must use a reparative strategy. Essentially, this involves assessing the relevance of the information for the unaware and, if it appears highly relevant, working out the best timing and circumstances for the secret-holder to disclose it to the unaware. The therapist insists, for ethical and practical reasons, that the secret be shared, but can be flexible concerning the best circumstances and timing for disclosure. The specific decisions reached on these factors will be designed to make it less difficult for the secret-holder to open up and to minimize possibly destructive outcomes.

For example, the therapist can offer to be present in a session to help the secret-holder with this task; or s/he can respect the latter's desire to do so in private with the unaware. S/he may offer extra sessions to help the secret-holder prepare for disclosing the secret. These sessions would be designed to support the secret-holder's courage and conviction that this is necessary and would help to anticipate and thereby minimize destructive outcomes.

If, in these cases, the secret-holder adamantly refuses to reveal the secret and continues to forbid the therapist to do so, the therapist may well feel that s/he cannot, ethically and practically, continue with the case. The client's refusal to consider ever disclosing the secret rules out more flexible responses from the therapist. Again, there may be exceptions to this rule, as in the case of potential crises or, perhaps, a circumscribed symptomatic problem expressed by a child which appears responsive to treatment without opening a possibly unrelated marital secret.

Finally, it should be made clear that all of these approaches rule out the theoretical option of the therapist's forcing a disclosure of the secret him/herself. If the secret-holder is unwilling or unable to face the consequences of disclosing the secret, the therapist cannot take responsibility for forcing the situation because all indicators are that the necessary resources for minimizing destructive consequences would be insufficient. The therapist can encourage (literally, give courage to) family members to face secrets. S/he cannot do it for them.

## References

Boszormenyi-Nagy, I. and Krasner, B. Trust-based therapy: A contextual approach. *American Journal of Psychiatry*, 1980, *137*, 767-775.

Karpel, M. Family secrets: I. Conceptual and ethical issues in the relational context. II. Ethical and practical considerations in therapeutic management. *Family Process*, 1980, *19*, 295-306.

**MARK A. KARPEL, Ph.D.**
*Private Practice and*
*Consultants in Family Therapy*
*Northampton, MA*

# 21. Persistent Jealousy Following the Termination of an Affair: A Strategic Approach

**Question:**

As a strategic family therapist, I find a spouse's persistent jealousy and distrust of the spouse who has apparently terminated an affair particularly difficult to treat. Although both partners voice a desire to manage the jealous behavior, the "green-eyed monster" rears its ugly head and devours hope for and progress toward resolution. I have tracked the sequence of the jealous behavior, gathered data on the attempted solutions, and have attempted to interrupt the sequence with substituting behaviors. When these efforts fail, I try paradoxical interventions but the distrust and withdrawal persist, despite my prescribing and predicting these behaviors. I have eventually abandoned the conjoint effort and worked with the jealous person on self-esteem issues. This effort becomes time-consuming, promotes the idea of jealousy as simply an individual problem, and is usually ineffective. Usually the therapy ends with the goals of jealous management unmet, and me and the couple exhausted. Do you have some suggestions in treating this particular problem?

**Discussion:**

Since my earlier work (Teismann, 1979), experience has helped me consider additional issues and procedures in the strategic treatment of jealous behavior. My answer assumes your assessment has eliminated neurophysiological complications and the potential for physical violence. The possibility of these factors being present would indicate a medical referral or crisis intervention, respectively, prior to formal treatment.

Some strategic family therapists, in their effort to efficiently engineer systemic change, bypass developing firm and trusting therapeutic alliances, especially with couples presenting persistent and escalating conflicts. First, find something you can appreciate about each partner. Try to understand the couple's paradox, that is, their desire to change and their fear of changing. Although important with all clients, this task seems especially important with a "gruesome twosome" embroiled in jealous conflict where distrust, disengagement, and discouragement abound. A collaborative team or *therapeutic triangle* will compete with the distrust inherent in a jealous triangle. Trust and confidence in the therapist becomes the prototypical experience for the couple to again trust in one another. The therapeutic triangle accents support, empathy, and structural stability and counters the unpredictable volatility. In addition to joining the couple, bring a respectful and serious playfulness to the dead serious and constricted struggling of the couple. As children, we solved problems with play and imagination, and these abilities are still available to us as adults and professionals. To me, imaginative play is the essence of enriched human contact, cooperative problem-solving, and hope.

Second, consider to what degree the affair has ended. Often the partner who has had the affair (AP) continues to be primarily bonded to the lover sexually and/or emotionally. Affairs are often extremely difficult to end when they are of extended duration and when the AP has been forced to end it. Given the premise that trust is founded on and supported by the structure of monogamous exclusivity, a contract for jealous management and marital reconstruction while an affair continues is contraindicated. Often the jealous person's (JP) distrusting behavior is good reality-testing, not paranoia, and efforts to manage it become absurd. A significant and continuing bond between the AP and the lover has occurred often enough for me to assume that the affair is *not* terminated, unless given clear indication that it has before contracting for marital therapy. I try to discover the degree of bonding by empathically joining the AP in an individual session on how difficult it is to terminate the affair. For instance, I might say, "Mary, it is probably painful for you to say 'good-bye' to Mike. You may feel this pain of being apart acutely and you may want to see Mike again. I would not be surprised if you continue to see him even now and this makes it difficult for you to consider working with John on your marriage." This tack generally surfaces the degree of bonding and helps me to know with what I am working. When the attachment remains strong, I suggest that the couple contract for a number of individual and conjoint *assessment* sessions *prior* to any formal treatment intervention of the jealousy.

Third, consider how your problem is formulated (Teismann, 1981). "Jealous behavior" tends to be a poorly framed problem since it accents individual versus systemic operations. Help the couple move from conceptualizing the affair and the jealous behaviors as their problem to their *attempted solutions* of a previous problem. By accomplishing this temporal-conceptual shift, the couple moves from the current and volatile cycle of blaming, defending, and withdrawing to a more workable and rational perspective of the cyclic events of a mutually shared problem. Usually this mutually shared problem involves aborted efforts at intimacy.

For example, with one couple presenting a persistent jealous problem, I said, "You have both made a big step by coming today. Despite your pain you both want to deal with your marriage and this involves facing facts. You are realizing that your marriage has been in serious trouble for some time and that you have both used desperate and dangerous means to manage the pain from this trouble. These means have only made things worse. You could both justify your affair and your jealous behavior, but you are realizing they mask the real pain of longing for an elusive intimacy. You have used the affair and the jealousy as analgesic drugs which mask your real problem, that is, your stubborn refusal to share your needs for excitement, your joys, your sadnesses, your dreams, and your passion with one another. Your jealousy and your affair are avoidances, faulty solutions, and you have become addicted to their use. I suggest that you begin immediately to examine how it has come to be that you have stubbornly refused to share being intimate." After framing the couple's problem as a mutual avoidance of intimate behavior, track out the cyclic events surrounding this previous problem in which *both* partners mutually shared and which they can cooperatively attack.

During the tracking of many intimacy-avoiding cycles, I have noticed a high incidence of unshared and unresolved losses, including deaths, sudden and irreversible physical disabilities, job loss, and children leaving home, followed by the affair. The grief was unshared and unresolved for these couples. The affairs and the jealousy seemed to be attempts to make contact with a lover and conflictually with one another. These couples talked about how difficult it was to share and request comfort at the time of the tragedy, leading to an estranged disengagement. When this unresolved and unshared grief is present, the therapist can further the problem-formulation statement to include the avoidance of mutual grief as intimate partners. Further, this information helps the couple clarify and differentiate the grief related to the affair and the grief related to loss.

Strategic family therapy involves accepting the problem that is given and framing it into a workable reality. Often the framing or formulating of the problem is insufficient. What often happens is the following: When the couple fails to respond to straightforward interventions built on a poorly formulated problem, some therapists label the family as "resisting" and then use a heavy paradoxical intervention which often likewise fails. This is especially true when the therapist has learned techniques without developing strong assessment skills, especially problem formulation. Often paradoxical interventions are used when the therapist is frustrated with the family. When the family recognizes this frustration, its members will withdraw trust and confidence in the therapist. This is often devastating for the therapy of jealous conflict which requires utmost trust in the therapist. A systemic understanding of "resistance" must involve not only the family's, but also the therapist's, resistance. It may be that the concept of resistance has been developed by therapists to explain their own ineffective treatment procedures. It may also be that the reason why paradoxical interventions are successful is because the therapist has developed a strong therapeutic alliance and formulated the problem well.

Fourth, I begin treatment typically by encouraging the AP to *unilaterally* begin the change process with my promised support. I support the JP by saying that it is enough just to contend with the leftover jealous feelings and that since the AP broke the contract the AP should begin to take the risk of initially working on the marriage's reconstruction. One method of doing this is through "contentless imagery." With both partners present I have the AP silently imagine behaviors that the AP could perform that would lead to intimate outcomes with the JP. Next, the AP imagines how the JP could "unwillingly" undermine the AP's efforts, and visualizes the conflict that might ensue. Next, the AP pictures specific behaviors that would "transcend" the imagined conflict and lead to intimacy. Finally, the AP is asked to commit him/herself to achieving a specific number of intimate outcomes, at least one of which is to be followed by a typical conflict. Although directed to the AP, the JP typically joins the imagery experience. One advantage of the "contentless" approach is that it eliminates the objection that "you are only doing what the therapist told you to do." I spend a few minutes individually with the AP each week (and sometimes with the JP) reviewing the successes and problems of the task and conjointly repeating the contentless imagery with the new information in mind. Another advantage of this approach is that it produces mystery, a needed ingredient in intimacy. Eventually, the imagery exercise is incorporated into the lives of the couple, often by their taking a few minutes together and silently imagining ways of effecting intimate outcomes.

Having the AP unilaterally begin the change process has a subtle and important rationale. In a monogamous relationship, an affair, even when understood in its systemic context, remains a broken contract. The reestablishment of trust requires the JP's forgiveness and the AP's atonement, although eventually both partners must forgive and atone since both participated in the alienation process. Initially, it seems, the JP needs to experience the AP's efforts to heal the relationship and the AP needs an opportunity to effectively do so. This experience provides a basis for the JP's forgiveness and renewal of trust and a means for the AP to assuage moral guilt.

Punishing the AP, especially when the JP is the punisher, is clearly counterproductive. It reinforces the idea of the AP's disloyalty and the JP's righteousness. More importantly, punishment increases the AP's potential to renew the affair. As one client aptly put it, "Hell, I might as well go back to Jane; I'm being punished for it anyway!" When the therapist encourages and directs the AP's initial efforts at change, the JP can relinquish the punishing role and refocus efforts on developing intimate behavior more easily.

Another reason for unilaterally working with the AP initially is that often the JP is simply unable to control the jealous reaction, despite understanding it as an avoidance of intimate behavior. The triggers for the jealous reaction are ubiquitous and entrenched. It is easier for the AP to interrupt the reactions and establish new sequences than it is for the JP to control them, despite the therapist's best efforts to build self-esteem. The harder the JP tries to control the jealous reaction, the more the JP is reminded of the problem, and the more the triggering effect becomes entrenched. This seems to be the classic case of the harder one tries, the worse it gets.

If the JP is insistent on improving the intimacy in the relationship, I reemphasize the need for the JP's restraint at changing and then suggest *charting* all the opportunities the JP can create and gracefully receive intimacy, but not to act on them, since the action might be contaminated with inadvertent sabotage of the AP's efforts. The paradoxical reaction may result, but the restraint is based on the rationale given above.

This discussion has not included consideration of severely dysfunctioning systems where jealousy is the presenting problem. The couples interact in intense, survival-like ways reflective of the pseudo-complementary, pseudo-symmetrical pattern discussed by Selvini Palazzoli et al. (1978). Ironically, an actual affair is often lacking, but the perceived threat and extreme sense of abandonment and rejection are strong. These couples require an additional discussion of their dynamics and modification of specific treatment procedures not presented in this discussion.

## References

Selvini Palazzoli, M., Boscolo, L., Cecchin, G., and Prata, G., *Paradox and Counterparadox*. New York: Aronson, 1978.

Teismann, M. Jealousy: Systematic, problem-solving therapy with couples. *Family Process*, 1979, *18*, 151-160.

Teismann, M. Dysfunctional families and the homeostatic cycle: Assessment procedures. In L. Wolberg and M. Aronson (Eds.), *Group and Family Therapy 1981*. New York: Brunner/Mazel, 1981.

**MARK W. TEISMANN, Ph.D.**
*Associate Professor and
Director, Specialization in Marital and Family Therapy
Northern Illinois University
DeKalb, IL*

# 22. Dealing with Sexual Secrets in Conjoint Therapy

## Question:

The dilemma of how to deal with secrets in conjoint therapy has long been an issue for family therapists. The popular belief is that secrets "bind" the therapist and force him or her to collude with one person in the family. The partner often feels that disclosure of sexual behavior, having to do with infidelity, homosexuality, childhood experiences, or fantasies, is threatening or shameful. Should the therapist avoid hearing such secrets? Cannot, in fact, the therapist be better equipped to help couples resolve their relationships if s/he knows their secrets?

## Discussion:

I have never felt "bound" by a confidence disclosed during therapy and often find myself freed by learning a patient's secrets. The disclosure inevitably leads to finding missing pieces of a puzzle which then takes on a new shape. Confession in its simplest form is a purge or act which can offer great relief. However, it is not in this role that the family therapist may find secrets most useful.

The retention of an important secret can obstruct therapy and cause the therapist to work diligently on a pseudo-conflict when the real conflict is about something else. Most commonly I work with a couple, one of whom wants help to leave a marriage, while the other wants help to make the marriage work. This might involve a third person whom either spouse wants to keep secret. This person may never be revealed in conjoint sessions and if the therapist suspects that one partner does have a lover, that partner may even deny a direct question from the therapist.

After repeated experiences of this kind and the continuing impression that "something was wrong" I began, as a matter of course, to schedule in the initial phase of treatment (during the first three or four sessions) an individual hour with each partner. My question to each is something like, "Is there anything I should know about you in order to be of help?" This question itself yields important data about how the person sees himself as well as the manifest content. I will next ask the patient, "Does your husband/wife know about this?"; "If not—why not?"; "Do you think it could be talked about at some time in our sessions together?" Many of the secrets people feel need to be maintained, once told to the therapist, can then, with encouragement, be shared by a spouse. Secrets look considerably less dangerous once out in the air.

However, what about the patient who wishes to swear the therapist to secrecy? It is not possible to make such an agreement without losing control of the treatment. Therefore, the therapist must help the patient to understand that while the therapist respects the importance of trust and of being able to speak openly, s/he must reserve the right at some time in the treatment to ask the patient to talk about the "secret" with the spouse. If the therapist finds during the individual sessions that the hidden material has caused a problem in the therapy, it must be dealt with immediately.

For instance, the therapist might request the partner who is involved with a lover decide whether he/she wants to work on the marriage or on the affair. If he/she cannot make the choice, then that ambivalence needs to be shared in a joint session. It is almost impossible to work with a couple on their marriage while one or the other is involved in an ongoing secret affair. However, it is surprisingly simple to do so when the affair is discussed and becomes a permissible topic.

Attention should be given here to another kind of secret, i.e., sexual experiences or fantasies about which the patient has great pain and shame. Incest and childhood sexual experiences fall into this category. A poignant example is of a 57-year-old male patient whose complaint was premature ejaculation. His wife had not found this to be a problem but he felt tortured by feelings of sexual inadequacy. In individual sessions he explained that he had long been carrying the burden of a terrible secret and felt he wanted to talk about it, but feared that once I knew I would want to tell his wife. I assured him that I would not myself tell the secret, but I reserved the need to use my judgment about requesting him to do so in our conjoint sessions. After several minutes of silent struggle, he tearfully described having sex (not intercourse) to orgasm with his sister when she was five years old and he was 15 years old. This event occurred nightly for several years, always with a sense of shame and fear that his parents would discover him, hence the need for speed.

I felt that the telling of this secret was of great importance and asked why he had not felt able to talk about it earlier in his life. He explained that his shame was so great that, until he began family therapy and discussed his family of origin, he had never allowed himself to wonder how he and his sister had maintained the pretense that these events never happened. Neither he nor his sister alluded to it except for one time after her marriage broke up when she told him that it was "his fault." My patient found the courage to speak about his "crime" but did not feel that his wife needed to know, as she might use it as a weapon against him. I did not consider it important that his wife know the secret, perhaps ever, but certainly not at this time. I suggested that someday he might forgive himself enough to want to tell her. I then scheduled both partners for alternate individual and conjoint sessions. During this time their relationship improved, but he did not reveal the secret. Two years after therapy ended I received a note saying they were doing well together and seemed to have solved their sexual problems.

This discussion is meant to encourage fellow therapists not to classify a secret as either bad or something that necessarily needs to be shared. Further, it is hoped that therapists will have the courage to sometimes bear their own discomfort with secrets in the service of helping patients to put theirs in perspective. This might be accomplished by "confession," sharing, or simply accepting that the secret in itself is not the problem.

**ANN Z. KORELITZ, M.S.W.**
*Senior Training Supervisor*
*Ackerman Institute for Family Therapy*
*New York, NY*

# 23. Marital Affairs and Counteraffairs

**Question:**

How do you deal with a couple coming into therapy, when one of the spouses has been involved in an extramarital affair? What attitude should the therapist take, and are there specific interventions which may be useful in treatment?

**Discussion:**

A common marital crisis which precipitates a couple's request for psychotherapy is the discovery by one partner of the other partner's involvement in a sexual liaison with another, commonly referred to as an "affair." Usually, the "innocent" partner requests the initial visit and the other person in the relationship consents to enter treatment, often with the expectation of censure or, at best, condemnation for his or her actions. At this crisis point it is important for the therapist to have an understanding of commonly noted interventions to direct the crisis toward a resolution. To be useful, these interventions must avoid actions which intensify the problem, increase resentment, and provoke further guilt or anger.

In my experience many of the initial visits may be spent with both partners arguing and discussing broken vows, deceptions, and resentments. There may ensue discussion over the viability of the relationship as well as future plans. After the initial assessment it is first helpful for the therapist to directly or indirectly deal with the process by relabeling the situation. The affair can be redefined in a manner that allows the couple to confront serious issues which have been an underlying problem.

The affair can be seen as any prolonged activity which removes a majority of emotional involvement of a partner from the relationship. The sexual activity by one partner can occur in response to a loss of emotional concern by the other. The therapist redefines the crisis as an "affair of the relationship." By viewing this activity in systems terms, it must be emphasized that both partners begin to assume responsibility for the affair. Each partner in some manner has been engaged in behavior which removes a majority of affect—the "juice," so to speak—from the partnership. To be a significant loss, the activity usually occurs over a prolonged period of time, and the behavior may be sexual or nonsexual. At times the sexual acting-out is a response to a more extended loss of interest by the other partner. At this pivotal time the therapist redefines the activity as a relationship affair in which both people involved have participated in its construction, rather than the common idea that it is self-motivated, individual behavior. In this manner both partners become involved, though initially the behavior was seen as one partner's irresponsible action.

Redefining the affair in systems terms begins a therapeutic process which sets the stage for both partners to accept their part in the scenario. In this situation, responsibility must be defined as each individual's acceptance of the requirement to change the way he/she has been behaving, rather than accepting or placing blame and guilt for the affair. In many situations this may be a difficult task and can require many visits to accomplish. The therapist may initially request the "injured" party to ventilate feelings, while he/she supports the other partner. It is important that the support be in the form of the therapist's ability to empathize with the motivation of the behavior, i.e., "I can understand why you would behave or feel in that way . . . ." This intervention is in contrast with support which might be seen as an excuse for breaking marital vows and might further aggravate a tinderbox situation.

The "innocent" person is usually unaware that he or she has been involved in a "counteraffair." This is usually a nonsexual activity that has the effect of draining the relationship of passion. It may be a conscious or unconscious response by a partner to a variety of causes such as dissatisfaction with the spouse for the quality of the relationship; nonfunctional family of origin patterns; or unfulfilled expectations. The important point is that rather than blaming one partner, the couple needs to see that each one has been involved in outside-of-relationship activities (sexual or nonsexual). The actions have removed the vital core of aliveness from a central to a peripheral position, while placing affection on another person or activity.

The counteraffair can be described as the behavior of the partner who has been uninvolved in the extramarital relationship and considers himself or herself "innocent." This person may realize that the acting-out sexual behavior is a response to lack of involvement of the other. Frequently the counteraffair activities are behaviors not unusual in themselves. They are common activities carried to extremes due to their degree of intensity. These activities preoccupy the individual, often to the exclusion of the partner, and include excessive work involvement, overconcern with either parents or children, or possibly individual psychotherapy. The therapist needs to be aware that the counteraffair may be the primary presenting symptom in some cases. This can take the form of one partner's prolonged depression or chronic psychosomatic illness. It is important for family practitioners or individual therapists to be aware of this hidden form of presentation of the affair, thus avoiding the common problem of treating only one member of the relationship. If the partner with overt symptomatology is treated without the other, there is often symptom recurrence at a later time due to the presence of the hidden affair.

For example, a husband might start couple therapy with his wife, the presenting complaint being his discovery of his wife's affair with the neighbor. He feels distraught, hurt, and angry and is considering divorce. He sees his wife as being guilty of betraying him. Through the process of therapy the couple gradually becomes aware of his counteraffair. This has been his involvement with two jobs he has taken over the past three years to support the family. The husband has been unaware of the serious effect his absence has had on the family. Because he is working for the family benefit and survival, his wife has made the assumption that she cannot comment on her feelings of loss and resentment. She had harbored these feelings internally until the opportunity presented itself for her to sexually act them out and have needs met with the neighbor. Over time the relationship center has been eroded, and the wife, feeling uninvolved, has turned to another for closeness and intimacy. This is to replace what she experiences as having been lost. As both partners see their participation in the scenario, they can start examining rules and assumptions which preceded the acting-out behavior. Through this process they can start dealing more effectively with their needs, i.e., husband modifying work schedule or wife making her desires known directly.

A similar pattern can be observed when one partner may be involved in individual long-term psychotherapy. The person may be devoting a significant amount of his or her emotional energy to this process if it is taken seriously. This often leads to the other partner feeling jealous or emotionally excluded and eventually acting-out of feelings.

Obviously, in long-term relationships partners are temporarily turned away from each other for various periods of time. This requires a modicum of patience or maturity to accept this temporary loss. In the counteraffair, the significant factor is the amount of time and energy that the partner spends in outside activities. The commonly occurring nodal points in a family life cycle may become fixated and remain as a nidus for a counteraffair. These include events such as the birth of a child, the first years of the baby's life, job changes, and subsequent overinvolvement with a special child or chronic illness in a family member. Occasionally, a partner may have incompletely differentiated him/herself from the family of origin. He/she then spends an inordinate amount of time occupied with his/her parents' world to the exclusion of the primary relationship. This was well illustrated in Ingmar Bergman's film, *Scenes from a Marriage*. As the behaviors absenting one partner become excessive, the spouse's complaints about them may not be heeded. Possibly due to family rules which forbid commenting upon certain behaviors or expressing feelings, the frustrated spouse moves toward acting-out his/her feelings with another. Many times this becomes a systems problem of circularity, with gradual escalation of avoidance behavior by both partners, until one enters into a sexual relationship attempting to restore the homeostatic balance.

It is the therapist's task to attempt to turn this crisis period toward constructive goals, moving the relationship past the impasse without fragmenting. If the partners remain in conjoint psychotherapy, they can reexamine their relationship. They can begin to determine changes they would like to make and address issues they have been unable to effectively manage. The couple needs to be given encouragement and support for having the courage to look at themselves and examine their entrenched behaviors, fears, and resistances to change.

The more positive direction can be accomplished if the affair can be presented as a nodal or "opportunity-for-change" point in the natural history of the relationship. It is a time to move from a limited, restrictive way of relating to a more comfortable way to communicate. This is not an easy process but the couple can be encouraged to start the work of reexamining the values, needs, and motivations which originally brought them together and how these have changed over time. One person may have moved in a new direction and not really taken into account the effect of change upon the couple. Indeed, while examining the relationship, one spouse may determine that he/she has needs or desires the other cannot fulfil. Each partner may decide on alternative courses of action, such as dealing with needs in other ways or leaving the relationship. It is helpful at this time to emphasize the positive aspects of the relationship inasmuch as therapy may artificially highlight negative aspects and the couple may be ignoring significant gratifying qualities.

Many therapists may only try to weather the crisis and return the couple to their previous functional state, rather than use this time as a lever to deal with germane and central issues moving the couple to a more optimal functional level. This is the time the therapist can determine and change many of the previous restrictive and limiting assumptions and rules. At this crucial time, it is important to see both partners together and not fractionate them in separate sessions or individual treatment. If seen separately, often side-taking, misunderstanding, and alienation from one another can occur, leading to further deterioration of the relationship.

The present state of the extramarital relationship is another issue which needs to be addressed. Is the outside relationship still occurring or has it been terminated? If the sexual or outside relationship is still in progress, therapy is often difficult. It may allow some ventilation but few changes in the relationship. The ambivalence of the involved individual prevents therapy from progressing. In some cases it is nec-.essary to take a cautious approach by relabeling the situation in later visits. The therapist can assist the partner in examining motives, needs, and consequences. On rare occasions it may be useful to see all three individuals involved in the triangle. This can be helpful in select situations when all participants are known to each other and willing to interact together. It may overcome a therapeutic impasse, especially when multiple lives are involved. To aid in making a decision, the sexually involved individual can be made aware of the "split-transference" phenomena often noticed in affairs. In this situation many negative qualities are perceived in the spouse in the primary relationship, while positive qualities are projected upon the other person in the affair. If the sexually involved individual leaves the primary relationship on the crest of the affair, the negative qualities are now reexperienced with the new individual as a consequence of seeing that person in his/her totality, rather than a polarity of the spouse's behavior.

It is helpful for the therapist to avoid taking a "can this marriage be saved" approach. Any approach which tries to aggressively push the couple toward rapid resolution or staying together may paradoxically move the couple toward the direction of ending the relationship. A slower, more phenomenological approach, in which the therapist joins with the couple in eventually exploring the difficulties, dissatisfactions, and problems occurring prior to the affair, seems most effective. A useful tack is to ask the couple, "What were the conditions present which allowed or accounted for moving away from each other and seeking gratifications in other activities?" By encouraging these aspects and using restraint from rapid change techniques, the therapist minimizes resistances and avoids sidetaking. This allows the couple to determine their own direction.

The therapist constructs a situation that allows the pair to look at issues which could not have been explored or broached without moving toward a crisis point that allowed feelings to surface. The interventions can move the couple to a new way of relating and allow them in a supportive atmosphere to deal with previous inhibitions or restrictions in communication. The therapy is constructed to avoid the usual recriminations, destructiveness, and acrimony which are characteristic of dealing with the first moments of discovery.

The process of reframing the situation as an affair-of-the-relationship allows both partners to consider their participation in the occurrence. It also leaves them responsible for working in couple psychotherapy on the decisions necessary for changes, movement, and breaking the impasse in their relationship. It may help them deal realistically and constructively with themselves, rather than forcing them into premature closure without examining underlying issues. This is one approach to an exceedingly difficult impasse and crisis. The method is intended to avoid the personally destructive and irreparable aspects of the affair. The goals are to move the couple toward a more flexible, open, and personally satisfying mode of being together in which they may retain their individuality and self-respect.

**MARTIN H. BAUMAN, M.D.**
*Assistant Clinical Professor of Psychiatry*
*Family Therapy Section*
*Langley Porter Neuropsychiatric Clinic*
*University of California Medical School*
*San Francisco, CA*

# PART D

*Integrating Treatment Approaches*

## 24. Integration of Psychodynamic and Behavioral Techniques in Marital Therapy

**Question:**

Psychodynamic and behavioral approaches to marital therapy are usually presented as distinctly different, if not antagonistic, ways of working. Since the concepts and techniques of both these approaches seem useful to me, I am searching for a way to integrate them. Is this possible?

**Discussion:**

In my opinion, psychodynamic and behavioral approaches to marital therapy are complementary and synergistic. I conceptualize the dynamics of dysfunctional marital systems from an integrative psychodynamic-behavioral-systemic perspective (Feldman, 1976, 1979, in press; Feldman and Pinsof, 1982) and direct my therapeutic interventions toward changing both the interpersonal and intrapsychic components of the marital problem-maintenance process. Behavioral techniques are utilized to help couples develop more effective interpersonal skills. Psychodynamic techniques are utilized to reduce anxiety and defensiveness, correct cognitive distortions, and bolster self-esteem. The integrated use of both types of techniques creates a mutually reinforcing positive feedback process which promotes both interpersonal and intrapsychic change.

In the initial stages of my work with couples I make extensive use of the psychodynamic technique of empathic reflection and the behavioral technique of empathy training. In the former, I reflect back to each spouse my understanding of his or her feelings about whatever marital issues are being discussed. In the latter, I ask the spouses to reflect back to each other their understanding of the other's feelings about whatever marital issues are being discussed. The integrated use of these two techniques promotes the establishment of rapport, increased empathy between the spouses, and a reduction in each spouse's level of anxiety and defensiveness.

In the middle phase of therapy, I continue to use both psychodynamic and behavioral techniques. Of particular importance here are dream work and behavior rehearsal. Generally, I use the former during those times when there is relatively little overt conflict and the latter when disruptive conflict is actively present. In working with dreams, I have found both the psychoanalytic free-association method and the gestalt role-playing method to be useful. When I use behavior rehearsal, I concentrate on reinforcing constructive approaches to problem-solving and actively countering destructive ones. The integrated use of dream interpretation and behavior rehearsal, along with the continued use of empathic reflection and empathy training, promotes more constructive problem-solving, increased intimacy, and increased self-esteem in both spouses.

In the termination phase of therapy, I make use of the behavioral principle of intermittent reinforcement by tapering the frequency of meetings from once or twice a week to once every two weeks and, finally, once a month. During this period, I use psychodynamic techniques (primarily clarification and interpretation) to help spouses deal with their emotional and cognitive reactions to termination, and behavioral techniques (primarily behavior rehearsal) to help them rebound from temporary regressions.

It has been my experience that the integrated use of both psychodynamic and behavioral techniques provides for greater therapeutic leverage than the exclusive use of either of these approaches alone.

*References*

Feldman, L. B. Depression and marital interaction. *Family Process*, 1976, *15*, 389-395.
Feldman, L. B. Marital conflict and marital intimacy. *Family Process*, 1979, *18*, 69-79.
Feldman, L. B. Dyfunctional marital conflict: An interpersonal-intrapsychic model. *Journal of Marital and Family Therapy*, in press.
Feldman, L. B., and Pinsof, W. M. Problem maintenance in family systems: An integrative model. *Journal of Marital and Family Therapy*, 1982, in press.

**LARRY B. FELDMAN, M.D.**
*Associate Professor of Psychiatry*
*Northwestern University Medical School;*
*Chief of Research*
*Center for Family Studies/*
*Chicago Family Institute*
*Chicago, IL*

# 25. Using "Paradox" in Psychodynamic Marital Therapy

**Question:**

I've read a lot recently about the therapist's use of paradoxical interventions in marital and family therapy. I've also attended several workshops on strategic therapy where the use of paradox was discussed and demonstrated. From all of this exposure, I've gotten the impression that a therapist who works this way cannot also be thinking about couples in psychodynamic terms. Isn't there a place for paradoxical intervention in psychodynamically oriented marital therapy?

**Discussion:**

The use of "paradoxical" interventions assumes that a couple has such self-perpetuating properties that any changes initiated in the couple in psychotherapy will almost automatically be maintained after therapy. That is, such therapeutic approaches assume that what behaviorists call "natural reinforcement" will take over once the problematic interaction pattern has been changed, and will result in extratherapy generalization. For such therapists, then, skill training and interpretation of marital dynamics occur rarely.

By way of contrast, most marital therapists with a psychodynamic orientation (e.g., Framo, 1981; Gurman, 1981; Sager, 1981; Skynner, 1981) are concerned with what a couple takes away from therapy in addition to symptom reduction. Such therapists are also concerned that the therapist's use of covert and indirect influence may model such a style for the couple, and that such modeling is antithetical to the goals of clear and nondefensive communication, problem-solving, and general living in an intimate relationship. Like behavioral therapists (e.g., Jacobson, 1981), dynamically oriented therapists believe that durable clinical change is most likely when couples learn new and effective ways to achieve their relationship aims, and learn them in such a way as to promote self-change after therapy is over. Thus, "paradoxical" interventions are rarely central to the work of therapy.

Still, certain aspects of "paradoxical" intervention, which may be called "paradoxical commentary," e.g., "positive connotation" and "ascribing noble intention" (Stanton, 1981), may be used fruitfully and in full accord with the reintegrative goals of psychodynamically oriented couples therapy. The brilliance of therapeutic "paradox" in couples therapy lies not in its clever management of power relationships, but in its addressing the most basic, relationally central dimensions of the unconscious strivings of couples. Such interventions are "expressions of the most essential truth, which subtly break the rule that fantasy and reality must be kept apart, by relating the two in a disguised, seemingly innocent fashion which expresses only the positive aspects" (Skynner, 1981, p. 76). Perceptively arrived at, and sensitively presented, such interventions are not "paradoxical" at all. They express the most central and powerful psychodynamic themes, agreements, and self-definitions that relate to a couple's suffering and seeking help, and they reveal both the positive and negative elements of intimate collusion.

As Papp (1980) noted, "The target of the systemic paradox is this *hidden interaction* that expresses itself in a symptom" (p. 46, italics added). Psychodynamic models also assume that part of the hidden interaction is the complex of unconscious contracts, collusions, and mutual agreements not to emerge as whole persons. Thus, in psychodynamically oriented therapy, paradoxical commentary aims to make explicit the covert interactions which produce symptoms or marital distress, so that they may be better understood, and so that the conflicts they reflect surreptitiously may be handled by the couple overtly.

The use of paradoxical interventions very early in psychodynamic couples therapy is rarely appropriate. There are two reasons for this. First, paradoxical interventions are not the strategy of choice for couples who comply with the requirements of their patient role; they are to be reserved for situations of major noncompliance (Papp, 1980). Of course, "compliance" is a relativistic notion, and most couples will show at least some resistance to change in therapy. The crucial issue that the therapist must address is, thus, not whether noncompliance exists, but whether and how readily it can be overcome, especially by the use of more direct interventions, such as further development of the therapeutic alliance, confrontation or interpretation, or instructional reiteration of the importance of the couple's following the therapist's ground rules for therapy. As any experienced therapist knows, direct dealing with the couple's resistance to change often yields more therapeutic change and improvement than a single-minded focus on presenting problems, target complaints, and the like. Except in rare circumstances, it is unwise and probably countertherapeutic for the therapist to assume (based, for example, on the couple's previous treatment history or identified patient diagnosis) that noncompliance both is and will remain severe. Rather, a more experimental attitude is called for, whereby assessments and/or predictions of major noncompliance are tested in response to interventions aimed at overcoming such resistance. In general, at least a few treatment sessions are required in order to gather concrete, experiential evidence to either support or refute such predictions.

The second reason why paradoxical intervention is rarely appropriate in very early sessions is that, in order for the therapist to formulate accurately the paradoxical intervention, he or she must develop a penetrating understanding of the hidden dynamics and functions of the major presenting symptom or, where one spouse is not initially a symptom bearer, of the most salient distressing interaction patterns. While such a rich formulation may be easier to come by when a therapist operates as part of a therapeutic team (e.g., Papp, 1980), most marital therapists are not fortunate enough to have this advantage. Except in those rare cases of a very gifted therapist or in the presence of a couple whose dynamics are immediately obvious, such an understanding of the most basic hidden interaction underlying a symptom or interaction pattern is not achieved readily. Indeed, except in the infrequent circumstances just mentioned, it is probably a useful rule of thumb for the therapist to assume that when such a fundamental appreciation of the couple's hidden dynamics appears in the first session or two, it is probably either quite inaccurate or incomplete.

An additional issue in the timing of paradoxical interventions may be considered. Coppersmith (1980) usefully outlined the components and steps in the proper delivery of a paradoxical prescription in family therapy:

1) overt identification of the functions of a symptom (which, as noted, can also include the functions of a dominant interaction pattern);
2) positive connotation of the recurrent behaviors of concern;
3) attribution of volitional control of those behaviors; and
4) the prescription to continue those behaviors, or some variation thereof (e.g., to increase their rate, frequency, or intensity).

The first two components comprise the essence of what I referred to before as paradoxical commentary. The use of these two components in tandem calls for no observable behavioral action or change by the couple. Thus, even while the therapist's understanding of the hidden interactions and dynamics is still being formulated, as in very early therapy sessions, such paradoxical commentary may be offered tentatively, with a quality of working collaboratively with the couple to generate useful hypotheses about what maintains their dysfunctional and distressing behavior. But, as noted, progressing to using the third and fourth components as defined by Coppersmith (1980) should generally be delayed a while longer.

## References

Coppersmith, E. I. *Strategic family therapy: A team approach.* Workshop presented at the Ontario Association for Marriage and Family Therapy, London, Ontario, April 1980.

Framo, J. Integration of marital therapy with sessions with family of origin. In A. Gurman & D. Kniskern (Eds.), *Handbook of Family Therapy.* New York: Brunner/Mazel, 1981.

Gurman, A. S. Integrative marital therapy: Toward the development of an interpersonal approach. In S. Budman (Ed.), *Forms of Brief Therapy.* New York: Guilford, 1981.

Jacobson, N. S. Behavioral marital therapy. In A. Gurman & D. Kniskern (Eds.), *Handbook of Family Therapy.* New York: Brunner/Mazel, 1981.

Papp, P. The Greek chorus and other techniques of family therapy. *Family Process*, 1980, *19*, 45-57.

Sager, C. J. Couples therapy and marriage contracts. In A. Gurman & D. Kniskern (Eds.), *Handbook of Family Therapy.* New York: Brunner/Mazel, 1981.

Skynner, A. C. R. An open systems, group-analytic approach to family therapy. In A. Gurman & D. Kniskern (Eds.), *Handbook of Family Therapy.* New York: Brunner/Mazel, 1981.

Stanton, M. D. Strategic approaches to family therapy. In A. Gurman & D. Kniskern (Eds.), *Handbook of Family Therapy.* New York: Brunner/Mazel, 1981.

**ALAN S. GURMAN, Ph.D.**
*Professor of Psychiatry*
*University of Wisconsin Medical School*
*Madison, WI*

# 26. Paradox and Behavioral Marital Therapy

## Question:

Recently, I've heard a few behaviorally oriented marital therapists suggest that paradoxical techniques can sometimes be integrated into a basically behavioral treatment. Since behavioral methods are usually so aboveboard, with the clients being explicitly informed of the therapist's treatment rationale and techniques, whereas paradoxical techniques are rarely explained so directly, how can such an integration possibly work?

## Discussion:

Until the last few years behavioral marital therapists tended to discount the necessity, value, and effectiveness of paradoxical techniques. This view was determined by several factors. First, a reading of the family systems literature indicates that paradoxical techniques are specifically employed to counter the "almost inevitable" resistance on the part of partners to change their relationship. However, *resistance* itself was seen by behaviorists as essentially a phenomenon resulting from ineffective case management, a concept invoked to explain failure of clients to change only after the treatment techniques proved to be unsuccessful. Accordingly, behaviorists are generally taught to remediate poor therapeutic progress through the more effective use of *overt*, skill-oriented techniques, rather than having to resort to *covertly* manipulative strategic techniques, such as paradox. In addition, as the correspondent suggests, many behaviorists view covert manipulations as inconsistent with an aboveboard, social learning approach, if not inappropriate under any circumstances. Finally, behaviorists are trained to base treatment interventions on empirical data for effectiveness and the literature indicates little if any supportive evidence for the use of paradox. Groups which pioneered the paradoxical techniques or have since studied them intensively have not produced definitive studies. Thus, throughout most of the 1970s paradoxical interventions were viewed by most behavioral marital therapists as covertly manipulative, unsystematically and intuitively applied techniques of questionable necessity and effectiveness.

However, again as the correspondent notes, during the past two or three years especially, behaviorally oriented researchers such as Alexander, Barton, Birchler, and Weiss have increasingly concerned themselves with that phenomenon called *resistance*. Moreover, these investigators have described treatment approaches designed to combine certain strategic and behavioral interventions. The addition of the "strategic" techniques is, in part, a recognition of the inadequacy of the current behavioral model to effectively facilitate change in a high enough proportion of distressed couples and families. Now, having laid the groundwork, let us focus more on the point of this discussion: whether the use of one specific strategic technique, paradox, is compatible with a behavioral approach; when and why paradoxical techniques might be used; and how they should be applied.

First of all, when applied sparingly and judiciously, paradoxical techniques are quite compatible with a behavioral approach. One of the critical criteria for an effective paradoxical prescription is that the therapists' formulation be *accurate*. That is, although not recognized previously by the clients, the therapists' functional analysis of the symptom or interactional system must be conceivable, if not highly probable. For example, consider the case where a couple has repeatedly been given weekly communication training homework assignments, but invariably returns having bickered and argued all week without completing the practice exercises. In using paradox, the therapist could earnestly assign the couple to converse as little as possible or not at all the following week on the grounds that nonconflict communication represents intimacy and at this stage the couple is not quite ready to become more intimate. Their arguments keep them at a safe distance from one another. Therefore, if they must converse, it should be only to argue so as not to threaten the precarious balance in their relationship. Given that at least the short-term goal is to get the couple to stop bickering, such a paradoxical prescription has a chance of succeeding because it is both a plausible functional explanation of their system and it is probably unacceptable either to cease talking and/or to follow the therapists' directions. The point is, based on an accurate functional or systems analysis, it is possible to tell a couple quite openly and honestly why a certain assignment is being given. This is consistent with a behavioral approach. Obviously, the therapist does not indicate that the assignment is meant to be a paradox or have a paradoxical effect.

Concerning the question of when and why paradoxical techniques should be used, it is important to remember that they are complex interventions which take considerable skill and experience to apply successfully. Consequently, they should be used as a last resort. That is, in my view paradox is too frequently used before it is either necessary or appropriate. Following a behavioral framework, a therapist should certainly look first to proper case management according to principles of social learning. Quite often, clinical phenomena called resistance can be accounted for by technical factors which are external to the dynamics of the client's relationship. Examples are inaccurate assessment and identification of target behaviors and primary problems, too little behavior rehearsal, poor instructions, lack of therapist social reinforcement, modeling or shaping, and poorly planned homework or follow-up to homework assignments.

On the other hand, once the therapist has exhausted his/her repertoire of behavioral techniques and skill-oriented interventions, there still may be significant resistance which suggests a strategic intervention such as paradox. However, to reiterate, such interventions should be reserved for resistance phenomena which are persistent, repeated behaviors, which significantly obstruct the progress of therapy and which are unrelenting to the usual direct, educational interventions.

Within the context of practicing standard behavioral marital therapy (i.e., pinpointing problems, communication and problem-solving training, relationship enrichment activities, negotiation and behavior change strategies), observable indications of significant resistance phenomena or underlying issues fall into four categories:

1) *Clients' acting out between sessions.* There are unexcused, repeatedly missed sessions or chronic tardiness on the part of one or both partners. Clients fail to do or fail to complete homework or data collection assignments. Or, there may be minor crises between sessions which consistently prevent attention to a training agenda.

2) *Blocks to communication skills training.* In this category clients may manifest major difficulty in communication about very simple issues or in learning simple in-session skills (e.g., paraphrasing). There may be a constant emergence or generation of (apparently simple) conflict issues, even though the couple has previously demonstrated good basic communication skills. Finally, there may be an inability to thoroughly discuss specific issues and reach satisfactory solutions even though the couple has good communication skills. In these instances it seems that the couple is colluding to avoid the issue and yet appears frustrated, as if wheel-spinning.

3) *Regression: Emergence of original or new symptoms.* There may

be a return of the chief complaint or the original symptoms after significant progress has been made and temporarily sustained by new interactional skills. Or there may be a sudden emergence of entirely new symptoms of anxiety, depression, phobia, etc., after substantial therapeutic progress has been made.

4) *Lack of generalization and maintenance of treatment gains.* An indication of resistance here may consist of the consistent failure of one or both partners to support or reinforce formerly requested behavior changes in the other. The interactional pattern may even include evidence of mild to moderate punishment of the allegedly desired behavior. Finally, a nagging problem for behavioral marital therapists is the situation in which the couple manifests improved competence in communication and problem-solving skills, without positive generalization to exchanges of affection or increases in partners' subjective satisfaction with the relationship.

Again, once behavioral methods have been tried, any of the above clinical phenomena, when persistent, suggest significant resistance which is a candidate for strategic intervention. Unfortunately, inquiry into the potential reasons for such resistance phenomena is beyond the scope of this discussion.

Finally, a note about *how* to present a paradoxical prescription to clients. As Peggy Papp (1979) has suggested previously, one common error associated with the use of paradox is simply prescribing the symptom without verbally and logically connecting it to functional aspects of the marital or family interaction system. It is tempting and all too easy to make isolated paradoxical prescriptions without preparing the couple by providing a plausible, airtight rationale for the particular assignment. The necessity for the assignment should also be explained in the context of past failures of the couple to make the expected progress, using whatever previous techniques. It might be helpful for the therapist to encourage the couple to have an experimental cognitive set about the assignment and its outcome: "I think this assignment is very important. Whatever happens, it will probably give us invaluable information which we can use to help you improve your relationship. So it's important that you both give this an honest effort and then we'll see where to go from there." This "try it out and then let's evaluate" position is certainly consistent with the skill-training, social learning orientation of the behavioral approach.

In conclusion, there are increasing efforts to integrate interpretive/strategic interventions with existing behavioral approaches to marital distress. Paradoxical techniques, though lacking empirical support, may offer one way of helping the clinician to gain therapeutic leverage which is otherwise difficult if not impossible to obtain. While paradox should be applied very carefully and only when more direct approaches are unsuccessful, there are no particular problems in integrating it within the behavioral framework.

*Reference*

Papp, P. Paradoxical strategies and countertransference. *American Journal of Family Therapy*, 1979, 7, 11-12.

**GARY R. BIRCHLER, Ph.D.**
*Associate Clinical Professor*
*Department of Psychiatry*
*University of California Medical School*
*La Jolla, CA*

# 27. Assessment and Treatment of Low Sex Desire

**Question:**

Most of my work with couples deals with nonsexual problems, but occasionally I am referred couples who complain of low sex desire in one partner. At these times, it is often difficult to decide whether the focus, or at least the initial focus, of therapy should be on sexual behavior per se, or on other aspects of the marital relationship. Could an experienced sex therapist offer some practical clinical guidelines to help make this diagnostic decision that is so important for planning treatment?

**Discussion:**

This is a very pertinent question. In our experience with couples in which low desire is a presenting complaint, sexual and marital issues usually need to be addressed simultaneously. We often find that our standard sex therapy program of 15 sessions is not long enough to produce significant change. We routinely extend treatment to 20 or 25 weeks, spending a good deal of time in session and in our homework assignments on marital and individual issues.

Treatment planning for these couples involves a complex assessment of the etiological factors that have led to the low desire. We categorize the syndrome along three dimensions. The first two have also been described by Kaplan (1979). We note whether the low desire has been *lifelong* or *not lifelong*, i.e., intermittent periods of more desire, or a recent loss of desire preceded by higher levels. We determine whether low desire is *global* across partners and sexual activities, or *situational*. Thirdly, we check to see if low desire is the only sexual problem, or if there are other dysfunctions in either spouse.

Different combinations of these dimensions suggest different etiologies. For example, global low desire may be more likely to indicate a physical problem. Any debilitating illness may interfere with sexual desire by depleting the client's energy, causing chronic pain, being a source of anxiety, or affecting the client's self-perception as an attractive, sexual person. Medical conditions that may directly affect sexual desire include endocrine disorders leading to low circulating testosterone or high prolactin, and possibly temporal lobe epilepsy.

Another notorious cause of global loss of desire is depression. We find the Zung Scale (Zung, 1973) a useful, brief assessment tool with low-desire clients. If depression or a medical problem seems to account for low desire, the focus of therapy would obviously shift to ameliorating the primary problem.

In regard to the lifelong vs. not lifelong dimension, we see a number of clients who have experienced a lifelong lack of sexual desire which seems to be psychogenic. Some have never been very actively sexual people, reporting global low desire. Others have expressed their sexuality through masturbation, but have great conflict about being sexual with a partner. Some historical and current factors often associated with lifelong low desire include: severe parental disapproval of sexuality; a religiously orthodox (especially Catholic) upbringing; an early sexual trauma; a pattern of never having masturbated or of having discontinued masturbation; a very close and conflicted relationship with the opposite-sex parent; aversion to his/her own or partner's genitals; and an aversion to any body secretions that are wet or sticky. Perhaps due to cultural definitions of male and female sexuality, men who fall into this category usually present with a neutral lack of interest in sexual activity, while women more often express strong fear and disgust towards sex. For both sexes, a lifelong pattern of low desire is often accompanied by difficulty in becoming sexually aroused with a partner. It is important to assess sexual fantasies in these clients. A long-term lack of desire for the spouse may mask a primarily homosexual fantasy life or an unusual sexual preference.

It is very difficult to change a lifelong pattern of low desire. While we work on producing some insight into historical influences, and on resolving conflicts about being a sexual person, much of our effort goes into the homework assignments. We ask the client and his/her spouse to make sex more salient in their lives. We send them to erotic movies and ask them to look at sexy pictures and books. We work on increasing the frequency and richness of their sexual fantasies, sometimes assigning them to share their fantasy with their partner either verbally or by acting it out. We help clients identify activities such as sports, dancing, flirting, or even ways of dressing, that make them feel sexy. We may facilitate these assignments by having both spouses keep a "desire diary" that lists sexual thoughts, feelings, and fantasies along with the circumstances which elicited them. In session, we sometimes use gestalt techniques to work on the client's self-image as a sexual person. We also help the client devise coping self-statements to combat anxiety about having sex. We particularly try to get across the idea that sex is for his/her own pleasure, rather than being a task to perform in order to satisfy the partner or societal norms. We also may help the spouse of the low-desire client become more tolerant of the need for these "extra" sexual stimuli.

Marital conflicts, especially ones not acknowledged by the couple (LoPiccolo, 1980) are an important determinant of low sexual desire which has not been lifelong in duration. A sudden aversion to one's sexual partner, or just complaining of a mysterious lack of sexual desire, is a very safe and effective way of expressing anger. Another common pattern occurs in spouses who cannot tolerate the degree of closeness that sex entails. They may, more or less consciously, regard the bedroom as the only place in which they can win the fight to remain separate from their partner. Out of their ambivalence about intimacy, they marry someone who has a high need for closeness. The more this spouse pushes for attitude similarity, physical affection, and shared time, the more the low-desire spouse withdraws. Masturbation or casual affairs for this low-desire client may be the only situations in which they can let go without feeling trapped and overwhelmed. Other clients resolve their conflict by giving up on sex entirely.

Again we start by focusing on sexual issues in the homework. When we assign nongenital couple-pleasuring exercises, we look for diagnostic signs of the marital struggle. When asked to take the roles of giver and receiver of sensual pleasure, how do the partners handle taking and giving up control? Do they find either role erotic? Do they feel distant from their partner? Were they angry at any point? Who initiated the session? Was positive and negative feedback communicated?

We use some of the same additional assignments as were described above for the lifelong low-desire client. In addition, we may focus on sexual initiation itself if one partner has difficulty asking for sex or refusing the other spouse's invitations. We may assign one spouse to act out a sexual initiation several times, with the provision that it does not have to lead to sexual activity. When desire discrepancies exist in a couple, the partner who wants more sexual contact may really crave more affection or closeness. We point this out if we see it occurring.

Within therapy sessions we attend to relevant marital issues such as poor communication, covert anger, inequitable distribution of family responsibilities, poor problem-solving skills, and a lack of positive, caring, or romantic behaviors. We also give homework assignments that focus on these issues, usually following a behavioral marital therapy format (Jacobson and Margolin, 1979). Often the couple will have one sexual and one marital assignment in the same week. The predominance of sexual vs. marital treatment methods varies from couple to couple, and week to week.

Occasionally we see a couple in which low desire seems clearly secondary to other sexual dysfunctions which have made sex a frustrating and anxiety-laden experience. In these cases we follow a more traditional sex therapy format to see if the level of desire will increase once the other dysfunctions are ameliorated. If low desire remains a problem, we then switch the focus of treatment into either a marital or a more desire-centered mode.

Our treatment techniques for low sexual desire are less well-defined than those for the other dysfunctions. These suggestions summarize our current "state of the art." We are continually examining our therapeutic efforts in the hope that we can increase our effectiveness.

## References

Jacobson, N., & Margolin, G. *Marital Therapy: Strategies Based on Social Learning and Behavior Exchange Principles*. New York: Brunner/Mazel, 1979.

Kaplan, H. S. *Disorders of Sexual Desire*. New York: Brunner/Mazel, 1979.

LoPiccolo, L. Low sexual desire. In S. R. Leiblum and L. A. Pervin (Eds.), *Principles and Practice of Sex Therapy*. New York: Guilford, 1980.

Zung, W. W. K. From art to science: The diagnosis and treatment of depression. *Archives of General Psychiatry*, 1973, *29*, 328-337.

. **LESLIE R. SCHOVER, Ph.D.**
*Assistant Professor of Urology (Psychology)*
*University of Texas System Cancer Center*
*M.D. Anderson, Hospital and Tumor Institute*
*Houston, TX*

# 28. Treatment of Psychosexual Disorders in the Context of Marital Therapy

**Question:**

> As a marital and sex therapist in a psychiatric clinic, I see a great number of couples referred to the clinic whose chief complaints are specific sexual disorders, others whose complaints are strictly marital disharmony, and some others reporting mixed marital and sexual symptomatology. The major concern of our trainees is the question of the focus of treatment. Should couples whose chief complaint is sexual be treated by focusing solely on the sexual dysfunction while ignoring other marital problems? What about the treatment strategy to be used with the other two categories? Is it possible to integrate sexual and marital therapy?

**Discussion:**

Sexual problems are frequently the presenting complaint in a discordant marriage. For some couples, marriage is a source of love, security, pleasure, and sexual gratification; for others, it is a source of distress, pain, and sexual frustration.

Since marriage is, after the mother-child relationship, the most intimate relationship between two people, it is not surprising that sexual intimacy is uniquely sensitive to feelings of love, trust, anger, pain, and rejection. Given that, an important aspect in the treatment of sexual disorders is the exploration of the couple's ongoing relationship and the connection between their relationship and satisfactory levels of sexual intimacy. A basic principle of sex therapy with couples is that there is no such a thing as an "uninvolved" partner, with the marital relationship itself being the patient and not only the sexual dysfunctional partner. Couples are seen as sharing mutual responsibility for their present sexual conflict and one partner is not more responsible for the problem than the other. Therefore, the focus of therapeutic intervention attempts to alter the couple's pathogenic interactions. Most clinicians with a systems theory approach, like myself, make no clear distinction in treatment between sexual and marital symptoms.

In my experience, a very high percentage of couples present a combination of marital and sexual difficulties regardless of whether the main complaint is sexual or marital. Very seldom will I find clear-cut sexual or marital symptoms. Therefore, it is very important before selecting a treatment strategy to fully understand the dynamics of the couple's relationship and the link between the marital conflicts and the sexual disorder. This information is crucial to determining the initial focus of treatment. Couples seeking sex therapy usually present sex as the problem in their relationship because their sex life is not satisfying. Couples seeking marital therapy report dissatisfaction with their partner and their relationship. Sager (1974), in evaluating the factors involved in determining the focus of treatment, found that couples may be divided into three general categories depending on the origin of their marital disharmony and the extent to which the disharmony is secondary to the sexual disorder or vice versa:

1) When the sexual dysfunction produces discord in the marital relationship, sex therapy usually is the treatment of choice.
2) When couples have some marital problems which impair sexual functioning, sex therapy usually is indicated because of their desire to improve their sexual relationship. These couples usually have positive feelings toward each other that outweigh the negative aspects of their relationship.
3) When couples have severe marital problems and basic hostility, sex therapy is not indicated. With these couples the treatment will focus on their marital relationship.

In our work at the clinic we stress the importance of taking a multi-causal, eclectic approach in order to understand and treat sexual difficulties. It is apparent to us that the dysfunction itself is often only the tip of the iceberg and underlying the sexual difficulties are sometimes serious relationship problems and/or unconscious intrapsychic conflicts deriving from early family experiences of both partners.

Within this multi-causal and eclectic framework our program also emphasizes the need to adapt therapeutic techniques to the life-style and value systems of the patients. Our experience in working with different cultures and multilevel socioeconomic groups provides an extensive base of information regarding the varied range of sexual dysfunctions and the most effective class-relevant strategies for their treatment. From this clinical exposure we have developed a framework of considerations which every therapist should consider as he/she initiates contact with the couple. Before developing a strategy for treating any presenting complaint, the therapist must understand fully the sociocultural context within which the treatment methodology must fit. Most importantly, the following represent some of the major issues which require therapeutic attention: sociocultural norms, gender-linked role expectations, sex-linked traits, culturally imposed restrictions, and language expectation. The therapist must know the myths, beliefs and customs that influence his/her patients' behavior, for without this understanding, he/she may develop therapeutic strategies that conflict directly with the couple's personal attitudes and values regarding sex and marriage. Further, this becomes even more significant when working with multi-ethnic couples whose own mixed backgrounds may present a significant amount of cultural discord (Ficher, 1980).

The acceptance that sexual difficulties are often related to the hardship of the marital relationship and are not necessarily expressions of one person's intrapsychic conflict is one of the most significant advances in the behavioral sciences. There is no doubt that clinical interventions must be geared to change the dysfunctional marital and sexual system. Thus, in most cases marital and sex therapists work with couples in conjoint therapy rather than with the symptomatic patient alone. In the conjoint session, the techniques applied are the ones developed by marital and family therapists. The differences between regular marital and sexual therapy is that in the latter psychotherapy is combined with prescribed sexual experiences.

In summary, I see sex therapy with couples as a subdivision of marital therapy. The focus of treatment is determined by the nature of the marital conflict and the extent to which the disharmony is secondary to sexual disorder or vice versa.

## References

Ficher, I. V. Treatment of sexual disorders in a community program. In M. Andolfi and I. Zwerling (Eds.), *Dimensions of Family Therapy* New York: Guilford, 1980.
Sager, C. J. Sexual dysfunctions and marital discord. In H. S. Kaplan, *The New Sex Therapy*. New York: Brunner/Mazel, 1974.

**ILDA V. FICHER, Ph.D.**
*Professor*
*Director, Van Hammett Psychiatric Clinic;*
*Chief, Human Sexuality Section*
*Department of Mental Health Sciences*
*Hahnemann Medical College and Hospital*
*Philadelphia, PA*

# 29. Combining Family Therapy with Other Clinical Interventions

**Question:**

When is it useful vs. harmful to combine other clinical modalities of intervention with family therapy?

**Discussion:**

The answer to this question depends on the conceptualization of family therapy. This is a meaningless question if one considers family therapy as an epistemological way of thinking or adopts a world view in which the word "family" is almost redundant. Within such an ecosystemic way of thinking, there is no such thing as other modalities of clinical interventions (Keeney, 1979). There is only (family) therapy. As a family therapist, I find myself often thinking this way; when I do, the question of the other modalities becomes a non-issue.

However, at other times this is an unsatisfying perspective. It might be that I have reached an impasse in the therapeutic process, or a member of the family appears to have significant individual psychopathology (or perhaps even biological pathology with psychological manifestations) that is not improving or even worsening. Another example would be a system already involved in another clinical modality with someone else that comes to me for family therapy. In these situations, I am pushed to consider the question of family therapy as a "modality" among other modalities. I feel humbled by the fact that many other modalities or "schools" of clinical intervention existed long before family therapy and there is no clear evidence that family therapy is superior to them. There are many colleagues who have been doing successful work in the clinical field long before and after family therapy evolved.

Whitaker and Keith (1981) consider family therapy as one in a multitude of modalities. They view family therapy as a starting place for everyone since the therapist has more leverage when working with the entire system than with only one member of a system. Individual therapy, they feel, is more difficult early on because the therapist/patient team has to be powerful enough to change the patient, while simultaneously the patient must change his or her family. They consider individual change impossible without simultaneous change in the family relationships. For those to change, family members must change. In their view, individual psychotherapy becomes "a Ph.D. course in human relationships," worth engaging in only after graduating "high school" and "college" (i.e., after an individual has worked out the major interpersonal struggles with his/her family of origin and family of procreation).

Although this is a useful perspective, I find there are situations in which it is important to consider other modalities at a given point in a person or family's lifetime, rather than only longitudinally. When I see a new case not currently involved in other therapy, I tend to think about it in terms of Whitaker and Keith's (1981) conceptualization and start with family therapy. However, I will at times consider and add other clinical modalities to augment ongoing family therapy. Furthermore, clinical situations often arise in which a person and/or family comes to me asking for the addition of another modality. I will discuss this point later. Thus, although I start by thinking of family therapy as a world view or comprehensive epistemology, I find that in the real world it makes sense to consider it as only one of many modalities. The issue then becomes how to think about and, at times, use combined clinical modalities.

## Definitions

It is important to briefly comment on how I have been using and will continue to use the phrase "clinical modalities." I am using it to connote the broad division of all clinical interventions into various major subdivisions or "schools of thought" or "paradigms of thinking." Although there might be a question as to the usefulness of merging together these "different" concepts, I feel that their current connotations are wide enough to warrant consideration as a group in terms of their similarities. Various therapists have written on this subject but there is no current consensus on any subdivisions. Current divisions seem to have occurred, among other ways, along lines determined by basic Western ontological beliefs (e.g., mind-body dichotomy) and the historical traditions of various professional disciplines (e.g., psychiatry/medications, social work/family therapy). These include the traditional single separation into organic (drugs, ECT, etc.) and non-organic (psychotherapy and all other non-invasive treatments) interventions. Rabkin (1970), and recently Abroms (1981), have suggested that the major divisions might best be considered the biotherapies, psychotherapies and sociotherapies. Halleck (1978) has suggested a more extensive subdivision into the biological interventions, behavioral therapies, individual psychotherapies, group therapies, and family therapies. Havens (1973) has identified four major schools of thought including the objective-descriptive (which is somewhat synonymous with the biological school), the psychoanalytic, the existential, and the interpersonal-social school (which includes to a large extent the family therapies).

It appears that many of these "established" divisions are blurring in light of current theorizing. Pardes (1981) has commented that "the dualism between psychiatry and neurobiology will be a transient interlude. . . . The interaction and unity of mind and brain will be appreciated, ending this notion of a strict dichotomy." Karasu (1979) has suggested that at least the psychotherapies might well be unified, in which "*parts* of many therapies may be combined to produce the most important therapeutic regimes."

However, I am primarily addressing "formal" issues of modality combinations that are not intrinsically tied to the specific modalities and might well be applicable to any future divisions of the clinical field. Nonetheless, it is important to address the issue of the extent to which our present modalities pursue the same or different goals. Insofar as there is an agreed-upon, optimal "state of being" which is definable, one might consider various modalities as equally reasonable ways of getting to this universal end point. Thus, one sees experienced clinicians of different "schools" applying different clinical modalities to patients/families presenting very similarly, if not exactly the same. Another notion is that, although there might be generally agreed-upon optimum mental health, there are different problems which require different modalities. This is consonant with aspects of the psychiatric medical model suggesting that different modalities are appropriate for different "illnesses."

An alternative view is that the different clinical paradigms implicitly (or sometimes explicitly) generate different goals and/or different optimal states of being. For instance, Klerman et al. (1974) have discussed how both drugs and psychotherapy help depression but along "different dimensions." Abroms (1981) suggests that the biotherapeutic modalities promote cognitive and affective regulation of the individual, while (individual) psychotherapy is valuable in fostering intimate relationships. Sociotherapies (which include family therapy) are primarily designed to promote socialization "involving social belonging and obligation in terms of individual autonomy and freedom" (p. 387). There is the possibility that the optimal state of being (i.e., the end goal) of the family and individual family members is very different in, say, experiential family therapy (Whitaker and Keith, 1981) than in the rational emotive therapy tradition (Ellis, 1974). In the former, there is an emphasis on "craziness" and trusting one's intuition. In the latter, there is an emphasis on rational control and the ability to solve all problems by "thinking." It appears that the optimal state in either school of thought might be considered sub-optimal by the other. It is important to keep in mind the potential "apples and pears" situation of different modalities/different goals as one considers clinical combinations.

## Criteria for Combining Modalities

Any criteria at this point in time must be rudimentary and intuitive since most of the conceptual energy over the century has been focused on developing the specific modalities rather then the larger picture I am addressing here. What follows are my own criteria for thinking about this issue.

It makes sense to use combined modalities for the following reasons:

1) If it appears that different modalities would help significantly in different "dimensions" as described above.
2) If it appears that a given modality is either not helpful or of limited usefulness without the addition of another modality.
3) If there is significant motivation on the part of an individual and/or family to combine modalities.
4) If the modalities are synergistic, i.e., they enhance each other.

A case example demonstrates this point.

Family therapy was bogged down with the Rifkin family. Mother had a depression which did not seem responsive to any family therapy interventions. The family and therapist were losing hope in the therapeutic process. The therapist suggested the use of a tricyclic antidepressant for mother. She responded well clinically and within the next few weeks family therapy was able to progress again.

The following reasons should be considered for *not* combining modalities.

1) The cognitive and epistemological foundations of the various modalities are often based on contradictory assumptions. For example,

the biotherapies see depression as a reflection of aberrant neuro-chemical processes, while the family therapies view it as a manifestation of system dysfunction. Since one goal of therapy is to provide some coherent cognitive ordering of the world, combining processes can at times be unproductively confusing.

2) Additional time and money are involved that may be unnecessary since a single modality is often powerful enough to accomplish what is therapeutically necessary.

3) Different modalities can dilute the potential cathexis available for each separate therapeutic involvement. To the extent that there is meaning to the concept of psychic energy, it could be divided between the various modalities with not enough available in any one for the "critical mass" necessary to accomplish therapeutic work. This is similar to the concept of "diluting the transference" in psychoanalytic thought.

A case example may demonstrate this point.

The Smith family had been in ongoing treatment for about six months. The identified patient was the daughter who was acting out with promiscuity and drugs. After three months, her acting-out had stopped and the covert marital conflict emerged. Rather quickly Kevin, the husband, although active and involved in the family therapy, became increasingly anxious and stopped working. The therapist felt he needed more therapeutic intervention than could be provided in weekly family therapy and urged him to join a new group therapy that was just forming in the clinic. Kevin's anxiety lessened within a few weeks of starting group therapy and he restarted work. However, in the ongoing family therapy sessions he became angry and silent. The family continued for only another month before they dropped out.

On one year follow-up from an independent source, the couple had divorced and neither spouse was doing particularly well. Symptoms in the children had increased. According to the group therapist, early in the group Kevin had expressed a lot of anger about his wife and the family in general. Soon, however, his participation decreased and in spite of the urgings of the group, he remained uninvolved. Two months after starting the group, he dropped out of that therapeutic process also.

In this case, it appeared that perhaps the two clinical modalities sabotaged each other by allowing Kevin to withdraw necessary affect, at first from one process but eventually from both.

*Clinical Applications*

I will describe how these criteria may be used in clinical practice. I will not discuss in detail whether the same therapist should be using combined modalities or whether different therapists should be involved; or the further issue of how, if at all, the different therapists should communicate with each other. These issues have not been covered in any detail in the literature and need further exposition. In the discussion that follows in Section A, I will assume that the ongoing family therapist has started the therapy within a systems framework and is considering the addition of another modality. In Section B, I will consider the situation in which a patient comes to the family therapist in a different ongoing treatment with someone else and wants to start additional family therapy.

A. *Adding other modalities to ongoing family therapy.* I will separately consider two situations concerning the addition of another modality to family therapy. One is when the patient wants to add another modality and the other is when I consider adding another modality. If the patient wishes to add another modality, I usually discuss with the patient the pros and cons of adding the modality as embodied in the criteria described above. I suggest that the final decision rests with the family and/or individual family members. Just as I do not make decisions such as whether a couple get a divorce, I do not make the final decisions as to whether a family should add an additional modality. However, if they do start another modality and if the family therapy then goes dead or reaches an impasse, I reserve the right to suggest that it might well be because they started the additional modality and to suggest that they choose to discontinue either the family therapy or the new modality.

Situations in which I wish to add another clinical modality to the family therapy usually result because I feel we are stuck or when I feel that one of the family members is not doing well and would continue to do poorly or get worse. I first get a consultation from another family therapist and consider other family therapy maneuvers. These include, for example, adding additional family members or reformulating the issues in an attempt to break the transference/countertransference logjam.

B. *Adding family therapy to other ongoing modalities.* Occasionally, a family and/or family member who is in a different therapy with another therapist wants to be seen by me. For instance, if he/she is in individual therapy, he/she might want to add family therapy because he/she feels that the therapy with the other therapist doesn't appear to be helping enough. My first impulse is to send him/her back to the ongoing therapist with the comment, "Be sure to tell the therapist that you have come to me for a consultation and that you feel at an impasse. . . . If it is still not going well after you see him again, let me know and perhaps we can all get together and talk about the problem." I tend to view ongoing therapy in some ways similar to marriage. I feel that once a relationship has been established between a therapist and a patient and there is a bilateral investment, the best chance for growth is in working out that relationship and not diluting it at the first therapeutic impasse. My experience has been that the majority of cases that I have dealt with in this way have worked out well. The "one shot" consultation has broken the impasse and allowed further therapy to be helpful. There have been a few cases in which the patient/family has come back a second time because it "still isn't working." I usually tell them to have the therapist call me. If and when the therapist calls, I discuss the value of additional family therapy in terms of the criteria discussed above.

There have been times when a therapist has called me directly from the beginning of therapy suggesting that the patient would benefit from additional family therapy. I view this as being different from situations in which I get a referral from the patient him/herself. I tend to go along with the referral without viewing it as a therapeutic impasse. In my clinical experience, I have found it makes more intuitive sense to initially emphasize the transference aspects of a patient's request, deemphasizing the countertransference aspects of the therapist's request. The following case demonstrates a successful outcome of the above situation.

Jerry's father died when he was an infant; he had felt chronic guilt most of his life, related in part to not taking better care of his mother living alone in Texas 1000 miles away. After four years of working on oedipal and self-esteem issues in individual psychodynamic therapy, he was referred by a colleague who felt that "too much of Jerry's 'self' seems tied up in the marriage . . . and thus couples therapy seems like a necessary intervention at this time."

He continued his individual therapy during the first year of work in couples therapy. The couple's therapist did not make any effort to have him stop the individual therapy. It did not appear that his wife felt that the individual therapy was a stumbling block in their relationship. Rather, she felt it had been helpful to Jerry in reducing his depression and making him more accessible to work on their marital relationship.

Jerry reported that the first year of couples therapy seemed to "unlock additional material that made sense to talk about in the (concurrent) individual therapy." Also, it appeared that the individual work helped the couples therapy in the following way: Jerry's energy, interest, and wish to focus on the marriage increased as the issues with his parents resolved.

After one year of combined modalities, the individual therapy stopped; the couple continued for one more year in couples therapy. At termination, both the spouses and therapist felt that the therapeutic work was successful and that the combined modalities had been helpful.

## Summary

This is an exciting time in clinical work. The schools of clinical intervention have continued to refine and elaborate their own rich and varied development. Examples include self psychology and object relations theory within the individual psychodynamic school. Lithium has been a powerful addition to our chemotherapeutic armamentarium over the last decades. The clinician must continue to use these various perspectives for clinical work. Conceptual frameworks for integrating and combining these modalities, as discussed here, have begun to be developed. It is necessary for the feedback cycle between clinical work and theory to continue. Hopefully, the therapist will continue to learn from emerging theory and to add to theory-building by using his/her intuition, experience, and courage to attempt new combinations of the various clinical modalities.

## References

Abroms, C. Family therapy is a biomedical context. *Journal of Marital and Family Therapy*, 1981, 7, 385-390.

Ellis, A. *Growth Through Reason*. Hollywood, CA: Wilshire Books, 1974.

Halleck, S. *The Treatment of Emotional Disorders*. New York: Jason Aronson, 1978.

Havens, L. *Approaches to the Mind*. Boston: Little, Brown, 1973.

Karasu, T. Towards the unification of psychotherapies: A complementary model. *American Journal of Psychotherapy*, 1979, *33*, 4.

Keeney, B. Ecosystemic epistemology: An alternative paradigm for diagnosis. *Family Process*, 1979, *18*, 117-129.

Klerman, G. L., DiMascio, A., Weissman, M., Prusoff, B., and Paykel, E. Treatment of depression by drugs and psychotherapy. *American Journal of Psychiatry*, 1974, *131*, 186.

Pardes, H. The future of psychiatry—More unified, more innovative? *Roche Report, Frontiers of Psychiatry*, 1981, *11*, 10.

Rabkin, R. *Inner and Outer Space*. New York: Norton, 1970.

Whitaker, C. and Keith, D. Symbolic-experiential family therapy. In A. Gurman & D. Kniskern (Eds.), *Handbook of Family Therapy*. New York: Brunner/Mazel, 1981.

**STUART R. SUGARMAN, M.D.**
*Assistant Professor of Psychiatry*
*University of Connecticut*
*School of Medicine*
*Farmington, CT*

# 30. Brief Family Therapy Used to Catalyze Extended Psychotherapy

**Question:**

Many of my patients are young adults still without families of their own. Some of them are deeply troubled about painfully unsettled issues and relationships in their families of origin. More often than not, however, they are physically separated from their parents and siblings by hundreds or even thousands of miles. Isn't this a situation where working with the family, while it might make sense in principle, is simply out of the question?

**Discussion:**

No, at least in many such cases. The only cases in which I do not even *consider* family intervention are those in which literally no one in the family is still living and able to remember, relate and talk (Birk, 1978, 1982).

Before tacitly siding with the patient that family meetings are impossible, the therapist should remember how easy it is for people to engage in flights into resistance when it comes to "leveling" with family members—especially parents—with whom frequently he or she has had very little truly honest communication over the course of a half-lifetime, despite the overwhelming importance of each to the other. Typically, there are strong defensive "ruts" of noncommunication, or more accurately, selective partial communication. All members of the family, including the distant member now in the therapist's office for his/her own psychotherapy, have overlearned and practiced such defensive evasions for years.

It should therefore hardly be surprising that the patient him/herself almost never suggests meetings with the family as an option, and that, when the therapist first brings up the subject, a multitude of seemingly compelling objections emerge. Of these, one of the first and foremost is likely to be something like, "Oh, they live in Montana! I can't ask them to come all the way out here (Boston)." My answer to that is usually an immediate, "Why not?"

144

When more objections arise, I persevere:

But this is important; I see *many* people for family meetings who come that far, or ever farther. . . . What if you needed them to come for some medical reason? Would they come if you needed a kidney transplant?

I go on to explain that family meetings are not a necessary part of all psychotherapy, but that when they are needed and possible, they tend to accelerate and deepen the work of therapy:

Some psychotherapy must be finished with a handicap—not being able to actually talk with the "important others" who shaped a person's early life, experience, attitudes, and personality, because the important people are dead.

But you are lucky, your father (or mother) is alive; you have a real opportunity to talk with him now, before it's too late for that. . . . That could save you several years in therapy, as well as improve the eventual outcome of therapy considerably. Beyond that, you and he will have a real chance to be truly honest with each other; usually that makes for a much better relationship in whatever time you two have left. . . .

A next common line of defense is, "Maybe in theory it would be a good idea, but he (she/they) would *never* come. . . . They don't even believe in psychiatry . . ."—to which I reply that I see many families like that, and it almost always proves useful. Or the patient may say, "If he (she/they) did come, you'd never even see what they are really like. They would put up such a front. . . ." I usually respond by saying that this is not my general experience, which comes from many, many families (including many where this has been predicted), provided I as the therapist come to the first meeting forearmed with enough preliminary information from the patient, about what his/her family—especially his/her parents—were and are really like, and what some of the crucial events and issues in the family are. (This "preliminary information" is derived from between six and 12 months of regular work in psychotherapy, most often in twice weekly group psychotherapy.) There are those rare cases where I find that even as an outside family therapist, amply informed in advance about people, events, and issues in the family, I also "cannot get to first base" during the meetings. In such cases I point out that, if that should happen, you still will have gained something of value, because in that case you will be working with a therapist who knows firsthand how "tough" your family is, and what formidable problems you have had and indeed still have in trying to relate meaningfully to people so rigidly resistant to authenticity and honest communication.

I have gone to such lengths in overcoming realistic barriers and resistances to family work in no more than a third of my cases in which geographical separation complicates matters. But when I have deemed it important enough, I have introduced the idea early in therapy, "for later," and I have kept at it, not unremittingly, but tenaciously and recurrently, typically over many months and with the strong support of many of the patient's peers in his/her therapy group. This happens because nearly all the members of my groups have either resisted and then done, or witnessed others first resisting and then doing, useful family work. Frequently, the idea of family meetings is in fact first brought up by other group members, and not by me.

Once the issue of family meetings has been joined, in one way or another, I have succeeded in getting the patient and his/her family to arrange a series of meetings in well over 90% of the cases where it becomes an issue. And with well over 90% of those patients, the eventual meetings prove highly useful.

The family meetings themselves—discounting preparation time before, and integration time after—may amount to as little as only three-to-six hours, out of a psychotherapy duration of 200, 300, or more hours. Yet overall, the meetings for everyone concerned seem to be very much "worth it."

Why? First, because as soon as I suggest the idea (or another group member suggests it), *therapy is never again the same.* Even if for particular reasons no family meetings ever occur, therapy is never again dry or theoretical. Also, the patient is thereafter much more likely to get beyond mere recitation of grievances, and to make a real effort to be balanced and honest about what he/she says about his/her old hurts, angers, and grudges at people in his/her family of origin. After all, accuracy is now crucial, because one day I might just meet "them" and hear the other side of the story!

Second, even if my original patient and his family can succeed in experiencing together only one session during which both are authentic in what they say and what they feel with each other, the patient undergoes a permanent, reality-based change in the way he/she perceives his/her family. Behaviorally, both original patient and family may regress—almost inevitably of course they do regress, at least in part—but they cannot but be lastingly affected by what they have seen and participated in. A person might mistake a motionless, closed-up terrapin for a lifeless stone. However, once there has been a glimpse of the "stone" moving, creeping on four legs, craning its neck, peering about with two beady eyes, there is no going back to the stone concept. Even though subsequently the terrapin may close up again and look like (behave like) a stone, it will never again be seen and thought of as a stone.

Third, although we still lack rigorous scientific evidence to document it, as in most areas of psychotherapy, I do really believe what I tell my patients in my admittedly hard-sell approach to setting up family meetings: that such brief adjunctive family work does materially accelerate psychotherapy, as well as deepen the significance of the benefits that result from it.

Such a "blitzkrieg" approach to family therapy does, however, carry its own special problems, risks, and cautionary notes, a few of which I will list:

1) While it can often be better to meet with the original patient and part of his or her family rather than only with patient, there are problems in being too ready to compromise the ideal of seeing the whole surviving family. It may not be necessary to see every living sibling, but in my experience it can be a real blunder to agree to see the original patient only, plus his or her parents, unless he or she is an only child.

2) If the parents are divorced—sometimes long-divorced—I believe it is important to see both parents plus at least one sibling, but wise to set up alternating meetings, rather than meetings all together, with the mother and the father.

3) If one of the parents is both at a great distance and severely disturbed, with a history of recurrent psychotic episodes for example, I believe it is ordinarily unwise to press for family meetings to include that person.

4) For patients with healthier families, the therapist should be sensitive to and anticipate the fact that the meetings may usefully stir up interest in or need for couple therapy or psychotherapy for some of "the folks back home." My own practice is to mention that fact in the course of the brief series of family meetings, and to offer myself as a resource person for helping to arrange an appropriate referral in the distant city, should that become a practical need.

## References

Birk, L. Behavior therapy and behavioral psychotherapy. In A. M. Nicholi, Jr. (Ed.). *The Harvard Guide to Modern Psychiatry*. Cambridge, MA: Harvard University Press, 1978.

Birk, L. Psychotherapy within social systems. In A. Jacobson and D. Parmelee (Eds.). *Psychoanalysis: Critical Explorations in Contemporary Theory and Practice*. New York: Brunner/Mazel, 1982.

**LEE BIRK, M.D.**
*Associate Clinical Professor of Psychiatry*
*Harvard Medical School;*
*Director*
*Learning Therapies, Inc.*
*Newton, MA*

# 31. Choosing Between Individual Therapy and Marital Therapy

**Question:**

> I've heard some people argue that it is important to keep an eye out for the possibility that some patients will request marital therapy as a defense against examining their own individual problems or pathology. Can some guidelines be offered about how the therapist can assess such a situation so that the proper modality of therapy is offered?

**Discussion:**

The request for marital treatment may indeed serve to defend against patients' examination of their "individual" problems. Conversely, and far more frequently, patients seeking individual therapy wish to avoid their intrafamilial conflicts (Whitaker and Miller, 1969). Further, the request for child or adolescent therapy often facilitates the denial of parents' marital *and* individual problems (Freud, 1905; Montalvo and Haley, 1973; and the current film, *Ordinary People*, 1980). Thus, we may safely say that the *request for any particular modality can serve defensive needs*.

All of this underlines the axiom that almost all presenting clinical situations partake simultaneously of individual (intrapsychic) as well as interpersonal (systems) dynamics. As the Heisenberg principle in physics suggests, methodology is crucial. Light, depending on how we study it, can be viewed as made up of either "particles" or "waves." This relativity is all the more true in the mental health sciences. In addition to methodology (individual or family observation) determining what is seen, the particular perspective of the observer is also critical. A symptom from the perspective of individual theory may be seen as encompassing maladaptive learning (behaviorism) or a compromise formation between unconscious impulse and defense (psychoanalytic), while family theory will tend to see the symptom as serving a homeostatic function for the family unit.

The demarcation between an "individual" and his/her

"marriage/family" is thus somewhat artificial; indeed, where there is poor mutual self-object differentiation (object relations theory), an undifferentiated family ego mass (Bowen), or an enmeshed family (Minuchin), the pathological boundaries between individual and family are what need therapeutic attention. They can be attended to in either modality if the therapist is so oriented. The distinction therefore between individual and family therapy is also somewhat arbitrary and reflects theoretical and political divisions, as well as loyalties within the mental health disciplines. Such parochialism, needless to say, distorts the reality of interlocking individual and family dynamics.

Where does this leave us? What guidelines can be offered in the midst of such indeterminacy? First, an awareness of these defenses and boundary issues is as important as the "offering of a proper modality." It is more a question of the therapist's perspective: Individual problems can be explored within the context of marital treatment just as marital disturbances can be explored in the context of individual therapy. An individual psychoanalytic patient of mine deplored what he thought to be his wife's disparagement of a recent personal success of his, thus making her similar to his critical mother and contributing to his sexual impotence. A query as to how he was so sure she was disparaging led him to ask her directly what her reaction was. This led to a declaration of her pleasure, albeit subdued in expression, with his success and to a more reality-based interaction between them. This in turn fostered his gradual appreciation of his wife as different and separate from his mother.

In my recent book (Sander, 1979), I described the case of a wife (Mrs. B) who was dissatisfied with her husband's "workaholic" habits. She had had two individual therapies with no change in their 15-year marriage. Her last individual therapist referred them in the hope of getting some change in the marital relationship. Her husband, with obvious "individual" problems, experienced no pain other than the referred pain of his wife's "unhappiness"; individual therapy was inconceivable and unacceptable to him. Marital therapy was barely tolerable and made possible, at the start, only by his wife's threat of divorce. After over a year of once-weekly marital sessions, Mr. B reported a dream in which he was being chased by a threatening group. He put half a cantaloupe on his head and everything turned out all right. Though still pursued by his wife and me, he was no longer able to "elope" from his marriage and the therapy. He had begun to accept responsibility for their marital impasse and to realize that his own compulsive and detached behavior had limited his own pleasure at work and at home. Some months later, with eagerness mixed with trepidation, he accepted a referral to group therapy for himself. This outcome was made possible by two years of therapy which prepared him to work on his more "individual" difficulties. Returning to the presenting question, this vignette illustrates that we must start with an attitude *and* modality that respect the defenses of a patient or family. With the reduction of these defenses, individuation can emerge with either modality.

## References

Freud, S. Fragment of an analysis of a case of hysteria (1905) *Standard Edition*, Vol. 7, 1-122. London: Hogarth Press, 1953.

Montalvo, B. and Haley, J. In defense of child therapy, *Family Process*, 1973, *12*, 227-244.

Sander, F. *Individual and Family Therapy: Toward an Integration*. New York: Aronson, 1979.

Whitaker, C. and Miller, M. A re-evaluation of "psychiatric help" when divorce impends. *American Journal of Psychiatry*, 1969, *126*, 611-616.

**FRED M. SANDER, M.D.**
*Assistant Clinical Professor of Psychiatry*
*Albert Einstein College of Medicine;*
*Director of Family Therapy*
*Long Island Jewish-Hillside Hospital*
*New York, NY*

# SECTION III

# Treatment of Severe Disorders

# 32. Treating the Alcoholic Marriage

**Question:**

Like many areas of mental health practice, there seems to be an enormously wide range of beliefs about the "alcoholic personality" in general, and its relationship to marital problems in particular. Even supervisors of mine who generally share the same theoretical persuasion disagree a lot in this area. I would like to know something about the scientific status of the answers to these questions: 1) Are there real interaction differences between "alcoholic marriages" and other distressed marriages? 2) Do the spouses of alcoholics show a very common personality style? and 3) What implications for conjoint marital therapy of the "alcoholic marriage" can be pulled from our scientific knowledge in the first two areas?

**Discussion:**

These three questions have plagued alcoholism treatment and research professionals for at least 40 years. Currently, many therapists believe that alcoholic couples have poor communication and problem-solving skills. They engage in few positive interactions, and have developed a style of interacting characterized by coercive control, threats, and nagging. Communication is seen as ambiguous, vague, and inconsistent. In these ways, alcoholic couples do not appear to be dramatically different from other distressed couples. However, alcohol then enters the scene. Often, when conflict arises, the alcoholic will flee the scene and drink. This perpetuates the conflict and probably creates new problems, since the couple has to now attend to all of the concomitant difficulties that arise when one person is drinking and the other is trying to cope with it, control it, or ignore it. For many couples, the drinking may also serve positive functions in the relationship, in that the couple may be better able to express affection, attention, or anger while one partner is intoxicated.

Many studies support this view. Some have found that there is a high probability of drinking following interpersonal conflicts, and that increases in assertiveness, amount of speaking, or affectionate displays occur consequent to drinking. Observational studies have in general found high rates of hostile and coercive interactions, low rates of friendly or affectionate interactions, and low rates of discussing relationship issues.

Your second question, about personalities of spouses of alcoholics, has also generated a great deal of research and comment in the field. Virtually all of the work in the field has been on wives of alcoholic men, so I will limit my comments here to female spouses. Early clinical reports described wives of alcoholic men as riddled by neurotic conflicts, ravaged by sexual fears, dependency conflicts and poorly controlled aggressive impulses, and desiring to dominate a weakened male. Basically, these women were seen as being fixated at a particular psychosexual stage, and, as adults, as continuing to experience conscious and unconscious conflicts as a result of this early fixation. Marriage to an alcoholic or potential alcoholic was seen as a neurotic resolution of this conflict. Some of these early authors also stated that alcoholic men unconsciously marry these women to meet their own neurotic needs.

Studies designed to test this view of spouses of alcoholics have utilized general measures of psychological disturbance, such as the MMPI or the Psychological Screening Inventory, or have measured specific traits, such as "dependency" or "dominance." Taken as a whole, this research suggests that wives of alcoholics show some generalized increases in psychiatric symptoms when their husbands are drinking but that these symptoms generally decrease if the husband stops drinking for a period of time. The research has also found that alcoholic men tend to perceive their wives as dominant, although this term is generally quite loosely defined.

Rather than viewing these women as having common personality patterns, many in the alcoholism field have accepted a more sociological perspective. This view suggests that living with an actively drinking alcoholic is a stressful situation and that the disturbances observed in these women, and their perceived dominance, are typical responses to dealing with this stressful environment. Studies which find decreases in these symptoms accompanying abstinence tend to support this view.

There are several treatment implications of the findings about patterns of interaction in alcoholic marriages, and the lack of findings of common personality profiles among wives of alcoholics. First, it appears that many behaviors that spouses engage in represent attempts to cope with the drinking itself. Some of these attempts may in fact contribute to further drinking. Thus, repeated comments about the person's drinking, questioning the alcoholic about his plans and actions, or checking up on his or her whereabouts may actually cue further drinking. Removing aversive consequences of drinking, by cleaning up messes, calling the boss when the drinker is unable to get to work, or lying to friends and family, may also maintain the drinking behavior. Some spouses may actually be more positive and attentive toward their alcoholic partner when he or she is drinking, thus inadvertently reinforcing drinking. Thus, one component of treatment should probably address specific ways to teach spouses more effective ways of coping with these situations. The second logical component of treatment is specific interventions directed at the marital relationship. These interventions follow from the communications findings, in that couples need to learn more positive ways of responding to each other and need to learn more effective communication and problem-solving skills.

While these treatment interventions follow logically from the previously described findings, one important question must be raised. We do not know how much marital interaction skills improve as a natural consequence of abstinence. If couples can acquire or reacquire these skills on their own, it may be that no specific marital interventions are necessary and that all treatment should focus on teaching the alcoholic how to maintain abstinence and teaching the spouse how to respond to drinking and to nondrinking. This is an empirical question which is currently under study. Until this question has been addressed, it appears that the initial focus in treatment should be on the actual drinking behavior, involving both the alcoholic and spouse. Consequent to this phase of treatment, the focus of treatment should probably shift to general interactional patterns and problems which the couple exhibits.

**BARBARA S. McCRADY, Ph.D.**
*Associate Professor*
*Section of Psychiatry and Human Behavior*
*Butler Hospital/Brown University*
*Providence, RI*

# 33. Family Dynamics and Interventions in Alcoholism

## Question:

It appears that alcoholism is often involved in family dynamics. Are there any specific family dynamics associated with the development of alcoholism? On the other hand, how does alcoholism affect family structure and function? Where and how can family therapy be used in the treatment of alcoholism? What are the special problems facing the family therapist, and what modifications of treatment technique are involved in alcoholism treatment?

## Discussion:

Since at least 1940 there has been recognition of the significant interactive relationships between alcoholism and the family (Kaufman and Kaufman, 1979; Pattison and Kaufman, 1981; Pattison, Sobell, and Sobell, 1977; Steinglass, 1977). Yet the family therapy field has relatively ignored alcoholism-related family problems, while alcoholism treatment programs have been slow to incorporate family therapy methods. I have observed that family therapists often assume that alcoholism problems can be treated like any other family problem—which ignores the special complications of alcoholism. While alcoholism personnel often view alcoholism as solely an individual problem, rather than a reflection of family system dynamics, I believe each field has much to learn from the other before family therapy will become a major treatment modality in alcoholism treatment programs.

There are four major psychodynamic themes in the interaction of alcoholism and the family.

First is the effect of alcoholism on family dynamics. An alcoholic family member creates a major stress on the structure and function of the family. Economic losses strain financial stability; legal problems may create loss of family social status, family esteem, and family morale. Drinking behavior often interrupts normal family tasks and creates functional conflict. It may evoke structural change in family roles to cope and adapt to the drinking behavior as well as changes in usual performance of the drinking member. In brief, an alcoholic member usually impacts heavily on family dynamics, leading to gradual deterioration and disintegration of the family system.

Second are the effects of the family on alcoholism. This is the other side of the coin of the first dynamic. Marital and family conflict may evoke, support, and maintain alcoholism as 1) a symptom of family dysfunction, 2) a coping mechanism for dealing with family stresses, and 3) a consequence of dysfunctional family styles, rules, and patterns of alcohol use and abuse. In each case, we are confronted with family dynamics which contribute to the development and maintenance of alcoholism in a family member.

Third are the dynamics of the family and alcohol abuse as a system. Alcohol use in the family is not just an individual matter. Drinking behavior is purposeful, adaptive, homeostatic, and meaningful. Alcoholic behavior influences and is influenced by the system functions of the family. Further, alcoholism is embedded in generational and kinship relations. There is psychological transmission of alcoholism dynamics from one family generation to the next and between kinship associations. Alcoholism families breed alcoholism families in their children and their relatives. Children of alcoholics are more likely to marry alcoholism-prone spouses, whether male or female.

Fourth are the implications of family dynamics for treatment of an alcoholic member. The family is a critical factor in impeding or promoting definitive treatment for the alcoholic member. Family involvement throughout the treatment process significantly improves treatment participation and treatment response. Family involvement in community aftercare programs significantly influences long-term treatment success. Therefore, where there is an intact family with an active alcoholic, I believe it is imperative to include family therapy as part of the overall alcoholism treatment program.

However, family therapy is not a panacea for alcoholism. I find it the unusual case where family therapy alone can be employed to treat alcoholism. The alcoholic person ofter suffers from major physical, emotional, social, and vocational impairments, which require additional specific treatment or rehabilitation measures. So, I consider family therapy as one of several necessary treatment interventions.

Further, there is a major pitfall in treating alcoholics that centers on the need to focus on the drinking behavior per se. I have found that any type of psychotherapy with alcoholics will usually fail if the drinking behavior is only viewed as a symptom which will disappear when the neurotic conflicts are resolved. It is difficult if not impossible to achieve meaningful therapeutic interaction with a drinking or drunk person. Further, the drinking behavior per se assumes functional autonomy apart from the psychodynamics that generated the drinking. Therefore, therapy must address the drinking behavior directly and interrupt the drinking so that the alcoholic can participate meaningfully in psychotherapy. I must emphasize that even after two-to-three weeks of sobriety, major cognitive impairment and affect instability are evident in most alcoholics.

The family therapist is faced with two kinds of systems—the *wet* family system and the *dry* family system. In a wet system, the alcoholic member is actively drinking and may appear for family sessions in some degree of intoxication. Initially, this may be used therapeutically to observe how the family copes with the intoxicated member. Usually the family has ineffective coping responses, which either exacerbate the drinking or minimize the impact of the intoxicated member. The task of the therapist commences with the identification of these ineffective family styles.

Then the therapist must confront the family with the need to change their coping response to drunken episodes and behavior. The therapist must be careful not to side in collusion with the family against the alcoholic. Rather the therapist must help the family to develop limit-setting responses that incorporate the alcoholic into the family. At the same time, the therapist must reduce the destructive impact of the alcoholic on family function. This may include direct interaction with the alcoholic to keep him/her within a reasonable family role, modeling appropriate responses to the alcoholic, and teaching family members how to appropriately protect themselves. These are all initial steps in converting a wet family system into a dry family system. If the family is unable to achieve a stable dry system, it is usually necessary to temporarily isolate the alcoholic from the family until short-term sobriety is established and constructive family therapy with a dry system can be instituted.

There are typical family dynamic problems encountered in alcoholism. Disengagement-enmeshment conflict is often seen. The alcoholic feels guilty and provokes family guilt. This leads to enmeshment, overprotection, and collusion with the alcoholic. When this fails and drinking again ensues, the family may then disengage, extrude, and isolate the alcoholic from family life. The result is a series of polar family-alcoholic stances of overinvolvement alternating with hostile extrusion. The therapist must identify both patterns and modify these polarities. The symptom of drinking behavior can be either ignored or set on center stage as the sole issue. Again, either polarity is dysfunctional. The meaning, function, consequences, and responses associated with drunkeness must be examined by the family in terms of how drinking fits into family system dynamics. Here, relabeling and reframing techniques can be useful. Family roles tend to be blurred or mixed. Therefore, role definition and role clarification are usually necessary. Family communication and family decision-making processes are usually dysfunctional. So, the family therapist will have to engage in family communication learning skills and guide the family into more effective decision-making processes.

In the above synopsis, I have assumed a primary focus on the here and now of family dynamics and family function. Because of the immediacy of the drinking symptoms and drinking behavior, the family therapist does not have the luxury of gradually exploring the background of family development and the dynamic progression of the alcoholism. The problem is before you: Direct and rather immediate changes in family function must be achieved. The therapist must be active, decisive, and constructive. The therapist must direct, guide, model, teach, instruct, and supervise the family. Only in unusual cases can a more interpretive, explorative, and developmental technique be used.

Finally, we need to consider different types of family alcoholism patterns which dictate different types of family treatment interventions. I shall illustrate with four types of family systems and corresponding family interventions.

First is the functional family system. Here, we have an intact family; the alcoholism is primarily isolated to the alcoholic member, with drinking apart from the family which minimally impacts on family operations. These families tend to have high denial levels accompanied by low psychological-mindedness. Such families operate on a surface level of life, albeit with good adaptive and coping strategies. These families often resist direct psychotherapeutic approaches. However, they may be receptive to initial family education methods, including didactic information about alcoholism. This can lead to family communication and family decision-making sessions. These are often good-risk families in which these surface-level intervention techniques may be successful and sufficient.

Second are the neurotically enmeshed family systems. These families demonstrate the ravages of years of existence as alcoholism families. There is deterioration of family structure and function, yet because of enmeshment and collusion the family remains intact despite the alcoholism. Here, the more direct and active restructuring of family process from a wet system to a dry system and consequent reorganization of family function as described are most appropriate. In these families it is usually necessary to also engage the alcoholic member in individual rehabilitation as well.

Third is the disintegrated family system. Here, the family and kin relations have been severed. The alcoholic is usually seen first in a hospital or halfway house. Initial treatment must proceed until the alcoholic has achieved sobriety, emotional stability, and some reintegration of his/her life. Only at this point will the family usually consider contact. Here, family sessions need to focus on evaluation of the alcoholic-family relationship. This may lead to reconstitution of the family unit or resolution of permanent family separation.

Fourth is the absent family system. Common among skid-road alcoholics and some halfway house and mission habitués is relative loss of all family and kin contacts. Here, reconstitution of new social networks which offer family and kin types of social relationships has proven useful.

To conclude, alcoholism is not one problem, but a set of multiple problems. Family therapy alone is appropriate for only a small group of alcoholics; yet family therapy, I believe, should be a part of most alcoholism rehabilitation programs. However, the family therapist must address the unique problems of alcoholism in the family with appropriate modification of techniques to address these special circumstances.

*References*

Kaufman, E. and Kaufman, P. *The Family Therapy of Drug and Alcohol Abusers*. New York: Gardner Press, 1979.

Pattison, E. M. and Kaufman, E. Family therapy in the treatment of alcoholism. In M. R. Lansky (Ed.), *Family Therapy and Major Psychopathology*. New York: Grune & Stratton, 1981.

Pattison, E. M., Sobell, M. D., and Sobell, L. C. *Emerging Concepts of Alcohol Dependence*. New York: Springer, 1977.

Steinglass, P. Family therapy in alcoholism. In B. Kissin & H. Begleiter (Eds.), *The Biology of Alcoholism. Social Pathology*. Vol. 4. New York: Plenum, 1977.

**E. MANSELL PATTISON, M.D.**
*Professor and Chairman*
*Department of Psychiatry*
*Medical College of Georgia*
*Augusta, GA*

# 34. The Narcissistically Vulnerable Couple

## Question:

What is a narcissistically vulnerable marriage? What holds it together? Why is it important to distinguish a marriage characterized by narcissistic vulnerability from one that is not? What are the features of the narcissistically vulnerable marriage? What technical problems do these pose for the therapist?

## Discussion:

The narcissistically vulnerable marriage, typified by the full-blown chronically conflictual or blaming couple, is not organized around satisfaction, fulfillment, or desire within the marriage. Such marriages are organized around the containment and expression of rage by the collusive exchange of projective defenses (Lansky, 1981). These maneuvers serve to ward off the experience of inadequacy and the humiliating realization that abandonment (or even the threat of it) results in debilitating anxiety and fragmentation experiences. Shedding light on the operations within the marriage risks exposing the partners as clingy, angry, envious, and intensely dependent on a spouse who is also held in contempt. The humiliation that comes with such awareness must be defended against by these patients who have usually been sensitized by actual experiences of humiliating dependency in their early nurturing relationships.

Often there is a history of: abandonment; neglect; physical or sexual abuse; or involvement in the parental marriage by being blamed, scapegoated or parentified. The humiliation-proneness may make even the simplest descriptive statement by the therapist appear as blame itself and, hence, intolerable. Interpretation of process, which with healtheir couples is best done by pointing out patterns of communication, may occasionally result in a transient subsidence of a crisis but without generalized learning or enduring change. In the narcissistically vulnerable marriage, the therapeutic activity of pointing out what the spouses actually do or what they communicate to each other is often

humiliating to the point of endangering treatment. The model of me-
tacommunication as the essence of therapeutic intervention is insufficient for the treatment of narcissistically vulnerable marriages.

Distinguishing a marriage that is characterized by narcissistic vulnerability from one that is not is of central importance not only in
overtly conflictual marriages, but also in clinical situations that may
find expression in other types of symptomatology that resonate to the
tensions in such a marriage. Such situations include alcoholism and
depression in a spouse; underfunctioning, aggressiveness or promiscuity in children or adolescents; sexual dysfunction; behavior disorders;
addictive disorders; and a host of apparently straightforward psychotherapeutic situations that end in a stalemate if the marital dynamics
are not appreciated. For a couple without narcissistic vulnerability of
clinical significance, many types of therapeutic experience, and even
nonprofessional growth experiences, may be helpful. For those marriages where narcissistic vulnerability is in evidence, understanding
of the features of this vulnerability is essential in adapting technique
so that it minimizes narcissistic injury to the couple in the treatment
process itself, and provides an experience in which truly generalizable
emotional learning takes place.

The more overt type of chronic conflictual narcissistically vulnerable
marriage can be easily recognized in the initial interview with a couple
presenting with marital difficulties. Such marriages are easier to spot
than when difficulties are covered over by overt symptoms in one
spouse or in a child who is identified as the patient. In marriages free
of narcissistic vulnerability, anger generally resides in a specific situation and diminishes with the resolution of that issue. Disagreements
are capable, at least in principle, of resolution. In vulnerable marriages, disagreements serve as opportunities to express infantile rage
and vengefulness in the form of blame. The surface issues serve as
justification for defensive operations usually projective in nature and
allow the blamer to voice fears of being let down, left alone, not being
taken care of, and disappointed. In more normal marriages, spouses
progress to the point of asking for what they want. Characterologic
demandingness and a sense of entitlement typify vulnerable marriages
so that nothing seems capable of fulfilling the spouses' omnipotent
expectations of each other. In normal marriages, disputes based on
differing preconceptions of the marriage can often be illuminated by
appreciating what it is about their parents' marriage each spouse
wishes to preserve or modify. The differences can often be negotiated.
In vulnerable marriages, there is usually an obvious trauma in upbringing with derivative themes from the parental marriages replayed

in the current marriage and unresolvable in principle. Such trauma results from character pathology in parents, manifested by gross defects or sudden changes in parental nurturance; parentification or blame by parents; triangulation of the child in chronically quarrelsome or vulnerable marriages; or physical or sexual abuse by a parent or with parental knowledge.

In normal marriages, ignorance of intimate situations is often resolvable by better communication and goodwill, once major conflicts near resolution. With vulnerable marriages, feelings of emptiness and preoccupation with disappointments early in life leave in both partners a feeling of incompleteness, inadequacy, and shame, making intimacy a terror to be warded off. The very awareness of that terror becomes yet another humiliation requiring vigorous defense.

In vulnerable marriages, low-level projective mechanisms accompanied by vengefulness and self-righteousness leave the blamer immersed in so much of the issue at hand that his or her observing ego is lost during the blaming. A completely different ego state is present when the couple is not in conflict. In more normal marriages, it is clear what areas of richness hold the marriage together. Vulnerable marriages have spouses with either limited capacities for satisfaction or so much that is disowned by the couple's need for each other that it is difficult to see what holds the marriage together. The discourse of narcissistically vulnerable patients is replete with complaints about the unhappiness of life, described as though they emanated solely from the shortcomings of the spouse. This style of blaming and complaining is the extreme of unempathic relatedness.

Narcissistically vulnerable marriages that are less typified by overt conflict may be more difficult to recognize in the consulting room or in the history of patients who do not appear to have been the offspring of traumatic marriages. Symptomatic dysfunction of a spouse in the form of substance abuse, a behavior disorder, or an affective disorder may alert the therapist to the presence of such vulnerability. More subtle are situations that present as loyalty conflict between family and job, between family of origin and family of procreation, and between marriage and children. Such preoccupations may not superficially differ from normal complex loyalties but often cover up preoccupied states of mind and a complete inability to engage emotionally in the marriage. The use of some special status or overriding loyalty serves to disguise the difficulty of bonding in the marriage by justifying attention to more pressing demands. Other clues are the character traits of contempt, self-righteousness, self-pity, blaming, debunking, or undue suspiciousness of any context. In a family with an identified dysfunctional member, narcissistic vulnerability in the nuclear marriage may evince none of these features. This concealing of the feeling of defectiveness by projection onto a spouse or a child who acts dysfunctionally in a field of seemingly normal family members is recognized by experienced family therapists as the purportedly individual disturbance that is found to serve the need of the entire family system.

Family therapists of any persuasion are familiar with the ability of families to give the appearance that symptoms reside only in one member. It is common for overt narcissistic vulnerability to appear (often explosively) if such an identified patient improves and begins to find freedom from the demands of the system in which the patient serves as the focus for projections of inadequacy. As long as this function is performed by the identified defective, there is some feeling of well-being in the rest of the system. Other systems aspects of the narcissistically vulnerable marriage are the clinginess and fear of abandonment that may be inferred from the symptomatic behaviors that reassert the unstable dyad. Moves of independence by one person are met with behavior on the part of others that reestablishes even an unsatisfactory dyad as the primary focus of its members' attention. The behavior is usually felt to be symptomatic, antisocial, or frankly psychotic: infidelities broadcast to the spouse, drinking, suicide attempts, and so forth. These give one party the chance to demand, to uncover, to blame, or to feel exploited—preoccupied states manifesting themselves and offering relief when that split-off part of the personality is allowed to express itself. The other spouse has a chance to inflict punishment by the symptomatic behavior. Both resume an unpleasant bonding, attachment to which is disowned but attention to which is undivided and unremitting.

The collusive defenses, often obvious if the couple is observed over even a short time, are difficult to bring to their attention; they are lost in projections and actions—invitations to blame, provocations to act up, and what become predictable responses that reestablish the blaming equilibrium. Blaming behavior or provocative blame-inviting actions are difficult to get into therapeutic focus, because the ego state that blames or provokes blame by drinking, gambling, acting undependably, and so forth is split off from the more usual state of consciousness which is the one that presents to the therapist. At such time, when the usual state of consciousness is present, the patient may be bewildered by the behavior, oblivious to it, ashamed of it, but in any event, not in control of it. This combination—split-off ego states accompanied by low-level projective defenses and actions—makes appeal to an observing ego most difficult. The same difficulties oppose the chance for therapy to become a situation where an effective therapeutic experience serves to generalize learning from the session to other situations. Hence, there is difficulty in establishing even that a patient or a couple is defensive, much less how they are defending or why. Narcissistically vulnerable marriages are characterized, not simply by conflict, but by actual deficits emanating from the shortcomings in genuine, protective, empathic nurturance early in life.

The techniques of treating the couple with narcissistic vulnerability should be aimed at collusive defenses; humiliation-proneness; fear of abandonment; massive rage with the specific flavor of injustice; vengefulness; excessive gratification from aggressive discharge in the act of blaming; splitting of the ego and low-level defenses that interfere with an effective observing ego able to learn from the therapeutic experience; and a history of unsatisfactory nurturance gathered directly, or inferred, from repetitive themes in the patient's life that repeat in derivative forms the traumata of childhood.

*Reference*

Lansky, M. R. Treatment of the narcissistically vulnerable couple. In M. R. Lansky (Ed.), *Family Therapy and Major Psychopathology*. New York: Grune & Stratton, 1981.

**MELVIN R. LANSKY, M.D.**
*Adjunct Associate Professor of Psychiatry
UCLA Medical School;
Staff Psychiatrist and Chief
Family Treatment Program
Brentwood VA Medical Center
Brentwood, CA*

# 35. Conjoint Marital Therapy and Spouse Abuse

**Question:**

More and more, I am seeing couples for whom spouse abuse (usually of the wife) is the presenting problem. Since the abusing spouse sometimes has clear individual pathology, but not always, I am unclear as to when individual therapy of the abusing spouse is called for, and when conjoint marital therapy is the treatment of choice. Can you suggest some guidelines about how to make this decision?

**Answer:**

The treatment of spouse abuse is extraordinarily difficult and the therapist must be flexible in regard to the decision of the appropriateness of individual or conjoint marital therapy. It is often sensible and practical to treat individual members of the couple for a period of time before beginning conjoint marital therapy. This allows for the individual members to discuss in an open fashion their chief concerns about the marital situation and to be honest with the therapist without fear of either verbal or physical retaliation.

Oftentimes it is not possible to do conjoint marital therapy because one member of the dyad is unable or unwilling to tolerate therapy. However, in my experience, abusing husbands are very much like the "fathers who never came to child guidance clinics." That is to say, fathers were not part of the treatment dyad because therapists did not attempt to do active case-planning and engage them in therapy. It is my belief, therefore, that the therapist ought to make extraordinary efforts to engage the abusing spouse in a therapeutic interaction.

After an initial period of evaluation and individual therapy, conjoint therapy may be appropriate. Spouses have suggested that often the verbal interactions in the office are followed by an increase in physical abuse at home. If this is so, it is probably wise to terminate the marital therapy. However, in my experience, the expression and fantasy of aggression are often very helpful in stopping, or at least minimizing, the cycle of violence.

If the cycle persists and seems to be resistant to any sort of change, it is probably best to switch back to individual therapy with the goal of helping the abused spouse take more active steps to restructure her environment. Such steps might include a consideration of further education and employment to establish a financial base from which she can contemplate leaving the marital relationship. Such changes will be slow and trying to the patience of the therapist. Working with abused spouses can be compared to working with autistic children. The gains are slow, steady, and difficult to achieve.

In this situation, the therapist may be at risk for the rage of the abusing spouse. It is important not to deny concerns articulated by the abused spouse about the safety and welfare of the therapist. She often has assessed reasonably well what the potential for danger is, both to herself and to others, as she has experienced danger and threat. It is important for the therapist not to minimize threats from the spouse abuser and to take adequate protective measures.

**ELISSA P. BENEDEK, M.D.**
*Center for Forensic Psychiatry*
*State of Michigan—Department of Mental Health*
*Ann Arbor, MI*

# 36. Treating Abusive Parents in Groups

**Question:**

Child abuse is a complicated family problem with each of the family members experiencing serious psychological stress. Most professionals agree that it is ideal to treat abusive families as an intact unit whenever possible. Only in extreme cases is it recommended that a member of the family be removed from the family unit in order to provide treatment. However, it is frequently not possible to treat a family as an intact unit for a number of reasons. For example, when the abusing parent is the only family member who sees the violence as a problem, the rest of the family may not choose to engage in treatment. How should I provide treatment that can benefit both the parent(s) and the child and how should I structure immediate relief from the violent interaction so the family can remain together while resolving their problems?

**Discussion:**

The model I use for working with abusive parents provides a supportive environment that can lead to changes in both cognition and behavior for the parent. It is designed for working with the abusive parent for the benefit of both the parent and the child. The child is being seriously hurt, both physically and psychologically, by the existing abusive behavior. The prime goal of treatment is to stop the abuse by changing the parental behaviors and cognitive structures. The first step in treatment is to help the parent reduce any active physical violence and then to begin the process of helping the parent learn new ways of parenting.

*Response to Crisis*

Most parents seek some type of assistance with their abuse problems in a crisis situation; when a child has just been hurt, the parent is scared, anxious, and more receptive to help than he/she will be later.

At this time it is important to stress nonjudgmentally some ways in which the parent can behave to stop the feelings of guilt and self-outrage which tend to keep the abuse cycle in place. If the parent is allowed to believe that he or she is an awful and monstrous person, the belief will lay the foundation for the next episode of abuse.

The parent should be offered some concrete suggestions regarding his/her behavior with his/her child and other family members. I usually prescribe a sequence of behaviors that will keep the parent occupied and detract him/her from thinking about him/herself. The emphasis is on what the parent can do, not on what the parent is feeling. It is important not to escalate any emotions during this crisis contact, but instead give the parent some sense of control over him/herself and the situation.

After responding to the initial crisis, the parent is referred to a support group to begin treatment. Abusive parents are lonely, isolated individuals who have very little psychological or social support for themselves from either their families or their communities. Because most of them experienced abuse or some type of maltreatment as children, they are likely to see themselves as unworthy of love and respect. These beliefs have kept each them from engaging in meaningful communication with their partners and other adults, resulting in a sense of isolation which is often overwhelming. Becoming part of a group allows abusive parents to view themselves as part of a community, thus reducing their sense of isolation. As they recognize that many other people share their thoughts, behaviors, and feelings, the parents begin to relate positively and without fear of discovery to other adults. The support system inherent in the group model provides the parents with:

- distraction from themselves and their problems by involving them with other people;
- someone to talk with who is perceived to be like them and thus will understand their anger and violent behavior; and,
- a reference point for understanding themselves as acceptable human beings who can change their behavior.

## Therapist Role

The therapist functions in two specific ways in this model. First, he/she provides guidance and direction to the group process to ensure that the participants interact in ways that are helpful to each other. When group members are unable to be empathic or helpful, it is the role of the therapist to both model and teach them how to help each other, so that the parents will begin learning to look to each other for support rather than relying on professional intervention. Second, the therapist gives specific information to the parents about child development, normal behavior patterns for children, and the linkages between parent and child behaviors. Abusive parents typically place unrealistic demands on their children, often expecting them to act in a much more mature way than their years. They also are unable to identify the ways in which their behavior can reinforce the very behavior in the child which they dislike. Abusive parents cannot be expected to gain insight on these matters unless they are given some concrete information to experiment with in their homes.

## Treatment Model

After the crisis has been responded to and the parent is referred for treatment, there are three steps which the therapist can use to help an abusive parent make and maintain changes. Although the steps are presented sequentially, they can also be used concurrently. Cognitive restructuring is designed to eliminate the sense of aloneness and uniqueness which the parent has about his/her abuse problem. The parent is encouraged to expand the range of perceptions about his/her own behaviors by learning to think about his/her situation in different ways. While not encouraged to rationalize abusive behavior, the parent is encouraged to understand his/her life situation and accompanying realities which cause stress and discomfort. In most cases the parent begins to recognize that the feelings he/she has are legitimate, but the method of expression of these feelings is not helpful to him/her.

A parent who is abusive is typically operating on some common myths about parenting. Other parents are perceived as being able to accomplish the task of parenting with ease and joy. The abusive parent believes that he/she has failed at a task which everyone (especially mothers) in our society is expected to achieve without difficulty and certainly without any help from outside the family.

During this phase of treatment, it is important for parents to challenge beliefs about themselves and others. They begin exploring thoughts and beliefs which may be keeping them from making better decisions about their life style. For example, a mother who thinks that leaving children in day-care to go work is a sign of "bad" parenting may be making inappropriate decisions based on this belief. She resents the child because she can't go to work when, in fact, it is her own thinking that is keeping her from working. The mother is trapped into a routine that is not best for her or the child. Whether the mother changes her belief or not, it is important that she recognizes that her belief is structuring her behavior and keeping her from exploring other alternatives. Once she accepts this, she can begin to learn new strategies for coping effectively with the existing situation. As a parent, she will have an increased sense of control and responsibility rather than perceiving herself as controlled externally.

Teaching is the next part of the treatment modality and is directed toward eliminating behavioral unpredictability by providing normative information regarding children and parenting. When abusive parents talk together about their children, the unrealistic expectations surface immediately: toddlers are expected to be neat and clean when eating; babies are expected to sleep through the night; elementary school-age children are expected to be loving and attentive. While all of these behaviors may be desired, it is not reasonable to expect the behaviors to exist without parental patience and modeling. Parents who believe that "good" behavior should exist as part of the package are angered when their child does not live up to such expectations. Unfortunately, many abusive parents interpret their child's "negative" behaviors as an intentional insult directed at the parent.

Parents are usually relieved to discover that not only do other children behave "badly," but such behavior is often normal. Young children require a consistent routine in order to interact most effectively. If a parent upsets the child's routine, he/she should expect the child to behave inappropriately and be prepared to respond to that behavior without anger.

Abusive incidents are frequently triggered by unexpected and unexplained behavior on the part of the child. Since many parents do reinforce the very behavior that triggers the outbreak of abuse, they have to learn how to stop their contribution to this vicious cycle. Parents can be taught how to break down each step in abusive situations so they can perceive their own role and understand how they are encouraging the undesired behaviors. The therapist elucidates the linkages since clarifying the cycle does not, itself, typically provide adequate insight for parents regarding their role. For example, a father who does not talk with his son, except to convey disappointment or criticism, may become angry when the child is noncommunicative or distant. He expects his son to treat him politely and respectfully even though he has not demonstrated that behavior to his son. Abusive parents often fail to recognize that their behavior will be mimicked and adopted by their children.

Consulting with parents about future treatment needs is the final part of the treatment model. Once the parent has made significant changes in the parenting role and the home environment is more controlled and stable, the parent is often ready to respond to personal concerns. It may be important for some parents to become involved in treatment which will focus on the past and/or the present relationship with their parents and siblings. Other parents may be interested in continuing to develop personal skills beyond those they have acquired in group treatment. Whatever the choice may be, it is important for the therapist to help each parent explore alternatives for future treatment.

Child abuse is a complex problem and for that reason parents will need the support group for a minimum of one year. It is also helpful for parents to remain in the support group while they are in individual treatment. However, the therapist's role is not as prominent during this phase. The relationships formed by parents within the group are generally very strong and positive by this time. They are able to help each other continue to grow, while at the same time providing support for maintaining a nonviolent home life.

**MARY L. OTTO, Ed.D.**
*Associate Professor*
*Oakland University*
*Rochester, MI*

# 37. Creating a Working Relationship
   with Abusive Families

**Question:**

> Over the years I have encountered a number of very angry, re-
> sistive families, usually referred by courts and child protective
> or child-placing agencies where multiple agencies are involved.
> There are often charges, countercharges and implied threats of,
> if not actual, placement and/or other punitive action. The referral
> for "therapy" is often seen as part of this punishment theme. How
> can the therapist establish and maintain a working relationship
> within this context?

**Discussion:**

Initially, be prepared for a prolonged burst of anger—attacks on the
agencies and professionals with, for example, charges of racism and
dishonesty. Have no illusions that you are exempt. When possible,
interject a question regarding specific dates, injuries, and so forth.
These, however, need to be reviewed at a later time to get a more
coherent picture.

Abusive families are usually looking for advocates or at least support
for their position. It is tempting to be seduced into that role, particularly since it is hard to identify with the way the "system" deals with
the problem. However, a neutral supportive stance weighing in with
both the "side" of the client and the "side" of society is essential. A
comment to the effect, "I don't know what really happened. However,
I basically believe that children should be with their parents and I'll
do all I can to help you get your lives together in such a way that we
can get your child returned to you," is helpful in getting through the
anger. This repeated stance usually leads to some "joining" or a beginning alliance. This helps make the conflict more acceptable to the
family.

At this point it is helpful to review the abuse or neglect, dates,
circumstances, and timing with other events. Recognizing that abuse
is a relationship event, you focus on understanding what was and is

going on between the individuals. Often the two parents are looking for parenting from each other. They may have been unable to work these issues out with their respective parents, so try to work them out with each other. They are mutually exploitative and if they are unable to get their needs met with each other, the family of origin exploitation and the marital conflict may get acted out on the child. If the parent was exploited, he/she feels justified in calling upon the child to make it up to him/her.

During this time the attacks on the system continue but tend to be interspersed with attacks on each other, raising issues of basic trust, different values, life-styles, etc. These both energize the dormant conflict and tend to lift the intrapsychic to the interpersonal process. My focus then is to help the individuals stand back and focus on these issues and what they can change in their lives and relationship. For instance, in a recent situation the paramour, a small feisty man with a great need to impress and feel important, rented an apartment for $600 plus utilities. His partner, who had been on welfare, was left at home to deal with the bill collectors. She took to the streets to avoid the situation. He accused her of drinking and being with other men and threatened to leave her. There was much rage expressed by each about their unmet needs.

After explosions in and out of the office and much discussion, they moved to an apartment renting for $150, allowing them to pay accumulated bills. She then for the first time took to domesticity—painting, making curtains, cooking—and there was no longer any discussion of her drinking and chasing. One of his big issues was "respect," i.e., her being where he could find her.

In the meantime she had bleached her hair and plucked her eyebrows in an attempt to get compliments from him. He disapproved of her efforts but had never been able to tell her he liked her "natural" look. This was discussed separately and together and he gained some appreciation of her need for approval. Time was devoted to helping each define his/her needs and learning to express them directly. In other words, there was a great deal of focus on the couple relationship with tentative attempts to relate this to the symptom, since this was the context in which the current "abuse" took place.

The more complicated and difficult next step was to help each partner look at family of origin issues. In this same situation mother had been abandoned by her mother at birth, betrayed by her father at age five and left to the care of a much older half sister who beat and humiliated her, eventually leading, at age 12, to a long series of juvenile arrests and placements and later to adult imprisonment, heroin addiction, and a current eight-year probation. However, she is now drug- and methadone-free.

Although this woman did not physically abuse her child, her rage at the system which deprived, abused, and depreciated her was so intense and her sense of her own entitlement was so high that her judgment about child-care arrangements, realistic expectations of children, etc. was at times impaired. Until recently she had trusted no one, and at this point, with the exception of a beginning trust in her paramour, her most solid relationships, ironically, are with three or four of the very agency people who precipitated the placement issue. Parents often parentify society by their delinquent behavior.

The paramour, in exploration of his family of origin, has begun to acknowledge some of his problems, and in hearing her story, has finally begun to express some empathy and some understanding of her anger and distrust. In consequence, his anger and rigid ultimatums have lessened. He has introduced her to his family and is moving toward a permanent commitment with her. The children both before and after the return of the "abused" child have been included in over half of the sessions. They have been very useful in clarifying the shifts in the family by both their verbal and nonverbal interactions. Initially they were very proper and keenly tuned in to the adult interactions. Early on, the five-year-old responded to a very angry session with the comment, "It's all I've ever known." Now she can play in the session with her seven-year-old sister or three-year-old brother. Both girls were very "mothering" of him when the brother was in placement, but now seem more interested in dolls or a neighbor's new baby. Both girls have been and are still "parentified" but that seems to be lessening as they see mother getting her needs met elsewhere. This "parentification" will probably have to be addressed more directly when the natural father is involved.

In addition, we have been dealing at the interfaces with agencies, neighbors, mother's half sister and her partner's family, as well as anticipating future interfaces, such as her daughter's school. Mother, in particular, is negotiating these with both ease and pride.

Throughout, I have been completely open with the family about my contacts with other agencies and have given them copies of reports. I went to court with them as did the director of the Day Nursery, the child protective worker and the attorney from Child Advocacy.

The two broken bones more likely resulted from neglect and poor judgment about the child's capabilities than direct abuse. Now that the mother has a support system including a probation officer, a social worker in pediatrics and a drug counselor, in addition to those listed above, she is much more available and accountable and can relate more appropriately to the needs of the children. She also has solid goals for herself and seems to see herself as someone with a future instead of just a sordid past. For example, she has a scholarship to attend college as soon as she can work out the reality problems.

I use this clinical example to point up some of the processes and pitfalls. Lest this sound too "pat," let me hasten to say there is much family of origin work yet to be done both with the two surviving half sisters and the two deceased parents of the mother.

The whole area of work with the natural father has yet to be addressed. At this point I have a solid enough relationship that it may be possible to risk raising the "side" of the children's natural father. He is being treated by the court and the agencies as a totally negative factor. He did attend the court hearing at which time I urged him to call me. The judge informed him of how to apply for visitation rights. However, to date he has not been actively involved by any of the agencies nor has he approached them.

This goes to the heart of the contextual approach (Boszormenyi-Nagy and Ulrich, 1981) and to child custody decisions. In that view, to which I subscribe, even though the parents have been separated for three years, the father should have been involved from the very beginning. Raising the issue of the non-custodial father will be done in conjunction with reraising the issue of mother's relationships with her mother and father and helping her reexperience her hopes and yearnings for a more meaningful relationship with them. She has to date only hinted at her deep sense of loss in not knowing her mother and losing her father. Then, we'll undoubtedly go back to some modified form of the rage and sense of exploitation that surfaced in that first session. However, she may now be able to experience that deprivation somewhat differently. We may even learn what happened to her mother and how her mother was exploited. We know that child neglect always involves at least three generations. From what little we know in this instance, it seems fairly certain that the fourth generation has also been exploited, as well as exploitive.

*Reference*

Boszormenyi-Nagy, I. and Ulrich, D. Contextual family therapy. In A. S. Gurman and D. Kniskern (Eds.), *Handbook of Family Therapy*. New York: Brunner/Mazel, 1981.

**JEAN BARR, M.S.S.**
*Department of Mental Health Sciences*
*Hannemann Medical College and Hospital*
*Philadelphia, PA*

# 38. The Straight Approach to a Knotty Problem: Managing Parental Guilt About Psychosis

**Question:**

> When schizophrenia develops in a young person, parents and other family members struggle to explain the illness to themselves, in a cognitive mastery process organized around the premise, "If I know how it happened, I can make it go away." In our society it is inevitable that most parents will blame themselves for the psychosis. The resulting guilt will play a significant negative role in subsequent family interaction. What can the family therapist do to minimize the development of pathological guilt reactions? What strategies will promote change in family interaction without activating or intensifying guilt in the process?

**Discussion:**

For over 10 years now, I have been deeply involved in the treatment of families of chronic schizophrenics. Early on, I began to wonder about the wisdom of family systems theory (FST) as applied to this work, especially as two weaknesses became apparent. First, FST placed undue emphasis on family interaction to the relative exclusion of psychobiological processes. Second, there were still numerous aspects of work with schizophrenics and their families that required a fully developed knowledge of individual psychology.

As my reservations grew, I turned to another strategy for treatment planning. Instead of coming from etiopathogenetic theory, I would begin with the observation that family interaction is heavily shaped by the presence of a psychotic member. And I would follow with the premise that a clinical approach acknowledging the schizophrenic's burden on the family would eventually lighten the load and attenuate destructive interactions. Asking what family members require in order to live with a psychosis-prone individual flowed naturally from this line of thinking. This strategy, of course, assumed 1) that family members knew and could articulate what they needed and 2) that their general welfare would improve if they got what they were asking for. Coming as I did from a tradition of strategic and counter-intuitive interventions, I was somewhat circumspect about such a straightforward approach. But it offered simplicity and an opportunity for me to unscramble the tortuously complex ideas about the relationship between schizophrenics and their parents.

In a study published privately by the National Schizophrenia Fellowship in England, Creer and Wing (1974) polled parents of British schizophrenics regarding their lives and needs. Hatfield (1979) paralleled this inquiry in a sample of American parents. Parents asked for detailed information about the illness itself and about the prevailing treatments. Additionally, parents wanted specific guidance in learning how to live with the schizophrenic on a day-to-day basis. These observations offered a much needed pragmatic basis for charting a general approach to the schizophrenic's family.

### Absolution: "First Off, You Didn't Do This"

One part of this approach is addressing the issue of parental guilt and blame. Since concepts like the schizophrenogenic mother and the double bind have become household words in recent times, it is inevitable that parents and therapists will grapple with these issues. What follows is a summary of the principles that are evolving in my practice applying to the management of parental guilt.

I regard dealing with the parent's tendency toward self-blame as a top priority in work with the schizophrenic's family. Twenty years ago it became fashionable to think of psychosis as an expression of intrafamilial processes. A whole generation of family therapists has grown up in the interstices of the epistemological revolution attached to this perspective. But while the evidence now at hand suggests that family interaction influences severity of symptoms and level of adaptive functioning in schizophrenics (Vaughn and Leff, 1976), it does not necessarily support the contention that family interaction contributes to the origins of the disorder (Hirsch and Leff, 1975).

Of course, in our times all of us have bought heavily into the family's influence on character development—so heavily that any encounter between a therapist and the family of a schizophrenic transpires under a cloud of covert blame and covert guilt. Because of this societal ambience, it is essential that the family therapist address the issue of the family's role in etiology in the first encounter. Guilt is the great enemy of curiosity. And without curiosity, observational and problem-solving skills of family members are sorely compromised. New interaction patterns are acquired at a snail's pace, if at all.

*1. Informing parents about the psychobiology of schizophrenia.* Most parents face the incoherence and mystery of psychosis with less information than a first-year medical student or social-work student. Their position is untenable. We expect them to be supportive, yet they lack basic concepts with which to reduce the staggering complexity of the schizophrenic's interpersonal behavior to manageable proportions.

My interest in the therapeutic use of information derives from its influence on my own approach to schizophrenic patients. In spite of a strong a priori preference for a social-interactional frame of reference, direct work with schizophrenic patients forced upon me the realization that neuroleptic medication had an indisputably beneficial impact on the course of psychotic states. From 1970 on, I followed the literature on neurotransmitter research suggesting that neuroleptics alter the activity dopamine receptors in the brain. I also followed the Danish adoption studies that brought us evidence for the genetic heritability of psychotic disorders. Then in 1978, I started to read seriously in the psychophysiology of schizophrenia (Wing, 1978; Wynne, Cromwell and Matthysse, 1978). As I delved into this material, linkages between clinical phenomena, psychophysiologic data, and pharmacologic responses began to appear in my own mental images of the psychotic process. I could now see loosened associations stemming from a defect in the regulation of focal attention. And the psychotic's penchant for withdrawal now made sense as a response to sensory overload in a person with a preexisting deficit in input screening processes. Rapid shifts in affect and attitude could be seen as the result of a defect in self-state regulation (Horowitz, 1979). I could imagine these defects originating in deviant activity of mesolimbic dopamine tracts. All this was quite speculative, of course, but clinicians have a certain license with the distinction between fact and hypothesis borne of the necessity to make the inchoate at least barely understandable.

It soon occurred to me that parents might also benefit from information about neurotransmitter imbalances, defects in focal attention, input screening dysfunctions, and the like. Upon sharing these ideas with parents, I found it even more useful than I had anticipated. When I wanted parents to pull back and give a schizophrenic space, I found it more compelling to talk from a biological base than to move toward the same end with a hierarchical or paradoxical intervention. Additionally, parents claimed that such explanations were very useful. They were strikingly appreciative of a psychiatrist who would explain something about psychosis, rather than insinuating that their questions were a defense against facing their own personal problems, etc. And they clearly picked up on the implication that if the disorder was fundamentally biological, they could stop their agonizing self-recrimination.

2. *Challenging the concept of the schizophrenogenic mother.* The second type of intervention is a rather direct and explicit critique of etiologic models based on family interaction. Most parents I work with eventually learn about the concept of the schizophrenogenic mother. But virtually none are aware of its lowly status as a scientific concept. Most exhibit tangible relief when I critique the concept. One mother broke into tears of relief when I challenged her Laingian ideas, remarking forcibly, "We've been waiting for years for someone to say that!"

3. *Challenging the parent's wish to be wrong.* The third intervention is the most interesting and challenging, requiring a thorough acceptance of a universal wish to blame oneself for any catastrophe striking one's child. When faced with an adult child's psychosis, some parents seem to reason that "if I made it happen, I can make it go away." The poignancy of this magical line of thinking was revealed to me by one mother who tearfully remarked, "I was even willing to be wrong if it would make Christine better." Maybe if Christine could blame her malady on maternal inadequacy, she could come to believe in her own adequacy. And maybe her mother could undo her imagined psychotogenic influence by more sensitive parenting in the future.

When the wish to be wrong is active, parents will ask how they have contributed to the psychosis, hoping to use my response to fashion a curative environment. If coldness and aloofness were invoked as explanations, the parents would take to ministering to the patient's every need. If it were marital conflict, they would close over their differences with each other. So strong is the need to blame self in some parents that they become impatient when I fail to find fault with some of their behavior. They lead me into identifying them as the source of the child's trouble, recounting anecdotes of bad parenting. Careful inquiry reveals that the parents are selectively inattending to those aspects of their experience with the child that would cast the relationships in a more positive light. This process recurs repeatedly in work with some families, leading me to suspect that families may bring accounts of the damage they have caused on the heels of inputs from some external authority who espouses the schizophrenogenic philosophy. Inspired by the authority's blameful perspective, the family challenges my will to absolve them, testing whether they are to believe me or the external authority.

In these families, the first and second strategies must be supplemented by direct confrontation of the magical aspect of the wish to be blamed. I always do this in tandem with an acknowledgement of the fundamental wish to make the child well again that is driving the whole chain of parental cognitions and behaviors. In some families, the soul-searching ends only after the parents are repeatedly confronted by their relative inability to alter the course of a chronic psychosis. That is, failure to cure the psychotic finally lifts the burden of guilt from their shoulders.

I have one final proviso. I do not mean to create the impression that classical family systems interventions hold no place in my work. Rather, I am saying that such work cannot go very far in producing useful long-term change in family interaction if the family retains a collective view that schizophrenic psychosis arises from interpersonal influence. Once parents and patient have acquired a recognition of the biological roots of schizophrenic experience, therapeutic attention to the details of family interaction can make a significant contribution to the quality of life for all.

*References*

Creer, C. and Wing, J. *Schizophrenia at Home*. London: Institute of Psychiatry, 1974.

Hatfield, A. The family as partner in the treatment of mental illness. *Hospital and Community Psychiatry*, 1979, *30*, 338-340.

Hirsch, S. and Leff, J. *Abnormalities in Parents of Schizophrenics*. London: Oxford University Press, 1975.

Horowitz, M. *States of Mind*. New York: Plenum Press, 1979.

Vaughn, C. and Leff, J. The influences of family and social factors on the course of psychiatric illness. *British Journal of Psychiatry*, 1976, *129*, 125-137.

Wing, J. (Ed.) *Schizophrenia: Toward a New Synthesis*. London: Academic Press, 1978.

Wynne, L., Cromwell, R. and Matthysse, S. (Eds.) *The Nature of Schizophrenia: New Approaches to Research and Treatment*. New York: John Wiley & Sons, 1978.

**KENNETH G. TERKELSEN, M.D.**
*Medical Director*
*Family Institute of Westchester*
*White Plains, NY;*
*Clinical Assistant Professor*
*Department of Psychiatry*
*Cornell University Medical School*
*New York, NY*

# 39. Marital Therapy with the Paranoid System

## Question:

Frequently a couple is referred for marital therapy with the presenting complaint that one partner is paranoid and the spouse has had enough and is threatening to leave. Questions arise regarding how "paranoid" is paranoid? What is the treatment of choice? Do you treat the individual psychopathology before going ahead with marital therapy? When you start with a systems approach, how does the therapist sustain a neutral position? Is the problem rooted in this particular relationship? If separation does take place, would the partners experience greater harmony in other relationships?

## Discussion:

In outpatient psychiatry, a large proportion of our referrals are for marital therapy. During Intake Rounds these are assigned to staff with a systems orientation. However, when the referral contains information that one spouse is paranoid, frequently there is a debate between those professionals who are systems-oriented and those who use the medical model.

When the "paranoid" spouse is found to have a fixed delusional system, chemotherapy is frequently the treatment of choice. Once the delusions are under control, therapy is offered to the couple but is rarely accepted at that time. Those cases which present with a psychotic reaction are rare. The majority of individuals who are labeled as "paranoid" are found to be overly suspicious without sufficient cause. This is usually because they are possessive, dependent people who become profoundly jealous when they sense any threat to the marital relationship.

The appropriateness of separation therapy is determined by the degree of danger to the family. When the "paranoid" partner has an impulsive need to act out and physically abuse the spouse and/or children whenever threatened, then separation should be quickly and aggressively sought by mobilizing community resources.

However, this situation is unusual. Most paranoid systems respond to a marital therapy when the focus is on biographical material which explains the couple's symbiotic relationship. These couples are usually immature and chaotic, rather than psychotic.

The therapist's main task is to establish an atmosphere of trust and neutrality. This is best done by taking a careful history which circumnavigates the primitive battle which could erupt at intake as the initial complaints are presented. It is well known that every paranoid individual is reacting to some basis in fact and it is easy to get into a situation of blame and counterattack with the therapist being cast into the role of the "judge." This is avoided by asking at the first appropriate moment how these two people met, what it was like during the courtship, and how their respective families felt about the relationship. The tension between the partners immediately subsides and it is then rather easy to examine their early background experiences. This process and the subsequent therapeutic sessions are described in detail elsewhere (Waring and Russell, 1980).

It is often found that each partner in the paranoid system was deprived of a relationship with a nurturing adult which enhances basic trust, intimacy, and separate identity. The child's growth and maturity were thwarted and often there is sexual confusion as well. Their parents were tense and anxious in their own marriages. The marital conflict in the families of origin resulted in the child's being smothered and overprotected by one parent and cruelly rejected by the other. The child usually gives up on ever receiving unanimous parental approval and rebels openly during adolescence by leaving home, participating in antisocial activities, and establishing numerous promiscuous relationships. When two such people eventually marry, the projective identification is dramatic. One spouse decides that whatever he/she does there is little trust or affection from the other partner, and therefore angrily begins to act in a provocatively insinuating way. The other spouse begins to believe that the partner, like everyone else in his/her life, is untrustworthy and it was a mistake to have married with so much hope that life would be different. The battle for power thus starts with a vengeance.

The therapeutic process begins to focus on the parental system in each spouse's family of origin. Many questions are asked regarding the reasons for the parents' behavior, how each parent dealt with the other, and why they married each other in the first place. As the couple works hard to understand the parental relationship, each partner is able to elaborate, support, or clarify the other's theories. For example, attempts to examine the grandparents' histories frequently explain mother's insecurities or father's temper.

As the sessions continue, there is a growing awareness that the wife and the husband, in actuality, are sharing their own frustrations and expectations in relation to each other. It soon becomes apparent whether this marital relationship has a future potential. Each partner now recognizes the strengths as well as the limitations of the union. The therapist returns to an earlier theme regarding what attracted them to each other. They are able to decide whether they can tolerate the negative qualities and make a real commitment to their marriage. They now understand and accept each other's vulnerabilities and are able to nurture the strengths in the relationship. If this is not possible, then they are in a better position to make a mutual decision to separate and "hopefully" avoid similar pitfalls in future relationships. In any case, there is a decision to change the destructive legacy of three generations in which a primitive battle for control is acted out in all of these marital dyads.

*Reference*

Waring, E. M. and Russell, L. Cognitive family therapy. *Journal of Sex and Marital Therapy*, 1980, 6, 253-273.

**LILA RUSSELL, M.S.W.**
*Department of Psychiatry*
*Victoria Hospital*
*London, Ontario, Canada*

## 40. Family Therapy and
## Anorexia Nervosa:
## The Hospital Phase

**Question:**

I have just started to do family therapy with anorexic teenagers who are hospitalized on a pediatric service. The ward itself impresses me as a caring, well-run unit that puts prime emphasis on weight gain by the application of behavior modification principles, but also sees the necessity for family therapy. The problem I am having is reconciling the medical-behavioristic approach employed on the service with my own interpersonal style of family therapy so that they are synergistic rather than antagonistic. I have also been troubled that few families seem interested in intensive work post-discharge. Can you give me any guidelines for how I might work in a medical setting—specifically what goals would seem realistic?

**Discussion:**

In the present-day hospital treatment of anorexia nervosa, it is common for multiple therapeutic modalities to be employed—for example, some combination of individual and group psychotherapies, family therapy, medical and behavioral management, dance and movement therapy. However, very little has been written about how to integrate these diverse approaches so that the best possible care is rendered. You are certainly right when you say that in such a setting it is important that a family therapist have a clear idea of what he or she is doing and what his or her goals are. Otherwise, he or she runs the risk of a sort of professional identity diffusion.

The most immediate and important focus in the medical setting you describe is the development of rapport with the family, or what Minuchin (1974) calls "joining" a family. The repeated experience of rapport between therapist and family members provides the groundwork for the eventual formation of a working alliance (Swift, 1981). The prompt help that the medical-behavioral model offers the family can be of immeasurable help in the development of rapport. To understand this, you have to realize what the family has typically endured in the weeks and months leading to hospitalization. They have invariably been in a prolonged state of exhausting crisis. As alarm about their daughter's weight loss grow, they have tried various maneuvers — exhortation, cajolery, benign neglect, bribery, and threats—but all to no avail. A course of outpatient medical and/or psychiatric therapy has probably been attempted but failed also. Fears about the death of their daughter arise as weight loss progresses, and are made even more frightening because of the mounting rage family members feel toward the anorectic. Family interchanges are confused and acrimonious, and the situation is quite beyond their control.

Hospitalization is offered at this point and is seen as a relief by the exhausted family. The groundwork for the development of rapport is laid because of the family's gratitude for the dramatic surcease of their suffering offered by hospital admission. Furthermore, as the identified patient slowly but inexorably gains weight in the setting you described—and the great majority do—the family sees the hospital as a potent force for change and again a debt of gratitude, mingled with awe, is felt. The gratitude, of course, is most strongly directed at the pediatrician and nursing staff, but if the family therapist privately and publicly identifies himself or herself as an integral member of the team, and is identified by the team as such, he or she will reap a halo effect. It is an instance in which the medical-behavioristic and family therapy models are clearly synergistic and will make the family therapy a much easier task.

Before considering what other goals are reasonable to pursue during hospitalization, it is useful to recall the structure and dynamics of a typical anorexic family. By the way, the sort of family to be described is certainly not type-specific for anorexia—it is also seen among many "acting-in" adolescent patients—but it is common enough to clearly represent a strong trend. Descriptively, we see families which are usually bright, middle to upper-middle class, polite, pleasant, conforming, perfectionistic, and achievement-oriented. They seem on first meeting—especially with the united marital front that they so often present—to be a collection of extraordinarily solid citizens. Dynamically, family members are overinvolved, enmeshed with one another's psychology, but at the same time emotionally cool (Minuchin et al., 1978). The emotional coolness is most graphically displayed by strenuous avoidance of intrafamily conflict or even the appearance of conflict. To caricature the situation only slightly, it seems that family members have been immune to normal developmental stress and strain, and have resided in a world that is as it should be rather than as it truly is.

Thus, after the development of rapport with all family members, the focus of work should shift to helping the rigid, emotionally constrained, "should-be" family to relax by creating an atmosphere that allows for the irrational, the humorous, and the less-than-perfect. Although this is far from an easy task, it is not as hard as it may sound. The family therapist is in a unique position because he or she will be providing the first opportunity for family members to sit down and talk to one another at a new, more meaningful level. This is, in itself, a very powerful force for change. How the therapist goes about attaining such an atmosphere of relaxed openness will largely depend on the style of the therapist and what techniques are comfortable for him or her. My work has especially been influenced by the symbolic-experiential style of Whitaker and Keith (1981) and the group-analytic object-relations approach of Skynner (1976). So I rely heavily on humor, paradox, confrontation, and judicious self-disclosure. Other family therapists, influenced by other schools, would undoubtedly use different techniques but I think the important common denominator underlying whatever techniques are employed is a sense of ease and comfort with a person's own irrational side and the ability to share it. An approach emphasizing insight as the primary factor for change is futile with anorexic families, but the modeling by the therapist of what they are missing (e.g., whimsy, openness, paradox) within the framework of good rapport can positively influence them and especially so early in treatment.

The third focus of family work during the hospital phase could best be subsumed under the rubric "educative/administrative." This focus is most marked at the beginning and end of hospitalization. In the early stages it primarily consists of educating unpsychologically-minded parents and siblings to see their critical role in the eventual success or failure of hospitalization. If there is resistance to this idea upon intake, you can insist upon a guarantee of family sessions as a precondition for admission of the identified patient. At the first appointment post-admission, you might more fully explain the reason for mandatory family involvement by stating, "It has been our experience that when we admit a teenager to the unit we find invariably that both the child and the family are in a crisis and thus the entire family needs to be involved." If enthusiasm for family therapy wanes as time passes, it is best to remind family members that long-term outcome of anorexia nervosa is highly variable, from total cure to death (Hsu, 1980), and that their active involvement may well play a significant part in the outcome. Of course, in such an approach we are initially accommodating to the family's focus on the identified patient and her body, but only in the service of eventually helping family members move toward a multi-personal, transactional frame.

The family will also have questions about unit regulations and procedures (weigh-ins, diet, passes, room restriction, etc.) that are, on the whole, best referred back to the medical/nursing staff—although the family therapist should make it clear again that he or she is part of the team and supports the refeeding and behavioral regimen. There is one administrative issue, however, that must be dealt with directly by the family therapist: the family's threat to remove the patient, often early in the hospitalization, against medical advice. This usually results because a symbiotic mother and/or father are unable to tolerate the physical and emotional separation that a hospital stay implies. This dynamic is hidden because the anorexic will be loudly demanding to be released, claiming that nothing is right with the unit, while the parents appear to be intimidated by her rage and weakly complying with her demands. However, at its heart, it remains a collusive act, as the child sacrifices herself and her health so that the parents do not feel grievously abandoned. This situation always warrants a crisis family meeting with both the family therapist and the medical staff present, at which an attempt is made to work through these difficult issues.

Near the end of the hospital stay, as previously mentioned, the educative/administrative focus again comes to the fore. Issues arise, such as, should there be outpatient weigh-ins upon discharge and who should do them? Should the family monitor the anorectic's eating? What should be done if her weight drops? Should family therapy continue and if so how often? Of course, when handling such concerns, the therapist does not tell them what to do but rather creates a forum where the pertinent issues can be discussed and an expert referee, the family therapist, is available.

The approach outlined here puts primary emphasis on the development of rapport with the family, with the hope that these constricted families can experience a sense of emotional openness and relaxation heretofore unknown to them. It is incumbent upon the therapist to model this sort of openness so that the family members can identify with him/her and also deal with the educational/administrative issues that invariably arise as the work proceeds. It downplays the role of insight in family therapy as a primary tool. We also expect few families to be interested in intensive work post-hospitalization. The fact is that the hospitalization experience does frequently help the family greatly and they are in less need of intensive work. Also, it has to be granted that as the child gains weight, family anxiety, and hence motivation for treatment, drops sharply, representing a "flight into health." However, the family therapist should not feel overly anxious about this and should remember that if sufficient psychological work has not been done, weight loss will follow and a second admission will be warranted. It has been observed repeatedly in the setting where I work that when a second admission is required the family is more emotionally available for therapy than on the first occasion, having relinquished the hope that the anorexia will "just go away."

The therapeutic foci and goals enumerated here may seem too unambitious to some but I have found them to be reasonable and reachable. What this approach lacks in therapeutic grandiosity I hope it makes up for in practical utility.

## References

Hsu, L. K. G. Outcome of anorexia nervosa. *Archives of General Psychiatry*, 1980, *37*, 1041-48.

Minuchin, S. *Families and Family Therapy*. Cambridge, MA.: Harvard University Press, 1974.

Minuchin, S., Rosman, B. L., and Baker, L. *Psychosomatic Families*. Cambridge, MA.: Harvard University Press, 1978.

Skynner, A. C. R. *Systems of Family and Marital Psychotherapy*. New York: Brunner/Mazel, 1976.

Swift, W. J. Availability for the working alliance. *Journal of the American Academy of Child Psychiatry*, 1981, *20*, 810-821.

Whitaker, C. A., and Keith, D. V. Symbolic-experiential family therapy. In A. S. Gurman and D. P. Kniskern (Eds.), *Handbook of Family Therapy*. New York: Brunner/Mazel, 1981.

**WILLIAM J. SWIFT, M.D.**
*Assistant Professor*
*Department of Psychiatry*
*University of Wisconsin*
*Medical School*
*Madison, WI*

# 41. Marital Therapy with Adult Psychosomatic Patients

## Question:

Is there evidence that the marriages of patients with chronic physical symptoms of obscure etiology are different from the marriages of patients with psychiatric problems or the marriages of non-patient controls? What is the clinical value of this information for the marital or family therapist or physician managing such patients? What specific techniques of marital therapy are the most helpful? And is there evidence of clinical efficacy for these specific techniques?

## Discussion:

Studies of the marriages of psychosomatic patients who suffer from such disorders as hypochondriasis, chronic pain, myocardial infarction, and masked depression with physical complaints have demonstrated greater marital and sexual maladjustment in the marriages as well as an increased prevalence of psychological depression in the form of dysphoria in the spouse of the presenting patient (Waring, 1980; Waring and Russell, 1980a).

In patients with chronic physical symptoms of obscure etiology, although marital adjustment, as perceived by patient and spouse, is similar to that of non-patient couples and an absence of overt conflict is demonstrated, these marriages are characterized by specific incompatibilities in intimacy, socializing, and self-disclosure.

The features of patients with chronic physical symptoms of obscure etiology include

1) a presence of their symptom for a minimum duration of three to six months with serious psychosocial disability;
2) medical model treatment failures;
3) lack of successful intervention in providing symptomatic relief, although a variety of predisposing, contributing, and perpetuating factors may have been identified;

4) features of abnormal illness behavior and demonstration of marital
   maladjustment.

I will discuss the implications of this research for the clinician responsible for managing such patients in three distinct areas: 1) the
engagement of the spouse in the evaluation process; 2) the evaluation
process itself; and 3) specific marital therapy. Although in the minds
of most psychosomatic patients and their spouses the relationship of
their marriage to the presence of physical symptoms seems remote,
most spouses are able to recognize that they have "suffered" with the
symptoms of their spouse who has chronic physical symptoms of obscure etiology. Thus, a simple statement to the spouse such as, "In my
experience most spouses suffer with the physical symptoms of their
spouse," and engagement of the spouses in ventilation of their feelings
of helplessness, and most commonly dysphoria, can engage them in
assisting in the management of their spouse's condition. Often there
is an underlying resentment towards the spouse with the physical
symptoms, but my experience has been in the initial engagement that
attempts to allow ventilation or recognition of such feelings lead to
disengagement and avoidance of evaluation by the spouse and should
be left until much later in the therapeutic management of the patient.
The evaluation of the couple's relationship in more depth is facili-
tated by the ventilation discussed above. I then do a comprehensive
marital history with the couple with their permission focusing on their
perceptions and observations of their parents' marriages, how they
met, their courtship, engagement, marriage, honeymoon, and a development history of their family up to the present with a specific focus
on their cognitive theories of why the chronic symptoms have persisted
for so long. In general, in this initial evaluation with these couples, I
avoid an evaluation of their current relationship since, as suggested
by the research, the couples usually perceive their marriages as well
adjusted and this is usually because of an absence of overt conflict or
arguments in their relationships. Thus, more pertinent information
about their level of intimacy and self-disclosure and specific deficien-
cies in these areas in the initial evaluation are obtained by the historical method rather than a confrontation, which again in my
experience leads couples to disengagement and the absence of a therapy
contract.
Finally, if the patient fails to show symptomatic improvement with
a variety of therapeutic interventions, I will meet with the couple for
a second interview in which I will suggest directly to them that we
have found that couples who suffer with chronic physical symptoms of

obscure etiology often are not as close as they wish they were and have difficulties in terms of sharing their private ideas, assumptions, beliefs, and values about their relationship. I continue to find it surprising clinically how many couples accept that these factors may play a role in perpetuating chronic physical symptoms of obscure etiology and are willing to participate in some sessions to increase their level of intimacy by facilitating cognitive self-disclosure.

What is self-disclosure? Jourard (1964) was the first to symptomatically study the phenomenon of self-disclosure which he believed was a "symptom of health" and "a means to interpersonal effectiveness." Self-disclosure is the process of "making ourselves known to other persons by verbally revealing personal information including: 1) expression of emotions; 2) expression of need; 3) expression of thought, attitudes, beliefs, and fantasy; and 4) self-awareness. I specifically define the latter two as "cognitive self-disclosure." Thus, couples where one spouse suffers chronic physical symptoms of obscure etiology embark on a structured technique of self-disclosure of relative assumptions regarding their marital relationship in a reciprocal manner to a supportive listener, with some evidence that this facilitates the couple's level of intimacy and reduces abnormal illness behavior and the sick role. In summary, the knowledge that the spouses of patients with chronic physical symptoms of obscure etiology experience considerable dysphoria allows for an engagement process to involve the spouse in a comprehensive evaluation of the marital relationship. Secondly, knowledge that the couple perceives their marital adjustment as satisfactory allows the avoidance of unnecessary confrontations in the initial evaluation interview which would undermine any future therapeutic potential with the couple. Finally, the ventilation of the dysphoria and the non-stressful nature of the initial evaluation allows in a significant proportion of cases explanation to the couple of the evidence regarding intimacy and self-disclosure which in most cases can lead to the use of brief cognitive family therapy (Waring and Russell, 1980b) as an adjunctive and clinically effective form of marital therapy for these patients.

Because the psychosomatically ill patient has difficulties in experiencing and expressing affects produced by becoming aware of unconscious conflicts which may play a part in the predisposition to his/her illness or produced by the confrontation of interpersonal difficulties, he or she is not likely to respond well to either insight-oriented individual therapy or marital or family counseling in which affect is stimulated or uncovered. Thus, a therapy such as brief cognitive family therapy, which focuses on the interpersonal, deals with the psychological strengths and motivations of the spouse as well as the patient, concentrates on facilitating the expression of cognitive material, and suppresses affect, has several advantages in treating the psychosomatically ill patient. First, I have observed that these couples are willing to accept that their difficulties in cognitive self-disclosure may perpetuate their physical symptoms. Second, the spouses of these patients are often highly motivated to listen to their spouse in the therapeutic situation and can act as a facilitating model. And third, the increased intimacy that develops allows the couples to give up physical symptoms as an attempt to communicate and allows them to understand and problem solve any marital maladjustment.

*References*

Jourard, S. *The Transparent Self.* Princeton, NJ: Van Nostrand, 1964.

Waring, E. M. Marital intimacy, psychosomatic symptoms, and cognitive therapy. *Psychosomatics*, 1980, *21*, 595-601.

Waring, E. M. and Russell, L. Family structure, marital adjustment, and intimacy in patients referred to a consultation-liaison service. *General Hospital Psychiatry*, 1980a, *3*, 198-203.

Waring, E. M. and Russell, L. Cognitive family therapy. *Journal of Sex and Marital Therapy.* 1980b, *6*, 258-273.

**E. M. WARING, M.D.**
*Assistant Dean,*
*Continuing Medical Education*
*University of Western Ontario*
*London, Ontario, Canada*

# 42. Bowen Theory and the Treatment of Depression

**Question:**

Many families approach me and want me to see just the family member who is depressed. They are very concerned but view the depressed person as "sick" or "having problems." How can I assist these depressed clients and their families when they are experiencing these intense reactions? I would like to utilize a family systems theory (the Bowen theory) frame of reference.

**Discussion:**

The root of many depressions is emotional isolation, and the depressed person is impinged upon by his emotional field. Depression is overpowering and it has the function of repressing our thinking structures—the depressed person is overwhelmed by his feelings.

There is some agreement that depression results from a combination of elements such as genetic factors, faulty child-learning, biochemical combinations, and environmental factors. All of these suggested causes have their basis in the family.

It is true that depression is experienced by an individual. A depressed person feels very down, unable to do anything about the problem, and is overtaken by a sense of despair. The focus in depression is on the self, and the depressed person keeps going down an endless black hole into himself and into emotional isolation. He withdraws from the people around him into his own inner world.

One's own inner world is an important aspect of a person—but if a person stays inside that inner world, he tends to develop a strong sense of unreality. The more he focuses upon himself to the exclusion of other people, the more his problems and feelings get out of perspective, and he experiences true emotional isolation. A depressed person's major mechanism for handling tension and stress is distancing. In depression, the person is withdrawing from the world to get more comfortable, but he goes too far and then has difficulty getting back.

Decreasing this isolation often decreases the feelings of depression.

Therefore, it is very important for people who are depressed to stay involved with other people, particularly those to whom they are closest. The people to whom they are closest are usually their family members. Family factors play an important part in symptom formation and maintenance of depression. Feelings of depression exist at some level in all human beings, but vary according to frequency and intensity and are based on what people have learned in their family. This means that it is important to view the depressed person as part of a family and ask certain questions, e.g., how does the family contribute to the phenomenon of depression?

The Bowen Theory, or family systems theory (Bowen, 1978) views depression as a symptom of family dysfunction, which is determined by a person's basic level of self-differentiation and the degree of anxiety in the family system. The symptomatology of depression is, in part, a learned response to anxiety and can be understood by exploring the family process and by identifying the behavior patterns existing in both the past and the present generations.

I believe that the family is the unit of treatment in depression. I would not single out any individual family member as the "patient." I would, instead, view the family member who is depressed as the "symptom-bearer" and would see that individual as reflecting the disturbances of the family itself. For example, if I am seeing a family in which the wife is depressed, the husband will frequently expect me to focus on her because she is the one with symptoms. However, rather than focusing on her, instead I would spend most of the time talking to the husband. Changing the focus in this way, I can often encourage the wife to shift her attention to the husband. She can get out of herself and start moving toward another person—and begin to move out of her depression. Recognition and awareness of feelings in self are useful and necessary for change to occur, but movement toward objects and others will assist the depressed person to attain connectedness and decrease the feelings of isolation and depression. Encouraging the depressed person to make contact with the extended family members is also very effective in alleviating these feelings.

I would also begin to ask questions such as, "What are the other people in the family doing?" I would give each family member a portion of the problem. If the wife is depressed, I would look at the husband's role. For example, he may be overly sympathetic, which is a very common reaction. He may overfunction and try to do everything for her and this may just increase her sense of helplessness and inadequacy. She, in turn, may get angry with him because overdependence sometimes leads to hostility. There are many different reactions that are possible. By taking a family-wide view of depression, a problem is taken from one person and distributed throughout the family system. One person is not fingered as the "problem" and as the one responsible for all the difficulties. There is usually a great sense of relief when the problem is distributed throughout the family. The depressed person can then say to himself or herself: "I'm not the whole problem—everyone else has a part in this too."

What is important is that each family member gain some awareness of the part he or she plays in the ongoing family process. Teaching motivated family members how family systems operate and assisting them to learn to control their reciprocal roles in the process is essential. Once family members recognize that their patterns have been learned through the generations and that they have the option of doing something different, change can occur. It is then that the family can begin to work together to solve the difficulties they all have.

Any family system strives to maintain a dynamic equilibrium among the various forces operating within and upon it. We may call this homeostasis, balance, or steady state. The family is always trying to maintain this balance and resists change whenever it is in homeostasis. When families are in crisis, and this is when helping professionals work with them, they have been knocked off balance and are in a state of disequilibrium. Whatever it is they are doing—whatever coping mechanisms or problem solving techniques they are using—they are no longer effective. For example, a family may have a family member who is chronically depressed. The family adjusts to this and maintains some sort of balance in the family system—the symptoms of chronic depression are part of that balance. They expect this family member to be morose, pessimistic, and glum most of the time. Then, all of a sudden, things change and the depressed member becomes acutely depressed, crying, withdrawing from everyone, refusing to eat, and making all sorts of references to suicide. The depression is suddenly much more intense and it throws the family members off balance—they are in a state of crisis. They don't know how to handle this new behavior. When a family is in crisis, there is an increased openness and a reaching-out for help. Intervention at this time will produce maximum results. Family members are not nearly as resistant to change and are looking for new ways of operating that are more effective.

This is the time when we can be of the most help to the family. Unfortunately, this is often also the time when people panic and, frequently, families want to get rid of the depressed member because they are afraid that he will commit suicide. If a diagnosis is made and the depressed person is placed in the hospital, it can do real damage in the family. From then on, the other family members look at it as if it is the hospitalized person's problem and many times that viewpoint is almost irreversible. This is exactly what you don't want to happen. Instead, you want the family to realize that the symptom in one person says something about the other people in the family. No problem is in just one person, it is a problem of the whole system.

It is my opinion that it is most useful at this time to support the family members, to see them on an outpatient basis, even if it is necessary to see them more frequently in order to keep their anxiety down, and to try to assist them in maintaining the depressed member at home. I have found it useful to take the position, and to assist the other family members to also take the position, as follows: to let the depressed person know that I cannot be responsible for his/her life or death, that s/he has control over his/her own life. I make it very clear that I don't think suicide is a good solution to any problem and that I would regret it if the depressed person took such action, but at the same time I grant him/her the freedom to make that choice for him/herself. I suggest that s/he not make a long-term decision on a temporary feeling basis. This may sound somewhat callous, but I do not believe that it is helpful to allow another person to use the threat of suicide as a weapon. I have found that taking a firm stand, and negotiating a contract between myself and the depressed person or between another family member and the depressed person, that requests that the depressed person notify us if he is feeling particularly bad, has stopped the process and has been very effective. The threats usually stop. I am a firm believer that the professional person is a role model for the family (Cain, 1981). If I can take a stand and state what I believe and what I will or will not do, family members can often do this, too. It is also helpful to indicate to the family and to the depressed member that depression is self-limited and that it will decrease in intensity, if not go away completely.

Bowen Theory describes the depressed person as representing the adaptive position in the family. When one member maintains the adaptive position for long periods of time, this person gradually loses self, and his or her ability to function is markedly impaired, as is evidenced in the depressed position. One family member becomes viewed as the "overfunctioner" or the dominant one, while another is viewed as the "underfunctioner" or adaptive one. Neither position is one that enhances growth within the family system. Unfortunately, once these positions become stable patterns of interaction, the process often becomes chronic and is extremely difficult to reverse.

According to Bowen, those individuals who are most likely to experience depression are those who fall in the moderate range (25-50) of the differentiation scale. These individuals have large amounts of pseudo self, and it is the pseudo self that engages in the fusion process and allows for symptom formation. The more pseudo self available, the greater the likelihood of loss of self and depressive dysfunction. Only a moderate amount of stress is necessary to trigger the adaptive individuals into dysfunction, due to their relationship orientation and their sensitivity to others.

Persons at even lower levels of differentiation would be the most likely to develop depressive symptoms that would last for very extensive periods or that would be a lifelong patterned response to stress and anxiety. These would be the severely, chronically depressed individuals.

Depressive symptoms can occur at higher levels of differentiation, and they may be quite intense. However, these individuals would have greater control over their emotional responses and would not be as easily stressed into dysfunction. These episodes would be less frequent and shorter in duration. This would be in contrast to individuals at a lower level of differentiation who experience repeated episodes of depression and whose lives are dominated by their symptoms.

Emotional isolation is a significant component of depression. Another concept of the Bowen Theory that can be applied to depression is the emotional cut-off. This concept refers to the way people handle their unresolved emotional attachments to their parents by cutting off from the past. The existence of emotional cut-offs increases the amount of emotional investment in the person's present relationships and the chance for fusion in the nuclear family relationships. The depressed person's relationships to extended family members can either perpetuate or decrease the depressive symptoms and, therefore, can have a great impact. If the depressed person's relationships to the extended family are open, this absorbs some of the intensity, helps lessen the fusion in the nuclear family, and assists in decreasing the depression. If extended family relationships are cut off, this increases the emotional investment or fusion in the nuclear family, decreases the personal connectedness of the depressed person, and perpetuates the depression. Thomas Fogarty (1976), a family systems therapist, believes that the signs of depression are closely related to the characteristics of what he calls "emptiness." He believes that the depression or emptiness "always goes back to the lack of personal connectedness on the part of everyone in the extended family."

Another important piece of learning for those who are depressed is to realize that they frequently talk themselves into it. It has to do with the way they think (Beck et al., 1979). My point is that no one at any time in any place can upset or depress anyone else unless that person allows it. Moods really do come from our own thinking. Depressed persons are programmed to think "automatic thoughts"—these are frequently thoughts of self-blame, self-pity, or pity for other people. Once the depressed person can recognize these automatic thoughts, he or she can assess their validity and be less influenced by them. Therapy is based on learning new ways to think and on finding new options.

Lots of things in families are "automatic" and family members are so close emotionally that they cannot see this easily. That is where an objective outside person can be of real help to the family—to help them identify the automatic circuits and break down the cycle—in order for family members to see how they operate with each other and to assist them in figuring out ways of changing their own behavior.

In any system people compensate for each other. If one person is underfunctioning in certain areas, someone else in the system will compensate for this by overfunctioning in those areas. People do not have to consistently underfunction or consistently overfunction—some people overfunction in one area and underfunction in another. What is important is that the family system maintains an equilibrium or balance. In a family with a depressed member, there is usually a seesaw relationship. By that I mean that some member or members of the family are overfunctioning just as much as the depressed family member is underfunctioning. As other family members take on more and more responsibility for family affairs, the depressed member decreases his responsibility and can become almost totally dysfunctional. The aim in working with the family would be to work with the members who are overfunctioning and try to get them to do less so that the depressed or underfunctioning member can take back more of the responsibility and gradually increase his functioning. This is quite different from focusing on the depressed member to "come up" in functioning—instead the focus is on other family members to "let go" or "come down." It is a real boner to do too much for someone who is depressed—the more you do, the less he will do. He is capable of more than that—if other family members will allow him to function at a higher level. He may well have a worse time of it for a while, but if no one will do it for him, he will begin again to do things for himself.

One suggestion that is often helpful to the family member who is depressed is aimed at reversing his inner-directed aggression. Individuals who are depressed can repress a lot of hostility and direct it inward against themselves. They need to be taught to express their anger constructively—to get it directed outside rather than inside. Physical activities are excellent for this—get them to jog, play tennis, or ping-pong, use a punching bag, or any other kind of physical exercise to help work some of it off. It is amazing how the depression lifts when they are able to do this. If they are not the athletic type, just suggest they pound on the bed with their fists or beat on something indestructible with a hammer!

It is important for those working with families to have enough distance from the family system to maintain some objectivity, so that they do not get caught up in the families' depression and so that they can encourage family members to observe and think as much as possible. They need to be sensitive to the feelings of family members and in charge of their own feelings. They can then assist the family members in looking at the positive aspects and the accomplishments rather than focusing on the negative aspects and the failures of life.

In summary, the efforts of the family systems therapist when working with depression are aimed at decreasing the anxiety in the system, increasing the level of differentiation of family members, and bridging the emotional cut-offs in the family of origin.

## References

Beck, A. T., Rush, A. J., Shaw, B. F., and Emery, G. *Cognitive Therapy of Depression*. New York: Guilford Press, 1979.

Bowen, M. *Family Therapy in Clinical Practice*. New York: Jason Aronson, 1978.

Cain, A. The role of the therapist in family systems therapy. In G. Berenson and H. White (Eds.), *Annual Review of Family Therapy*. New York: Human Sciences Press, 1981.

Colgrove, M., Bloomfield, H., and McWilliams, P. *How to Survive the Loss of a Love*. New York: Leo Press, 1976.

Fogarty, T. *Coping with Stress*. Chicago: Claretiar, 1975.

Fogarty, T. On emptiness and closeness: Part II. *The Family*, 1976, *3*, 39-49.

**ANN OTTNEY CAIN, Ph.D.**
*Professor of Psychiatric Nursing*
*University of Maryland*
*Baltimore, MD*

# PART A

## *Divorce and Remarriage*

# SECTION IV

# Special Areas
# and Issues

# 43. Divorce Counseling and Mediation

**Question:**

Increasingly I am seeing in my psychotherapy practice patients who are in a divorce crisis or about to enter into one. I have found it difficult to do divorce counseling when the domestic attorneys are engaged in a legal battle, frequently giving advice which is therapeutically counterproductive. I have heard of divorce mediation as an alternative to the legal system. I would like to know more about it and how this fits with divorce counseling.

**Discussion:**

Whether one views divorce as "disaster" (Epstein, 1975) or as "development" (Kraus, 1979), divorce is a crisis and should be approached accordingly. Past notions have viewed the divorce experience as pathogenic, ascribing to this value that divorce is a failure and the divorced person is living a damaged life (Freund, 1974). It is, therefore, not surprising to note that such research focuses on the relationship between divorce and psychopathology. This follows the assumption that the nuclear family is the normal and healthy choice of life-style. Conversely, the members of divorced families are then often perceived as "fragmented, neurotic, tragic, or socially destructive" (Gettleman and Markowicz, 1974). Currently, the trend is to view divorce as a form of emotional crisis that provides some unique opportunities for growth, as well as the development of positive outcomes. Crisis theory as defined by Rapoport (1965) and Sauber (1973) offers a conceptual definition of an upset in an individual's steady state. The individual's everyday equilibrium cannot be dealt with by usual coping mechanisms. The state of crisis is assumed to have growth-promoting potential, since one can develop new capacities in coping with life-change events. In the case of divorce, one's social roles, expectations, and network of associations are rapidly changing. Coping with such flux of experience involves a reevaluation of one's life-style that may lead to improved functioning (Wiseman, 1976).

Often, the tragic flaw occurs when our social institutions of justice, namely, the legal adversary system, predominate the divorce. Most often this system impinges on each party's development and capacity to cope with the natural emotional processes of marital separation. Consequently, the parents and children involved become the victims of the justice system. The family members become powerless, confused, and overwhelmed. Power and personal responsibility are turned over to the system and its representatives. When there is disagreement, as one might expect between divorcing partners, the attorneys take charge and define action according to the rules of the adversary system. The couple's ability to begin to cope with the changes in their individual lives and living are impaired with attitudes that support and enforce self-gain and self-protection against the other partner. The adversary system imposes game rules which never before have been part of family interaction; these rules are not designed for the family, but for the individual's rights. Hence, each individual's representative wages the war of enforcing individual rights over the integrity of the family itself. Typically, the attorney for the wife advises her to demand everything and expect more than she may feel she is actually entitled to. This is to be sanctioned as a practical strategic position for bargaining and negotiation. The attorney informs his client that her best weapon is the children in receiving financial support and control. Now the children are the objects of the individual rather than members of the family. The attorney for the husband advises him to give her as little as possible, because it sets a precedent in future alimony and child support, and to claim that he has as little money as possible in order to place him in a better position to avoid financial obligations that could become excessive.

The psychotherapist at best can be placed in a position of being understanding of the disruption, paranoia, and financially draining experience of his clients going through legal divorce. To the divorce counselor, his suggestions or interventions to facilitate communication and reduce tensions between the family members are compromised because any expressed communication is often exploited by the other partner to enhance his or her legal position in the divorce contest. It is difficult for the divorce counselor to work with both husband and wife simultaneously because of the potential for manipulation and the likely breakdown in any kind of therapeutic work that could be accomplished. As couples go through the legal separation process, it becomes increasingly difficult for the divorce counselor to restructure any relationship changes between the parents to help them in their new relationship with each other and with their children. Frequently, the goal is conflict resolution, problem-solving, and task-oriented interventions to facilitate their adjustment.

The divorce counselor must also be cautious of attempts at collusion when an attorney requests reports that are likely to be used against the other partner. Lawyers' requests may be in the form of child custody evaluations (see Chasin and Grunebaum, 1981) or mental status appraisals of the patient currently or previously in treatment. It is important to note that there is a difference between the kind of divorce counseling that can take place simultaneously with the legal adversary system and that which can take place when partners are not in an active, ongoing legal power struggle with one another during the divorce process.

With the divorce rate for marriages reaching 40% and, in some states, close to 50%—double what it was 10 years ago—and with three-quarters of these break-ups involving children, experts are looking for ways to get property and custody disputes out of the courtroom and to some degree out of the adversary system. "Because the financial, emotional and physical toll of the courtroom is so great," Montgomery County Juvenile Court Judge Douglas H. Moore, Jr. (1980) reports, "Everybody loses . . . and the children suffer most, especially in a custody battle." Some professionals believe that divorce mediation may be a partial answer. In the legal system, each advocate pursues the goals of one client, which often has a destructive effect on the other partner and the children. A mediator is the voice of reason, who works out an acceptable solution that each side can live with and that is beneficial to the child from both parents' perspectives. The pioneering work in this field has been done by Drs. O. J. Coogler, President of The Family Mediation Association in Washington, D.C., and John M. Haynes, who heads the Academy of Family Mediators in New York City. Each of these leaders has written excellent texts on divorce mediation (Coogler, 1978; Haynes, 1981).

These associations serve as clearinghouses for information in this rapidly growing field and as an advocate and stimulator of training for marriage counselors, mental health professionals, and attorneys in the techniques of family mediation. The underlying assumption of divorce mediation is that the family continues to exist after divorce. With this in mind, Dr. Coogler sees the divorce mediation process in private practice proceeding in two steps: 1) the meeting of the couple with trained behavioral scientists who mediate their differences and are task-oriented toward working out an agreeable settlement in a way that does the least amount of harm to the continued family (i.e., after divorce)—the father, mother, and children; and 2) In the second step, lawyers are requested to rewrite the mediated settlement in legal terms. It should be noted that the lawyers deal with "family as the client," not as two parties in conflict. This redirection is an important step in the changing attitude of the legal profession.

Dr. Coogler (1979) observes in the proposed new draft rules for professional standards of the American Bar Association a response to the growing recognition of public concern over the excessive adversarial zeal of many divorce lawyers. The proposed new code, with emphasis on conflict resolution and its condemnation of the use of procedures which "harass or intimidate others," together with its new definition of lawyers' roles as negotiators and intermediaries, is a promising and overdue sign of change. Divorce mediation can be structured for low-income families as well and it should not be limited in application to private practitioners only, but as a feasible public agency service, as some family service groups have already demonstrated (Coogler, 1979; Haynes, 1982).

Where a couple has decided that their differences are irreconcilable and that the marriage partnership must be dissolved, divorce mediation can help them make the process a constructive rather than destructive one. This is especially true when children are involved. Mediation services will help the couple work out living arrangements for their children that are supported by a cooperative relationship between the parents. Research continually demonstrates that the most significant factor in children's post-divorce adjustment is the post-divorce relationship between the parents. The goals of divorce counseling and mediation are the same: the need for family restructure. Families, as well as marriage partners, carry a burden of pain when divorce results in family disruption. This calls for a rearrangement or restructuring of family life post-divorce so that both parents can have a meaningful relationship with their children. The philosophy is that all of the problems of the family are shared by all of the family members in some way. The process of restructuring the family relationships includes finding ways for dealing with family problems on a mutually-acceptable basis with cooperative negotiation, clear communication, and openness in sharing information needed for problem resolution.

Mediation as counseling requires the voluntary participation of both parties. However, the issues or controversies that are to be considered in mediation must be agreed upon by the parties in advance. The mediator will not allow parties to coerce or blame each other in an effort to force agreement. By entering the mediation process, the parties agree that the mediator can exercise the necessary control over the negotiations so that each is assured of this protection. The agreement reached must always be the free choice of the parties, and must be based upon complete and valid information. Mediators are trained to help the parties collect the information they need to explore the choices available to them. The mediator cannot require the parties to cooperate, but the mediator can keep the parties from negotiating with each other in noncooperative ways. By giving the parties small specific tasks that involve cooperation, they gain insight into their problems and learn that they *can* cooperate with each other. Research and the practical experience of working with couples confirm the effectiveness of the methods of mediation. The four basic issues for a mediated agreement are as follows:

1) Division of marital property;
2) Spousal maintenance (alimony);
3) Child support;
4) Custodial arrangements for the children.

There are variations in the ways in which divorce counselors, mediators, and attorneys work together. An example of one approach is that of Drs. Walter Ambinder and Sandra Lynnes (1981) of the Civilized Divorce Clinic in Detroit, Michigan, in which they combine family therapy with divorce mediation. Dr. Ambinder is a psychologist as well as an attorney. In their team approach, they report, one person takes on most of the responsibility for mediating the legal and financial elements of the divorce, while the other continues to function as a family therapist for one or more of the parties involved. The objective is to have a coordinated effort that helps each party deal with the practical problems of divorce while, at the same time, diffusing conflict. In this way, they believe, there is a better chance that the rights and well-being of the children are preserved and the financial settlement is one that both parties can accept.

Other approaches include the processes of counseling and mediation as independent functions with very little or no interprofessional communication or collaboration. As one might expect, most referrals to mediators are from the helping professions seeking alternative ways to a destructive adversary system. In contract, domestic attorneys frequently believe that mediation is ineffective and does not legally "get the most" for their particular client. Or attorneys may simply feel that this new method intrudes on their own professional turf and, therefore, divorce mediation may be viewed as competition (Ambinder and Lynnes, 1981). Increased media coverage on television and radio and in newspapers and magazines of the mediation process is likely to make more potential clients aware of this alternative positive approach.

Dr. Coogler (1978) has indicated that asking a couple to engage in a rational, cooperative negotiation and decision-making process over apportionment of the tangible evidence of their shattered dreams may seem to be asking the impossible. The very thought of undertaking the task is viewed by some as so overwhelming that they feel utterly helpless and powerless. Unfortunately, the structure provided by attorneys in the adversarial legal system invites many clients to avoid personal responsibility and to look for "seemingly" easy solutions. This process serves to feed the destructiveness and anger already present in the dissolving relationship. While the legal process emphasizes a win/lose outcome, with each party striving to be the winner, mediation emphasizes a win/win outcome, with each partner emerging from the negotiations with possible gains, while recognizing the right and need of the other also to have gains.

The mediator carefully focuses on the couple's possibilities of achieving their goals. The divorce mediator establishes at the outset that it is not his or her role to represent either party but that his or her task is to achieve a settlement that involves both economic and emotional issues that are agreeable and reasonable to both partners. When the emotional blocks are so severe and seriously impede the couple's work on the separation agreement, the mediator may call for a "time out" from the mediation process and will either refer or request consultation from a therapist or, in some cases, may even switch from mediator to therapist. Once the couple have been helped by divorce counseling in overcoming and dealing with their emotional problems, they can begin once again to focus on the economic issues.

An example of the voluntary nature of free choice and assumption of personal responsibility that exists in mediation as opposed to the legal adversarial system has been stated by the National Organization for Women. They cite that in more than half of all alimony cases, "The man falls behind in payments within two years, often intentionally" (Vecsey, 1977, p. 26). This is likely to be a result of the husband's perception that the settlement was imposed on him from outside sources, such as the judge or the attorney's manipulations. The husband therefore becomes increasingly discontent with his forced compliance. Anger which was not resolved at the time of the divorce increases to the point that the husband feels justified in ceasing payments. The courts are notoriously slow in enforcing divorce settlements, and women frequently find the court agreements to be valueless.

The cost of mediation is certainly another variable to consider. The mediation process takes between eight and ten hours in total for the couple, as contrasted to the traditional steps of husbands and wives meeting individually with their attorneys and then the attorneys speaking to one another, which multiplies the amount of time and consequent expense.

## References

Ambinder, W. and Lynnes, S. Practice profile: Combining family therapy with divorce mediation. *Psychotherapy Finances*, 1981, *8* (2), 3-4.

Chasin, R. and Grunebaum, H. A. A model for evaluation in child custody disputes. *American Journal of Family Therapy*, 1981, *9*, 43-49.

Coogler, O. J. *Structured Mediation in Divorce Settlement*. Lexington, MA: Lexington Books, 1978.

Coogler, O. J. Divorce mediation for low income families: A proposed model. *Conciliation Courts Review*, 1979, *17*, 21-26.

Epstein, J. *Divorce: The American Experience*. London: Jonathan Cape, Ltd., 1975.

Freund, J. Divorce and grief. *Journal of Family Counseling*, 1974, *2*, 40-43.

Gettleman S. and Markowicz, J. *The Courage to Divorce*. New York: Simon & Schuster, 1974.

Haynes, J. M. *Divorce Mediation: A Practical Guide for Therapists and Counselors*. New York: Springer, 1981.

Haynes, J. M. A conceptual model of the process of family mediation. *American Journal of Family Therapy*, 1982, in press.

Kraus, S. P. The crisis of divorce: Growth promoting or pathogenic? *Journal of Divorce*, 1979, *3*, 107-120.

Moore, D. H. Divorce wars. *Washingtonian*, March 1980,

Rapoport, L. The state of crisis: Some theoretical considerations. In H. J. Parad (Ed.), *Crisis Intervention: Selected Readings*. New York: Family Service Association of America, 1965.

Sauber, S. R. *Preventive Educational Intervention for Mental Health*. Cambridge, MA: Ballinger, 1973.

Vecsey, G. The absent father, too, can wind up broke or inside a prison. *New York Times*, 1977, April 18, p. 26.

Wiseman, R. S. Crisis theory and the process of divorce. *Social Caseworker*, 1976, *56*, 205-212.

**S. RICHARD SAUBER, Ph.D.**
*Department of Psychiatry*
*Columbia University*
*New York, NY*

*and*

**DANIEL R. PANITZ, M.A.**
*Director*
*Manhattan Alcoholism Treatment Center*
*New York, NY*

# 44. The Role of Explicit Rule-making in the Early Stages of Remarriage

**Question:**

Many of the stepfamilies who seek therapy at our clinic are within the first year or two of their remarriage and are experiencing acute crisis. They describe serious symptoms experienced by one or more family members, but as the therapist begins to meet with the family, problems often arise which seem typical of this family situation. They have difficulty coming to a common agreement to work together, there is a sense of all family members going in separate directions, and the marital partners are especially fearful of looking at problems in their own marriage. They protest that having to discuss the "trivial" chores of everyday living signals a lack of love and commitment. As discussions move to the special difficulties of stepfamilies, they may withdraw from treatment prematurely. It seems clear that the individual symptoms need to be seen within the special demands of the stepfamily structure. How can a therapist help these families so that they can deal with their presenting problems?

**Discussion:**

The establishment of a new sense of family identity in relation to which each individual feels a part is a basic task of the early period of remarriage. Families in this early period of reorganization do not have time-worn strategies for working together, there is no sense of stability, and there are no rules for comfortable closeness or for reasonable distance. There are no predictable times of refueling or comfortable patterns for arguments. Consequently, family members feel overwhelmed and helpless, unable to take effective action. These issues influence both the family's day-to-day lives and their responses to therapy.

Every family has its own rules and traditions which regulate relationships within the family. These continuing patterns of relationship establish a sense of family identity which is stable over time and differentiated from the outside world. During the divorce period these everyday patterns are disrupted and the old rules break down. New family identity is gradually developed, as a "one-parent unit" or a "family with two separated households." Feelings of belonging and of stability are gradually restored during this period, only to be disrupted anew with the introduction of additional family members from the remarriage. The experience of disorganization and the clash of competing patterns of living, as well as the renewed uncertainty about who is "in" and who is "out," trigger strong emotional responses in all family members. All stepfamilies face the task of developing family rules that stabilize their relationships. In addition, some have the extra baggage of conflictful relationships with ex-spouses or ex-in-laws, insufficient preparation time for being together, and/or children only too ready to be available for scapegoating roles. When these families come for help, the therapeutic task is twofold: It is as important to attend to the goal of rebuilding as it is to attend to the goal of unraveling unresolved conflicts.

Two of the factors central to the task of rebuilding family relationships are those of developing cohesion within the new unit and establishing new relationship rules. For diagnostic purposes it is particularly important for therapy sessions in the first phase of treatment to include all family members. In planning interventions, the therapist should attend not only to family members' complaints, but also to descriptions of the routine and everyday patterns of the household and to accounts of ceremonies for holidays and special celebrations. In so doing one may find, for example, that there is no period during the week in which all family members are together. The mother and two of her children may eat dinner regularly together, but her teenage son is seldom home, and the father and his child fix themselves food when they feel like it. This may go along with complaints of intense rivalry between stepsiblings, a worry that the teenage son will run away, or the stepfather's complaint about being shut out and not cared for.

Developing cohesion and establishing new relationship rules can be addressed simultaneously through a variety of interventions. The therapist may intervene with a family task of working out a time during the week when all are involved in something together. Frequently, this task centers around gathering everyone together at dinner time, but the content of the activity is not essential and should be set by the family. Doing this, the family begins to develop an identity of the family as a group and to devise mechanics for decision-making which include all members. A number of practical suggestions have been mentioned by stepfamilies themselves. Families with teenagers seem to need regular family meetings where each person has a say, grievances are aired, and rules agreed upon.

Another possible intervention is a daily half-hour of strictly held couple time when the events of the day are looked at and evaluated, and plans made for change or for continuing what was successful. Whether this is a time for arguing, planning of logistics, or of celebration, couples emphasize the essential need for designating this time as one of their top priorities.

A third example—cited often by successfully established stepfamilies—is the involvement of new family subgroups, particularly the stepsibling subgroup, in pleasurable activities of relatively neutral emotional content. These are activities in which everyone has little to lose in terms of past loyalties, but something enjoyable to gain. In one family, for example, all the children joined a local swim team. In another, they began an acting troupe, performing religious plays. The cohesion and sense of union resulting from the successful experience of the group, as well as the gradual building-up of new patterns of transaction, establish a base from which the more difficult issues of living together may be approached. By its very nature, building new alliances makes old divisions less rigid.

Despite shared positive intentions and the seemingly obvious nature of such tasks, the implementation of plans to do something together may meet vehement resistance by one or more parts of the new family. Resistance sometimes comes in the form of expressions of discomfort about the explicit nature of the new decision-making rules. For example, the wife might say, "These little things in life are so obvious. If he really cared he would join in automatically"; or, "If the children were committed to the family, if they had been properly brought up, they would be helping out and respecting our wishes." It is the rules and patterns which usually are routine, automatic, and unseen that have been disrupted.

The early stages of reorganization of everyday rules must become explicit and consciously discussed. This process makes all the family members feel anxious and uncomfortable. They may feel that if all family unity and connection is discussable, it can be dissolved. Family members may feel separate and isolated. The "new family" may be perceived as an external burden. It may be feared that each person will look out only for him/herself. Explicitness, however, also has the positive potential for creating an openness to trial solutions and input from each family member. Discussing old patterns as just one option in the routine of everyday living may not only threaten hard-won stability carried over from the one-parent family, but also neutralize the intensity of loyalty to former identities so that new alliances may be begun.

Another source of resistance comes from the fact that success can be a double-edged sword. Any changes, even those with undeniably positive results, may bring up feelings of loss and conflicting loyalties. Growing feelings of attachment and affection carry with them fears of rejection once again. Families need the therapist's support in weathering the discouraging resistances, as well as help in realizing the paradoxically frightening implications of success. In addition, the new cohesion needs to be reinforced by the development of clear understandings about rules for keeping reasonable distance. Over time, new traditions are developed in the family about what is "too far," what is "too near," and what signals are used to regulate distance among all members.

Mourning of the old family unit and increased distance from the noncustodial parent are often mentioned as essential parts of the divorce process which must be accomplished before new relationships can be productively entered. On the other hand, it is important to be cognizant of the stabilizing function within the new family of the acknowledgment of historic threads from the former families. It is important to include the ongoing ties with all members of the divorced-remarried extended family. This can happen in small, automatic ways as well as in more formal, explicit interventions. As alliances between stepsiblings develop, one child fills in the background of an old (former) family joke. Some therapists suggest that time in the session be spent with each person introducing him/herself with relevant personal history which may not have been known before. This helps to place each member in historical context, making his or her actions more understandable, and works to build a common language and a common version of history.

Old family/new family relationships and traditions become particularly sensitive around times of festivity or ceremony. As discussed by Reiss (1980), family ceremonies embody a version of family history. Their reenactment plays a critical role in forming family identity and sense of stability. The theme of the remarried family ceremony simultaneously contains the narratives of the former families, their troubled times, the one-parent families, and the time of change into the new family. Burt (1981) gives examples of stepfamilies retaining enough of the old traditions from each former family to maintain the sense of the holiday "feeling right," yet developing new rituals (e.g., making new Christmas tree ornaments together) which emphasize the remarried family's theme of working together on a creative new venture. The therapist listens to descriptions of the ceremony with an ear to its symbolic meanings and to the implications for family structure which the various moves of the ceremony imply. Does the ritual perpetuate dysfunctional family solutions at a disabling cost, or does it confirm and enhance in a manner allowing for growth? In moving with the family through the process of explicit examination of interpersonal rules, creating a situation which can facilitate a joining process, and at the same time validating each member's history, the therapist can be instrumental in aiding a new family to build a family reality which will have the strength to deal with the enormous complexities of remarried daily life.

*References*

Burt, M. S. Making the holidays "feel" right. *Stepfamily Bulletin*, 1981, *1*, 4-5.
Reiss, D. *The working family: A researcher's view of health in the household.* Distinguished Psychiatrist Lecture, Annual Meeting of the American Psychiatric Association, May 6, 1980, San Francisco.

**MARY F. WHITESIDE, Ph.D.**
*Clinical Psychologist*
*Ann Arbor Center for the Family, Inc.*
*Ann Arbor, MI*

## 45. Therapy with Stepfamilies Involved in Joint Custody

**Question:**

Lately I have been seeing more and more divorced parents who have joint custody of their child or children. What special problems should I look for, and who should be included in the family sessions?

**Discussion:**

It is not surprising that the issue of joint custody should have become more prominent in recent years, since a number of state laws have been revised in order to make such an option more easily attainable. In some states, such as California, state law now presumes joint custody following divorce, unless the specific case contraindicates such a determination or the issue is contested in the court. Overall, the recent changes reflect the psychologically sound attempt to keep the natural father functioning as a parent and to avoid placing the entire child-rearing responsibilities on the single parent.

Help regarding custody may be sought before couples divorce or during the post-divorce period. In the former case, a family may appear to consult a therapist because they agree on joint custody and need aid in formulating plans before the physical separation; in actuality, they are often using the session to announce their divorce plans, expecting the therapist's support to soften the anticipated blow to the child. It is sometimes startling to the therapist to discover that the child may still be uninformed of the divorce plans. If this is so, the first treatment issue is to discuss the divorce openly, in order to help the parents deal with their concerns about possible damaging consequences to the child. Contrary to parental expectations, the children are usually less worried about the divorce than what is going on and what will be happening to them. Indeed, the real issue for most children is comprehending the uncertainty, confusion, tension, and hostility they have been experiencing at home.

Unlike the usual goals of family therapy, typically aimed at maintaining the family structure, here the therapist is working toward more limited objectives—reducing the anger, frustration, resentment, and conflict sufficiently, in order to insure a continuing post-divorce functioning relationship around the child. The clinician's goal is to reduce the tension between the divorcing couple to a manageable level and to help insure that the adults not use the children as conduits for their own emotionally unfinished business with one another. The therapist must make this goal clear to the couple. If they sense that the therapist is attempting to reach beyond that, and to reunite two people who at a great cost have decided to separate, they may resist any further interventions and refuse to work on the issues involved in custody. Whether a couple seeks pre-divorce counseling is usually a function of how far they have gone in the process of separating; while some are prepared to begin a life apart, others remain enmeshed, despite any protests to the contrary.

The therapist underlines for the parents, and helps them in turn to emphasize to the child, that they will continue to exercise joint responsibility. Whether the child resides physically in one place or the other, and for what length of time, becomes a secondary matter; what is paramount is that the child will continue to have two parents. At this point, children will frequently express their anxieties about never seeing daddy again, or that mother will no longer take any responsibilities for child-rearing. The guilt that attends the breaking-up of a family and which produces a pathological rigidity in the parents must be reduced by the therapist in his or her attempt to help them both continue the parenting process.

If the parents come in post-divorce complaining of problems surrounding children, it is incumbent upon the family therapist to understand who the major characters in the family conflict are and to be sure they are all included in the treatment. When custody is joint, then the stepparents or other adults living with the natural parents are part of the transaction, and may very well be part of the solution. There are often initial resistances by the parents to getting together with the new spouses, because of anticipated rivalries, but this initial resistance must be met firmly by the therapist with a statement that all persons involved in taking care of the children must have clear lines of communication and that joint custody implies their ability to work together. Usually after family sessions, fights between new spouses and living mates can be reduced with concurrent reduction of pressure on the children.

The family therapist must be careful not to be drawn into the mechanics of the arrangements between the two families as these are

idiosyncratic and should be directly dealt with by the families themselves. Differing attitudes and values, for example, need to be worked
out by those involved. The temptation to take over and become a supra-
parent above the two sets of parents is inappropriate. The families
sense a lack of control in their having to share the children and, if the
therapist takes responsibility for the parenting, they feel even more
the lack of control and their sense of inadequacy as parents. Major
differences in value system and child-rearing notions must be worked
out by the couples. Siblings and grandparents are frequently a part of
the struggle in the family, lending fuel or offering themselves as scape-
goats. It is very important that these people be included in family
sessions.

Custody problems that may be seen later in the post-divorce process
frequently occur after both parents have successfully made separate
lives and children have reached adolescence. With the concurrent
struggles that occur at adolescence, joint custody affords some temporary relief, if not solution, from the adolescent's problems. At this
point adolescent child may be shunted back and forth from one family
to the other, i.e., "Go live with your father. We are not going to put up
with you anymore." In this case, after the child has caused conflict in
both homes, the parents may agree that the adolescent is impossible,
and in a sense he or she gets extruded psychologically from both families. At this point it is extremely important that both sets of parents
assume responsibility to exercise controls, establish values, and develop a sense of commitment to the adolescent. The family therapist's
task is to see that the adolescent does not fall between the cracks of
the two-family systems. The therapist sometimes gets handed the adolescent to act as surrogate parent, both sets of parents having been
exhausted by the child-rearing process. Again, this is a mistake on the
part of the therapist as the child needs to be returned to the two-family
system which must work in concert to help him or her. The connections
that are made at this point with the families and the feeling that they
may not opt out of the struggle is extremely important for the future
of both the adolescent and the remaining family members.

**IRENE GOLDENBERG, Ed.D.**
*Neuropsychiatric Institute*
*University of California*
*Los Angeles, CA*

# 46. Stepfathers—Stepdaughters: Sexual Issues in the Remarried Family

## Question:

Sexuality and sexual feelings between parents and their children are facts of family life, but sexual issues between a stepfather and his stepdaughter, especially a teenage stepdaughter, seem to be especially salient, confusing, and anxiety-arousing. In working with stepfamilies, what is a helpful approach to take in regard to these delicate and strong feelings?

## Discussion:

For most families the emergence of their children's teenage years marks an era for heightened tensions, anxiety, and sexuality. In recent years it has become increasingly evident that the beginning of adolescence is significantly more complex in the remarried family that has as a member a teenage girl.

Classical Freudian theory holds that girls pass through an oedipal phase where they unconsciously try to seduce the father in order to humiliate their mother, because of her dominant position of authority. It is assumed that girls will resolve this conflict without actually acting it out and learn how to relate to one of the most important men in their life. In the ideal situation the daughter not only learns from this stage but also goes on to lead a well-adjusted, sexually satisfied life. This situation is not easily achieved even in the well-functioning family. It becomes progressively more difficult to achieve and creates increased tension in the dysfunctional stepfamily. Visher and Visher (1978) state that stepfathers may find their stepdaughters attracted to them and these feelings may be returned when things are not going well in the marital relationship. It has been noted that incest taboos are often weakened by the lack of biological relationships within families.

Our experience in working with stepfamilies with the presenting problem of an acting-out teenage girl leads us to explore the family's sexual feelings and sexual relationships. When a stepfamily, with an adolescent female, presents problems such as running-away, drug usage, dating, or acting-out behavior, the therapist needs to examine the stepfather's involvement, or noninvolvement, in the situation. Shulman (1972) noted that a great proportion of mothers were jealous of the relationships between their daughters and the stepfathers. In addition, she noted that the stepfather often compensated by becoming overcritical and overinvolved in the stepdaughter's behavior in order to reassure his wife that his interest was not sexual. The converse can be equally devastating, when the stepfather, who has had a good relationship with his stepdaughter, suddenly withdraws all affection and involvement when she reaches adolescence because of his fear of handling his own sexual feelings.

The overinvolved or underinvolved behavior of the stepfather leads his daughter to not only act out for individual recognition, but also increase her signals of sexuality to punish the father, frustrate the mother, and keep a semblance of power within the remarried family unit. Pincus and Dare (1978) state that incestuous fantasies are part of the secret life of every family. Actual enactment of sexuality between the child and parent is most common in families where there is a lack of sexual fulfillment in the marital relationship and where contact with the child is a displacement substitute for marital loving.

If the marital dyad is functional, a productive technique is to approach the sexuality issue on an educational level. When partners of the functional dyad bring up sexuality issues on their own, it is safe to assume initially that they are asking for reassurance. The therapist can greatly reduce the family's anxiety by giving them the reassurance they need by reaffirming that sexuality issues in the remarried family are natural. It is also productive to talk about, and normalize, sexual feelings children and adults may feel for each other in the remarried family and how these feelings may be expressed.

Another important area to talk about with the family is the new couple's sexuality and how it affects the children. The goal of these discussions is not to make sex a focal point for the family, nor is it a discussion to inhibit sexual thoughts or development. Rather, it is an educational approach used to discuss sexuality issues with the family on an abstract level. This approach allows family members to ventilate feelings and have questions answered without having to share intimate feelings or details. It is also an effective vehicle to explore sexuality issues with the nonverbal family in a nonthreatening way. Finally, it is an excellent intervention to provoke more detailed exploration of the stepfamily's sexuality when all members of the family can be reassured that this is an appropriate and natural area to work on in therapy.

For the marital dyad that is weak, nonfunctional, or dysfunctional, one may suspect that sexual feelings may have progressed to incestuous behavior. Baideme and Serritella (1981) have provided a description of how difficult it is to work with a dysfunctional remarried family. They suggest that the remarried family with one or more failed marriages behind it may be quite fearful of looking at the problems in its present marriage, especially those that revolve around sexual issues.

The therapist can proceed in several ways with the dysfunctional family where sexuality is an issue. The first is to attempt the educational approach outlined above in the hopes that it will provoke the family to deal with sexual issues in the open. The second is to explore with the couple on a very concrete level the sexual activity within the family. If attempts fail, the therapist needs to be aware of his or her legal responsibilities to protect the child..If members of the family are bringing up sexual issues and the marital dyad is weak or dysfunctional, refusing to work on sexual issues, the next step must be the consideration of contacting local child protective services authorities.

In working with the remarried family, therapists need to be attuned to many varied issues. Sexual issues in the remarried family is an area that is too often overlooked because of the complexities offered by such family configurations. Being aware, however, that this dynamic can be present gives the therapist one more diagnostic guidepost to help the remarried family deal with appropriate and functional parenting and marital issues.

*References*

Baideme, S. M., and Serritella, D. A. Planning conjoint family therapy with the remarried family. In A. S. Gurman (Ed.), *Questions and Answers in the Practice of Family Therapy.* New York: Brunner/Mazel, 1981.

Pincus, L. and Dare, C. *Secrets in the Family.* New York: Pantheon Books, 1978.

Shulman, G. L. Myths that intrude on the adaptation of the stepfamily. *Social Casework,* 1972, *49,* 131-139.

Visher, E. B., and Visher, J. S. *Stepfamilies: A Guide to Working With Stepparents and Stepchildren.* New York: Brunner/Mazel, 1979.

**DANIEL A. SERRITELLA, Ed.S.**
*Odyssey Family Counseling Center*
*College Park, GA*

# 47. Issues and Guidelines in the Treatment of Gay Stepfamilies

**Question:**

In my practice I am beginning to see increased numbers of gay men and women who are living with a gay partner and children in a stepfamily-like relationship. I have very limited experience in treating gays, both individuals and families, and my colleagues can offer little assistance. Can you identify some issues specific to the treatment of these types of families and suggest some guidelines for working with them?

**Discussion:**

This is a timely question since many formerly married gay men and women and their children who live in a stepfamily relationship are in increasing numbers seeking the services of marriage and family therapists. Therapy with these stepfamilies can be a challenging, demanding, and precarious undertaking. Many of the problems they bring to therapy are unknown to heterosexual stepfamilies. These problems are often complex and are affected by many factors. The most obvious factors are that:

1) Gay men and women are members of a stigmatized group and their life-styles and relationships are disapproved by a majority of the population.
2) The status and concept of gay marriage and family are neither legally recognized nor have any precedent in law.
3) Contemporary community standards have not evolved to the point where a homosexual life-style is acceptable for purposes of rearing children.
4) Society evaluates as unhealthy the rearing of children by gay parents. This evaluation is motivated by at least three fears:
   a) Fear that children might be sexually molested by the parent or the parent's partner.

b) Fear that children of gay parents are more likely to become gay adults or develop "improper" sex role behavior.

c) Fear that children will be harmed by the stigmatizing process that inevitably surrounds such life-styles.

5) Gay parents live in constant threat of losing their parental rights and must conceal their sexual orientation and life-style. Discovery or even suspicion that a parent is gay is often sufficient reason for either ex-spouses, grandparents, or even public agencies to force that parent to relinquish custody of children.

6) Because of the social stigma associated with homosexuality and the fear of discovery, leading to the need for secrecy, the normal problems of parenthood, whether as a single parent or as a couple, are compounded. Secrecy creates a self-imposed isolation for the family. This isolation tends to be more pronounced for children than for adults. The feeling of isolation separates the family from the community of heterosexuals, is in part a significant contributor to much of the family's relationship difficulties, and makes it more difficult for them to deal with conflicts that arise within the relationship.

## Therapy Issues of Gay Stepfamilies

From my experiences with gay stepfamilies I have found that, as with other types of families, although each family presents its own unique circumstances, adaptation, and difficulties, there are several commonly encountered issues which can be expected. In general, communication difficulties, sex roles, sexual exclusivity, or fidelity and issues pertaining to the children (stepchild-stepparent problems) are the most frequently emphasized. Although both partners in these families are of the same sex, they often tend to emulate the sex role patterns similar to those expected for egalitarian heterosexual couples in the society. However, sex role conflicts are many since partners often experience difficulty in living with another person who had been socialized for the same roles.

Among other important issues that these families bring to therapy are problems of parenting and problems specific to children in such families.

## Problems of Parenthood

I have observed that regardless of sexual preference and life-style, gay parents face the same hazards and problems of survival and caring for their children as is true for heterosexual parents. However, for gay parents, parenthood is further complicated by the realities that the partners are of the same sex, and that gay relationships and life-styles are disapproved by the society. Not only does the heterosexual society reject gays, but gays also often tend to reject other gays, especially gay males, who are parents. Non-parent partners often demand that the dyadic relationship be the primary relationship and that they be first in the other partner's hierarchy of relationships. Consequently, for gay fathers who choose to retain custody of their children, there is always the fear of being rejected by peers and a partner because they are a custodial parent.

Most of the issues tend to be the same for gay male parents as for lesbian mothers; however gay male parents face an additional burden. Society tends to view with suspicion two males who live together for an extended period. The presence of children in such households tends to increase suspicion. As a result, gay fathers who live in a step-relation are always in fear of being discovered.

## Children's Problems

I cannot overemphasize that it is not easy for children to grow up in a family that is disapproved of and is perceived as pathological or deviant by society. Consequently, children in gay families face many difficulties that often cause them to react with confusion, depression, and even open rebellion when they are unable to adapt and cope with the secrecy necessary to being a part of such families.

The issue of maintaining secrecy about the life-style of the adults is an important one for children. From their perspective the need for secrecy creates a closeted and isolated existence not only for the adults, but also for them. Children, especially adolescents, are often reluctant to bring home either friends or dates for fear of discovery. Visits to the homes of friends are also fraught with anxiety since there is always the possibility of being asked prying questions about one's family.

The feeling of isolation from peers and community seems to emphasize the sense of difference these children feel. It also accentuates the lack of a shared consciousness of a kind between the children, the custodial parent, and the stepparent. The absence of this shared experience leaves the children without a refuge to which they can turn for assistance in dealing with the societal hostility and pressures.

## Therapist Issues

Therapists who treat gay stepfamilies face many obvious and immediate complexities that are not to be found in treating heterosexual stepfamilies. The first of these pertains to the need to rethink the concept of the family since neither the gay stepfamily structure nor relationship fit the accepted views of the nuclear family. Second, there is the need to perceive the family as a unit and to see its problems as a family problem and not the individual problems of persons who share a common residence. Third, there is the need to overcome the suspicion of the family toward the therapist because he/she is heterosexual. I have found much of this suspicion to be valid. The therapist must communicate understanding and acceptance of the family. This will probably be effective in diminishing the family's initial defensiveness, suspicion, and hostility towards the therapist. Fourth, the therapist needs to deal with the fact that there are currently no models nor therapy guidelines for gay family relationships upon which therapists, heterosexual or gay ones, can draw to guide interventions with gay stepfamilies. Moreover, although a family therapy orientation similar to that used with heterosexual stepfamilies can be useful, the techniques of conventional marital and family therapy must be modified to the special situations of gay stepfamilies. Finally, the therapist must deal with atypical forms of transference as well as rejection, resistance, and competition between partners for the therapist's favor. The therapist must also be prepared to deal with each partner's subtle attempts to both psychologically and sexually seduce the therapist. Such behaviors are a part of therapy with gay families.

*Therapy Guidelines*

Despite the difficulties in working with gay stepfamilies, heterosexual therapists can be successful with such families. Over the years I have found that a systems model that incorporates conjoint family therapy using behavioral techniques to be successful. The initial focus of therapy is on the family and understanding that system. The second phase of therapy incorporates the insights into the family system by means of a behavioral approach.

To be effective with these families, the therapist needs to be clinically skilled in working with stepfamilies in general, and gay couples with or without children, in particular. The therapist also needs to be sensitive to his/her own attitudes, feelings, and beliefs about homosexuals, homosexuality, and homosexuals as parents, and be especially cognizant how these may intrude and affect both the therapeutic process and its outcome.

Additionally, the following guidelines can be helpful:

1) The therapist must be knowledgeable of and comfortable with

homosexuality as a sexual preference and life-style and must have freed him/herself of the conviction that a gay orientation is either pathological, regressive, or immature. Therapists who have a deep conviction that the heterosexual life-style is superior to all others, and conduct therapy with gay families from that value premise, will not be of any help to gay stepfamilies.

2) The therapist should not be overinquisitive or patronizing, or treat the gay partners as though they were a laboratory specimen. The inherent assets of both the couple's and the family's relationship should be emphasized. Overabsorption in the pathology of the adults' life-style or family relationship can result in the therapist's ignoring these assets.

3) The therapist must be prepared to deal with his/her fears of being stigmatized or of compromising his/her reputation by working with these families. Often, therapists who treat gay families are accused by some peers and others of encouraging homosexuality, or even of being gay, if their goal is not to change the sexual orientation of their client(s).

4) The therapist must avoid the pitfall of "pseudo insight." He/she should avoid attributing all the family's problems, especially those involving children, to the fact that the family is a homosexual one. Many of these problems may be unrelated to the sexual preference and life-style of the adults. Likewise, many of the children's problems may stem from either normative developmental issues or concerns common to stepfamily living, regardless of the adults' sexual orientation.

5) The therapist should follow the family's own sense of need and let that guide the therapeutic process rather than redefine the therapeutic goals from the therapist's own value position. However, therapy must also deal with the typical kinds of marital conflicts that are found in heterosexual marriages—initial and remarriage. Clinical strategies must also include an ability to identify and deal with other relationship issues specific to gay persons.

*References*

Baptiste, D. *Treating gay stepfamilies: A challenge for marriage and family therapists.* Paper presented to the American Association for Marriage and Family Therapy Annual Meeting, San Diego, CA, October, 1981.

Walker, J. and White, N. The varieties of therapeutic experience: Conjoint therapy in a homosexual marriage. *Canada's Mental Health*, 1975, June, 3-5.

**DAVID A. BAPTISTE, Ph.D.**
*Counseling Psychologist*
*University Counseling Center*
*New Mexico State University*
*Las Cruces, NM*

# PART B

*Multigenerational Issues*

# 48. Family/Marital Therapy with Second Generation Holocaust Survivor Families

**Question:**

Ten to 15 years ago Holocaust survivor families presented in clinic and private practice settings with an identified patient who was a decompensating adolescent and whose defenses, as well as the family's coping mechanisms, were unable to work through the very traumatic experiences and losses suffered. Therapeutic efforts focused on extrication and separation of such identified patients from the enmeshed family system. Parents were helped to mourn, to abreact and restitute, etc., in an empathic relationship. The family therapy interventions at that time resulted in an improvement in 40% of cases, measured in terms of separation/individuation of the identified patients. Some second generation young married couples now present themselves with echoing problems. Is family therapy indicated again? What else is indicated?

**Discussion:**

The problems presented by such couples, now in their late twenties or early thirties, reflect themes already apparent in their adolescence—some conflicts unresolved, appearing anew, or displaced. Some couples, individual members of which I had seen long ago and who had managed to break away and had married each other, are presently functioning well, which gratifying result will also be discussed.

In addition to the usual marital problems presented by young couples (e.g., power and control struggles, dependency/independence conflicts, poor communication, lack of intimacy, loneliness, sexual dissatisfactions, and a poor problem-solving repertoire), this particular "different" group report added guilt feelings about having "abandoned" parents, not having lived up to the (frequently unrealistic) parental goals, which these already high achievers had vainly tried to satisfy before. They complain of failing in fulfilling "memorializing missions" burdened on them (often by themselves), which might justify their own, or the family's, survival. They also feel isolated and often lack the ability to trust, seeing the outside world as dangerous and hostile. Strong separation anxiety persists. Intergenerational conflicts continue to bind; there is clinging, manipulation, and interference, frequently preventing the development of clear generational boundaries or of real autonomy of the second generation members. These couples often assume a nurturing, parenting, protective role vis-à-vis their dependent parents, a phenomenon observed severally and cross-culturally (Davidson, 1980). The long-range effect of disturbed parent-child relationships in survivor families has been described elsewhere (Barocas and Barocas, 1979; Russell, 1980; Sigal et al., 1973).

I considered family therapy the treatment of choice for such cases, originally. Together with Davidson (1980), working in Israel, I still consider family therapy to be the treatment of choice of dysfunctional survivor families, for reasons outlined. The couples seen are still entrapped in their family systems. Four to 10 family sessions are needed in order to intervene effectively, following an initial assessment interview with the couples alone. A decision is then made whether to bring in one or both spouses' families, or involve significant others and which, if any, additional interventions might be necessary. In this particular series of cases I treated, no other individual or group therapy was involved, though such interventions should be used if indicated. Most of the couples were referred by physicians, other mental health professionals, community agencies, or the clergy, "who had given up on them." The others came through word-of-mouth networks or were self-referred.

My general therapeutic approach is empirical. I mostly used a highly structured, cognitive method described elsewhere (Russell et al., 1980). Hard work is needed to establish a crucially important therapeutic trust relationship—especially with the parents, who will have to give "permission" to effect a true separation from their children. The parents often dread this, because they fear losing their children "finally," or again. When complete separation is not yet (or not) feasible, family sessions are frequently very helpful in bringing about the acquisition of more appropriate ways of coping with loss, in a supportive setting. This brings about other growth. In my experience, several parent couples could then tell their children about their experiences in nonthreatening ways, which was identified as an important means to effect desirable conflict resolution in the latter. Such techniques are helpful to negotiate some of the factors causing considerable difficulties and obstacles in individual psychotherapy with survivors, as reviewed by Chodoff (1980) and others, which led them to be pessimistic with regard to outcome and prognosis, and to pronounce psychoanalytic treatment to be "inapplicable." Certain cases may benefit from abreactive or cathartic techniques in a supportive atmosphere. Understandably, survivors resent being described in clinical terms anyway.

In a typical case, a survivor couple's son and only child married the only child of another survivor couple. They met in university, became professionals, and then married. The wife's parents lived in an apartment next to their own, and fought incessantly, being overheard by our couple through the wall. His parents lived in an apartment across the street. Yet neither spouse was "permitted" by his/her own parents to communicate with his/her in-laws for various bizarre reasons. This led to side-taking, loyalty conflicts, and marital battles. The hostile-camp atmosphere blocked efforts to break out; it prevailed for years. The in-laws never acknowledged each other or talked. The birth of the first grandchild upset this "frozen" balance. The young couple decompensated, the wife developing severe psychosomatic symptoms, while the husband was so depressed he could not function adequately in his profession. As their sexual relationship was still fairly good, they decided not to separate but referred themselves instead.

When I first saw them, they had been married for seven years. Following assessment, I saw them separately with their families of origin, then prepared them for a joint meeting with both families, having made preparatory home visits. To everybody's surprise, all came. After a fairly dramatic initial session, contracts were negotiated, while extended family members were brought in to "help" overcome the considerable difficulties present. Some came from far away. Community resources were also mobilized. I used psychodramatic techniques and paradoxical instructions, as well as humor and reframing. Six (part and global) family sessions were needed, as well as 10 sessions with the couple alone. I made myself available to them under strictly controlled conditions, on the telephone, for about three months. Three years later this couple functions fairly well; no one has asked for the follow-up session offered. The husband went back to working effectively; then the couple moved to the suburbs. Their parents still live in their old quarters and are being taken out in turns or they visit, an unheard-of event previously. The parents still do not talk to each other directly, but occasionally on the phone, when "matters concerning the grandchild" are involved. The wife's psychosomatic symptom has almost disappeared, the infant is symptom-free so far. The grandparents work (half-heartedly) in survivor organizations. For this kind of case

I believe the techniques described above to be the most effective available, though far from entirely satisfactory.

Finally, I would like to emphasize the pressing need to avoid reinforcing already-existing negative, pathologizing stereotypes and myths concerning such survivor families as invariably damaged and traumatized and necessarily in need of therapy—family or otherwise. Several mental health professionals, such as Pilcz (1979), Davidson (1980), myself (Russell, 1980) and others believe it is time to recognize that the effect of the Holocaust on the second generation was not always traumatic and debilitating, but often provided a foundation for strength and stability of individuals and family. Various aspects of survivor skills have been identified and described (Pilcz, 1979). Some survivor families clearly function successfully in terms of raising children, as well as in other respects, and continue to do well—no mean achievement for survivors, as Rakoff puts it. The factors which make for a healthy, as opposed to a dysfunctional, family functioning merit further study. A systematic study of a nonclinical survivor population is also needed in order to try to discover adaptive patterns and to identify protective factors in various psychosocial environments, including cross-culturally.

In general, I, in concert with several second generation family therapists, prefer not to stress pathology and maladaptive vulnerability, but to emphasize adaptive patterns, growth, and strength found, thus shifting our clinical perspective. For dysfunctional individuals or couples of the second generation, family therapy sessions of the kind described provide an opportunity to connect, or "reconnect," with their family "crucible," to recall Gus Napier and Carl Whitaker's (1978) telling description. A "going home," in Bowen's or Framo's sense, presents the optimal forum for conflict resolution, for becoming autonomous, and for eventual adaptive functioning. Appropriate mobilization of psychological, social/community, and environmental resources, as well as of extended family and peer group networks, should be used judiciously. I emphasize ego- and family-syntonic activities as useful counter-pathogenic agents. Therapeutic results so far, while not overwhelming, appear to be better than other clinical approaches previously used.

## References

Barocas, H. A. and Barocas, C. B. Wounds of the fathers: The next generation of holocaust victims, *International Review of Psychoanalysis*, 1979, *6*, 331-340.

Chodoff, P. Psychotherapy of the Survivor. In J. Dimsdale (Ed.) *Survivors, Victims and Perpetrators: Essays on the Nazy Holocaust*. Washington, D.C.: Hemisphere Publishing Corp., 1980.

Davidson, S. The clinical effects of massive psychic trauma in families of holocaust survivors. *Journal of Marital and Family Therapy*, 1980, *6*, 11-21.

Napier, A. Y. and Whitaker, C. A. *The Family Crucible*. New York: Harper & Row, 1978.

Pilcz, M. Understanding the survivor family: An acknowledgement of the positive dimensions of the Holocaust legacy. In L. Y. Steinitz and D. Szonyi (Eds.), *Living After the Holocaust: Reflections by Children of Survivors in America*. Second edition. New York: Bloch Publishing, 1979.

Russell, A. Late effects—Influence on the children of the CCS. In J. Dimsdale (Ed.), *Survivors, Victims and Perpetrators: Essays on the Nazi Holocaust*. Washington, D.C.: Hemisphere Publishing Corp., 1980.

Russell, A., Russell, L. and Waring, E. M. Cognitive family therapy: A preliminary report. *Canadian Journal of Psychiatry*, 1980, *25*, 64-67.

Sigal, J. J., Silver, D., Rakoff, V., and Ellin, B. Some second generation effects of survival of the Nazi persecution. *American Journal of Orthopsychiatry*, 1973, *43*, 320-327.

**AXEL RUSSELL, M.D.**
*Consultant in Psychiatry*
*Oxford Regional Centre;*
*Department of Psychiatry*
*University of Western Ontario*
*London, Ontario, Canada*

# 49. Parentification and Deparentification in Family Therapy

**Question:**

Contextual family therapy as developed by Boszormenyi-Nagy is a therapeutic approach that has been receiving increased attention in recent years (e.g., Boszormenyi-Nagy and Krasner, 1980; Boszormenyi-Nagy and Ulrich, 1981). Questions of technique often arise in discussions of the contextual approach. Of frequent concern are questions about the application of the key notions of parentification and de-parentification. What is parentification and when does this become a pathogenic process? How can parentified family members be helped? Are there specific parentified roles? What are the specific steps a therapist should take in moving toward de-parentifying family members?

**Discussion:**

The notion of parentification has been defined as the "subjective distortion of a relationship as if one's partner or even children were one's parent" (Boszormenyi-Nagy and Spark, 1973, p. 151). Parentification represents recreation of one's past relationship with one's parent in a current adult relationship or/in a relationship with one's children (Boszormenyi-Nagy and Spark, 1973). This process is important because in a sense parentified relationships comprise the essence of intergenerational family therapy, not unlike how transference relationships comprise the essence of individual psychodynamic therapy.

The parentification process becomes pathogenic when it impairs the growth of one or several family members at any of the life-cycle stages. For instance, if a young adult had extreme difficulties in separating from his/her parents, the overriding sense of indebtedness for having abandoned or rejected his/her parents may be expressed by extreme devotion to his/her child, as if the child were the parent. In this manner, the adult both attempts to remain loyal and to reduce the indebtedness to his/her parents through the extreme devotion to the child. The child is thus placed in an impossible exploitative predicament where she/he is expected to behave both as an obedient child and as a nurturing or protective parent.

As may be apparent, parentification is the process element of what keeps families "fused," "enmeshed," or "undifferentiated." While parentification as process may be identified through the internalized expectations and commitment characteristics of the various family members, it may also be identified by the often obvious structured relational patterns or roles. Three roles are most common: 1) the caretaking role, sometimes referred to as the "paternal child," though not necessarily restricted to a child who takes on parenting responsibilities; 2) the sacrificial and/or scapegoated role; and 3) the neutral role.

Deparentification is the ongoing work of the family therapist to reverse the pathogenic family situation via a series of steps to rebalance the ethical structure of family relationships. Since parentification has its roots in the previous generation, often to work effectively at deparentifying a family, several generations must be involved in the treatment. In distilled form, the basic elements in the deparentification process are: 1) acknowledgment of the parentified member's positive contribution to the family; 2) a period of examination and reflection with the parents as to how they may have been parentified in their own families of origin; 3) an action component which connects the acknowledgment of the parentified family member(s) with the experience of the parent's parentification; and 4) an emphasis on how each family member can work toward rebalancing relationships, and specifically underscoring how all family members can act decisively in improving the family situation. This last step holds accountable all individuals, including the parents or the parental surrogates, to make the needed changes in the family.

In a case that involved mobilizing the sisters and brother-in-law of a 17-year-old young man who was psychiatrically hospitalized, parentified relationships were evident not only for the 17-year-old identified patient but also for most of his sisters. While the parents had died, the marital relationships of the sisters paralleled one another. They each related to their spouses "as if" they were their father. In the context of examining current relationships in light of the past, one older sister was able to discuss her extreme difficulties in expressing love toward her own spouse and in-laws; this she viewed as a reenactment of how she related to her father. The pattern had been one where she withheld love and affection.

The "identified patient" was often treated as a "monster" by members of the family. It was as if the 17-year-old were paying for the faults and/or shortcomings of the deceased father who apparently severely mistreated his wife and children. Paradoxically, while at times the identified patient acted in "bizarre" ways, at other times he was clearly a parent. This was graphically evident when one sister talked of how she was helped by her brother who told her she started to look "like them girls at the psychiatric hospital." Deparentification began to take on powerful effects when sister, who was the surrogate parent as well as the legal guardian, "acknowledged" her brother's helpfulness to her. Sister was able to thank her brother and offer him help. Other family members were willing to help in caring for him and to give in meaningful ways, establishing genuine human reciprocity. The family members were able to reflect, then critically examine, painful unfinished issues related to their parents; these issues were affecting not only their filial relationships but also their relationships with their own children. Based on such reflection and acknowledgment, a specific plan of action was designed by the family with the assistance of the therapists.

The essence of deparentification involves a dialectic between action and reflection. Acknowledgment to a scapegoated family member about his or her contributions without a connection to what can be done differently in the family is an empty sort of acknowledgment. Similarly, to engage in reflection about past injustices in the family devoid of a focus on how to correct current injustices is a false reflection. Conversely, to focus on changes and modes of action without an understanding of current conditions, past injustices, or of the contribution of various members is a myopic sort of activism. Action and reflection must be carefully interwoven in order to establish dialogue and thereby transform parentification in familial relationships.

*References*

Boszormenyi-Nagy, I. and Spark, G. *Invisible Loyalties.* New York: Harper and Row, 1973.
Boszormenyi-Nagy, I. and Krasner, B. R. Trust based therapy: A contextual approach. *American Journal of Psychiatry*, 1980, *137*, 767-775.
Boszormenyi-Nagy, I. and Ulrich, D. N. Contextual family therapy. In A. S. Gurman and D. P. Kniskern (Eds.), *Handbook of Family Therapy*. New York: Brunner/Mazel, 1981.

**GUILLERMO BERNAL, Ph.D.**
*Assistant Professor of Psychology*
*Department of Psychiatry*
*University of California*
*San Francisco General Hospital*
*San Francisco, CA*

# 50. The Role of Forgiveness in Family Therapy

**Question:**

In contextual family therapy (Boszormenyi-Nagy and Ulrich, 1981), the therapist must often guide adult family members toward rebalancing their "accounts" with their families of origin. Stagnant or broken relationships in one generation tend to replay themselves in the next generation. What is the role of forgiveness in this task?

**Discussion:**

Forgiveness is a core dynamic in healing stagnant or broken relationships. To the degree that genuine forgiveness for real injury or injustice is possible, trusting relationships can be actualized. Conversely, situations in which forgiveness is not possible result in relational stagnation. A person's legacy becomes imbalanced by a chronic sense of being wounded or by a chronic sense of guilt for inflicting wounds. In the context of relational stagnation, trust is an empty, meaningless word. Without trust, human freedom to relate is diminished and with it the capacity for personal responsibility. For example, the capacity of parents to give to their children is shaped to a large extent by the quality of parenting they have received. If individuals feel cheated of rightfully deserved parenting and resentful toward their parents, their strongest inclination will be to rebalance their felt injustices. Without reworking the relationships in which injustices are perceived to outweigh fairness, each of us tends to hold our children, our spouses, and the world at large accountable for what was not received from our own parenting resources.

In my practice, I frequently work with adults whose experiences with their parents are marked by a deep sense of injury and exploitation. They do not want to reopen the past, yet they are stuck at the level of their felt loss. Guiding them back to their own relational context is a beginning step in the process of forgiveness: "Did you ever ask your father (mother) about that? Do your parents know how those things have affected you? Can you imagine talking to your parents about that? If you could have it your way, what would you ask for from your parents? Is there something you would like to do to help them?" The therapist presumes that there are still resources for healing even in the midst of pervasive mistrust. Family members are encouraged to face their ambivalent feelings by attempting to rework the balance of give and take that exists between them.

The path toward forgiveness involves the following components:

1) *Reexamining the relationship* by going back to face their parents with a sense of having been cheated or exploited. When they can make a claim for consideration from their parents in the present, they are helped to face and overcome feelings of guilt, shame, and resentment. Making a personal claim is a relational strength and builds trust.

2) *Extending concern* by trying to imagine and eventually to understand how it was for parents in their own lives: Did they experience loss or deprivation? How did they struggle? Giving due consideration to their side is not an attempt to "wipe the slate clean" but rather to humanize a shared experience in the hope that new options for caring can be found.

3) *Reclaiming the relationship* by identifying past and present resources in the parent-child relationship. Developing the ability to acknowledge what was, in fact, given and gained, even as one challenges distortions and myths, signals renewed trust.

Forgiveness is a healing rather than a feeling act. It is not dependent on happy results. The therapist can help family members by stressing that claiming and extending consideration in an injured relationship carries more weight than a successful outcome. When individuals can be freed from a position of one-sided blame and lack of forgiveness by finally being able to face their part in an injured relationship, they experience the beginning of liberation. Sometimes the visible result of returning to the parental relationship may well be rejection and continued intransigency on the part of the other. Nevertheless, by making the attempt, family members are relieved of the burden of guilt that comes from wondering what could have happened if they had had the courage to risk one more time. Being able to act fairly, regardless of what anyone else chooses to do, is always freeing.

Sometimes a person's wounds are too deep to be healed. He/she is still entitled to a fair hearing from the sources of his/her injury with a view to examining what, if anything, can be done. If that is not possible, there may be no other option but to let go of the investment. Letting go should be presented as a moratorium, without blame or guilt, in the hope that resources for a relationship may be present at some future time.

Conflicting tendencies may remain even when attempts to repair an injured relationship have been well received. While it is true that a person is no longer bound by the same degree of guilt or fear, freedom is limited by the extent to which trust can be restored. Restoration of trust is a process and requires time.

The following questions frequently come up in discussions about the role of forgiveness in family therapy.

*Can forgiveness take place if parents are dead or unavailable?* In my experience, it can and does. The process is still the same but the therapeutic work is harder. In such situations, the therapist can guide family members back to siblings or to other relatives, such as aunts, uncles, and cousins, to learn about their parents' side.

*In order to work on forgiving one's parents, do they have to be present in the therapy?* In my experience, the work of forgiveness is primarily dependent on what people do outside the therapy room. The therapist may work with one family member or in conjoint sessions. However, both the therapist and the family can learn more about family loyalty dynamics, the ambivalent feelings of both parties, and how each person's actions affect the other through the process of live relating. In return, the therapist has something to teach family members about the integration of personal claims and consideration for others. It may well be the therapist's own ambivalence that prevents him or her from asking adults to ask their parents to come to therapy. In my experience, there have been few instances in which adults have been unwilling to make the attempt once they have experienced the therapist's concern for all the relationships in the family. On the other hand, the therapist who fails to consider family loyalty dynamics and inadvertently sides with a person against his or her parents will have a difficult time gaining sufficient trust to work effectively in conjoint sessions.

A strategy session in preparation for a conjoint session helps to manage anxiety. Concerns such as how to raise the question of therapy with parents, what might happen during and after the session, and needs and expectations, among others, can be thought through in advance with the therapist's help. I stress that the session is a commitment to explore the relationship and nothing may really change. I work to keep the sessions as low-key as possible without evading difficult or painful issues.

Guiding a family member toward forgiveness in an injured relationship depends on three components: 1) what action a person is willing to take on his or her own behalf; 2) whether a person has enough resources to care about the relationship; and 3) whether the therapist has the conviction, vision, experience, and skill to help a person mobilize his/her own trust resources to return to the relationship with a view to repairing it.

*References*

Boszormenyi-Nagy, I. and Ulrich, D. Contextual Family Therapy. In A. S. Gurman and D. P. Kniskern (Eds.), *Handbook of Family Therapy*. New York: Brunner/Mazel, 1981.

**MARGARET COTRONEO, M.S.N.**
*Instructor*
*Psychiatric-Mental Health Section*
*School of Nursing*
*University of Pennsylvania*

# PART C

## *Ethnicity and Family Therapy*

# 51.  Ethnic Differences and Family Therapy

**Question:**

> I have been a family therapist for some time and am aware that most family theories are written as if they were "culture-free," i.e., they describe processes that go on in all families. It seems to me that families of different ethnic groups have some differences in process or at least have their dynamics, patterns, issues, etc., influenced by their ethnicity. What do you think? What difference does culture make on the family's problems and my treatment of them?

**Discussion:**

It has also been my experience that ethnicity does affect family dynamics, patterns, major issues, and life-cycle rituals. In addition, a family's ethnic origin also seems to influence the types of problems with which they present themselves for treatment, their use of mental health services, and their methods of problem resolution. Traditionally, the mental health field has left the study of the effects of cultural differences on emotional functioning mainly to anthropologists. The major models of family therapy have made little reference to ethnic differences in the application of their method to treatment situations. Although Minuchin et al. (1967) have developed some specific techniques to work with lower socioeconomic families, the other major models (communications, strategic, and Bowen systems) do not mention ethnicity as an aspect of the family's context.

Only recently have we begun to consider ethnic differences when developing and examining different models (e.g., McGoldrick and Pearce, 1982). My own recent contribution has been to study the American Jewish family (Herz and Rosen, 1982). In order to examine how ethnicity influences family process and treatment, let us first define what we mean by ethnicity. It has been defined as a sense of "commonality or community derived from networks of family experience" (Feinstein, 1974). As such, it appears to be an essential determinant of values, perceptions, needs, modes of expression, behavior, and identity. It fulfills a deep psychological need for identity and a sense of continuity with the past. It is transmitted from past to present generations by the emotional "language" of the family and its surrounding community. Furthermore, there is increasing evidence that ethnic values are retained for many generations after immigration (Greeley, 1969, 1978) and that they continue to play an important role in family life and personality development.

The definition of a problem or dysfunction is affected by the norms and frame of reference of the individual(s) seeking help. Symptoms and the definition of illness differ greatly among ethnic groups. For instance, in Jewish families who view education and "the children" as central issues, it may often be some achievement difficulty in a child which gets defined as a problem. Members of Jewish families often refer themselves for treatment, while the Irish, who tend to view their problems as a consequence of their sinning, will generally come for treatment only at the suggestion of an outside source such as the school or the clergy. Partly because they tend to wait a long time before seeking assistance, the Irish rarely seek help for neurotic disorders, but rather have a very high rate of psychoses and addiction, primarily alcoholism (McGoldrick and Pearce, 1982). On the other hand, Jews tend to be overrepresented in "neurotic disorders" and underrepresented in hospital admissions for psychosis and addiction disorders (Rinder, 1963). As is evident, the definition of a problem tends to derive from a combination of the values, characteristics, dynamics, and issues central to a particular ethnic group.

Seeking help for problems depends greatly on one's attitude toward the "helper." This attitude is partly determined by one's ethnic origin. For instance, Italians tend to rely on the family and turn to an outsider for help only as a last resort (Gambino, 1974). Black Americans have traditionally distrusted the help they receive from traditional middle-class help-givers (Hines and Boyd, 1982). Several cultural groups, e.g., Puerto Rican, Chinese, and Iranian, tend to somatize when they are under emotional stress and therefore tend to seek medical rather than mental health services. It appears that a rather large number of potential clients either do not experience the need for mental health services or strongly doubt the value of therapy.

In terms of family therapy, there is little research suggesting ethnic differences in attitudes toward seeking such treatment. However, studies of ethnic differences in response to physical illness have implications for family therapy practice (Zola, 1966). Jews and Italians tended to complain about their pain, but Jews appeared to distrust simple solutions, while Italians looked for an immediate remedy (Zborowski, 1969). The Irish did not expect "cures"; they did not complain or mention their pain. WASPs were more optimistic, expecting science to discover cures and striving in the meantime for self-control.

From my clinical experience it generally appears that ethnic groups who value family expressiveness and who have intense interactions will tend to seek family treatment more frequently than those who do not value these characteristics. Therapeutic problems may develop when a therapist from a culture that values the former is confronted by a family who is more reserved or vice versa. In the first instance, the therapist may try to increase the emotional involvement and expressiveness of the family. In the second instance, the therapist may try to suppress such behaviors. Therapeutic problems may also result when therapists confront families with the same background as theirs. For instance, an Irish therapist may be hesitant to ask an Irish family members questions regarding their "personal life" as not "proper," because the therapist shares the family's inhibitions and sees their lack of expressiveness as normal. Or an Italian therapist may go along with the "secrets" of Italian families because he/she knows how strong Italian family loyalties are. Or a Jewish therapist who comprehends the need for insight and understanding does not "push" Jewish families to make a needed behavioral change.

Now this answers the first part of your question. The second part of your question regarding the application of this information to treatment planning is intricately related to our previous discussion and has already received some attention. However, there are several general ideas regarding ethnic differences which make sense in terms of your family treatment planning. It is important to have a framework for examining families, and ethnicity is one important aspect of a framework.

In performing a family evaluation/assessment, I always ask the ethnic background of both spouses. I am also interested in the following factors which influence the degree to which ethnic patterns surface in a family (McGoldrick and Pearce, 1982):

1) The reasons for immigration.
2) The length of time since immigration and the impact of generational acculturation on the family.
3) The family's place of residence—whether they live or have lived in an ethnic neighborhood.
4) The order of migration (e.g., Who came to America first?)
5) The socioeconomic, education, and upward mobility of family members.

6) The political and religious ties to the ethnic group.
7) The language spoken by the family.
8) The extent of intermarriage.
9) The family's attitude toward the ethnic group and its values.

Often, assisting a family member to explore and/or strengthen his/her cultural identity helps that individual develop a broad understanding of the current problem and patterns in his/her family. Grounding the problem in the complex family history decreases the family's intense anxiety about the current problems and broadens its frame of reference for understanding.

To function without some knowledge and sensitivity to ethnic differences is to remain ignorant of an important aspect of any family's context. By remaining open to new experiences one can often avoid negative stereotyping. By realizing the relativity of one's own values, one can be free to examine the values of others and to develop paradigms for organizing and exploring necessary ethnic information.

## References

Feinstein, O. Why ethnicity? In D. Hartman (Ed.), *Immigrants and Migrants: The Detroit Ethnic Experience.* Detroit: Wayne State University Press, 1974.

Gambino, R. *Blood of My Blood: The Dilemma of Italian-Americans.* Garden City, New York: Doubleday, 1974.

Greeley, A. M. *Why Can't They Be Like Us?* New York: Institute of Human Relations Press, 1969.

Greeley, A. M. *The American Catholic.* New York: Basic Books, 1978.

Herz, F., and Rosen, E. Family therapy with Jewish Americans. In M. McGoldrick and J. K. Pearce (Eds.), *Ethnicity and Family Therapy.* New York: Guilford Press, 1982.

Hines, P., and Boyd, N. The Black American family. In M. McGoldrick and J. K. Pearce (Eds.), *Ethnicity and Family Therapy.* New York: Guilford Press, 1982.

McGoldrick, M., and Pearce, J. K. (Eds.), *Ethnicity and Family Therapy.* New York: Guilford Press, 1982.

Minuchin, S., Montalvo, B., Guerney, B., Rosman, B., and Schumer, F. *Families of the Slums.* New York: Basic Books, 1967.

Rinder, I. Mental health of American Jewish urbanites: A review of the literature and predictions. *International Journal of Social Psychiatry,* 1963, *9,* 214-220.

Zborowski, M. *People in Pain.* San Francisco: Jossey-Bass, 1969.

Zola, I. Culture and symptoms: An analysis of patients' presenting complaints. *American Sociological Review,* 1966, *5,* 141-55.

**FREDDA HERZ, R.N., Ph.D.**
*Director of Graduate Studies*
*Department of Nursing*
*Herbert H. Lehman College*
*New York, NY;*
*Director of Training*
*Family Institute of Westchester*
*Mount Vernon, NY*

# 52. Working with Families
## Cross-culturally

**Question:**

What are the critical dimensions that make it possible for you to see, treat, and consult effectively about very diverse families from different ethnic, religious, and cultural heritages? What ways do you utilize to comprehend and transcend such extreme life-style differences?

**Discussion:**

During the 1960s and into the mid-1970s, there were various arguments advanced advocating that the therapist should share a common racial, religious, and cultural background with his/her client population, for, the logic went, only when they were products of a similar tapestry could the clinician understand and identify with the dilemmas of the "consumers of the service" (Richan, 1977). This lexicon and the thinking it reflected were popular during the first decade-and-a-half of the community mental health movement and the pioneering days of the "war on poverty" with its store-front clinics in urban areas providing ready access to services for neighborhood residents. Often staffs in child welfare and public assistance agencies and community mental health centers underwent radical transitions in order to better match the staff to the racial, ethnic, and religious composition of the patient population.

Such an endogamous, homogeneous model for delivery of services can, and sometimes did, reach absurd proportions. Some agencies tried to use percentage formulas to derive a proper ratio for patient-therapist match on background variables, but found that there was an insufficient number of well-trained clinicians who were Chicano, Oriental, Hispanic, Black, or whatever the prevailing need was in a given locale. Often, briefly trained paraprofessional workers were utilized to fill the gaps. In actuality this often meant the most distressed, multi-problem individuals and families received help from the least-trained worker whose primary qualification was similarity in ethnic or racial origin rather than the usually requisite theoretical knowledge and therapeutic skill.

Many questions arose as to which were the really significant variables for such a match—should someone be the same sex, similar in age, in gender identity, in educational and socioeconomic status, as well as ethnic and religious background? When would a shared heritage lead to overidentification and loss of necessary therapeutic objectivity? And at what point were indigenous workers likely to seize the opportunities provided, become upwardly mobile and "co-opted by the agency," thereby adopting a different value system and ceasing to be identified with the very population they were hired to serve and represent (Richan, 1977)? These noble experiments did serve a purpose—democratizing some agencies and forcing highly trained professionals to become more attuned to the specific needs, attitudes, potentials, and goals of the community they served.

What became clear, however, was that the essential ingredients for therapeutic effectiveness do not lie in similarity of background. Rather, the therapist must be thoroughly imbued with a rich understanding of those aspects of the human experience that are universal, for this is what undergirds the ability to adopt a multicultural perspective and touch the lives of seemingly vastly different people. Those feeling states that approximate universality include pain, grief, sorrow, hunger, fear, anxiety, hope, joy, ecstasy, and sensuousness. Common factors which produce high levels of stress and tension in individuals throughout the world include death, divorce, war, relocation, job loss, and severe physical and emotional illness. It is my belief that a highly skilled, sensitive, empathic therapist can transcend religious, ethnic, and racial differences and enter the family system by recognizing the universality of the turmoil, pain, indecision, and repressed or exploding longings in whatever verbal or nonverbal ways they are expressed. This makes cross-cultural consultation possible.

In addition, since the patients' emotions may be communicated through different masks and gestures in various cultures, it is incumbent upon the therapist-consultant to learn the characteristics attendant to the particular subcultural group to which his or her patients belong. For example, how do they view closeness and distance; formality and informality; male-female relationships—as needing to be dominant and submissive or equalitarian; the role of therapist as expert, soother, provocateur, analyst, healer, problem-solver or explorer; the attitudes toward candid revealing—or hiding—of feelings and desires to strangers and to their significant others? The therapist-consultant must also quickly attend to the nuances and idiosyncracies of the specific and unique family he or she has been requested to see—for the assessment consultation usually lasts but an ephemeral hour.

The families brought for the consultant's evaluation are usually those that a local therapist has found extremely perplexing, and what is hoped for is a dramatic breakthrough to get the family, the therapy, and the therapist unstuck. Allowing one's own primary process thinking to freely float so that it connects to the patient's primary, primitive thought processes facilitates tapping into the realm of the collective unconscious (Jung, 1933), thereby shortcutting much unnecessary verbiage in arriving at a dynamic assessment of the patients, their situation and interaction. Simultaneously, the consultant utilizes secondary process cognitive thinking to connect with the patients' verbalized conscious thought, integrating the two levels of awareness as the session flows along.

Thus, the preparation for practicing and consulting cross-culturally includes:

1) The education and training plus years of solid experience to become a highly competent, skilled, knowledgeable and articulate therapist. (It is an added bonus if one is artistically gifted as a therapist, as well as theoretically wise and technically proficient.)

2) Being willing to read about and become conversant with the attitudes, values, folkways, customs, and mores of the people of the subcultural group or country one is to become engaged with as the visiting consultant. In my own professional experience, I have found this to be imperative whether I was to interview a Pennsylvania Dutch-Amish family, a Mormon family in Utah, or a newly arrived Cuban family in Miami. In addition to preparatory reading, I find it enlightening to ask my local hosts to provide me with a verbal briefing—to tell me as much about family life in their locale (the expectations, dynamics and functioning) as they can before the actual interview, workshop, or symposium takes place.

3) Being willing and flexible enough to utilize an interpreter if it appears that the language differences are great and could become an obstacle. For example, I found this necessary when serving as a consultant on cases of marital conflict at the Family Court in Tokyo. The gentleman who had invited me to visit was a marital therapist who had taken some training in the United States and spoke a passable English. The other therapists and judges in attendance did not understand English. Thus, everything was relayed through my bilingual host, and although this slowed up the interchange and inhibited spontaneity of the dialogue, the day was none-

theless quite fruitful and satisfying for all involved. In grappling together to communicate, consultant and participants share some humorous moments and this enlivens and enriches the interaction.

4) Becoming comfortable in the limelight "on stage," and being video-taped, since many consultations are done as live demonstrations and are simultaneously transmitted on video.

5) Being able to map out, in the post-session discussion, what one has done and why; being able to tactfully and cogently discuss with the primary therapist and his/her ongoing supervisor the probable impact of the consult and the direction the treatment should now take.

6) Enjoying transcending one's own ethnocentricity in order to be able to meet each situation afresh in its own terms—adapting one's framework to the ethos in which one is working while retaining one's own integrity, professional sense of self and theoretical orientation, and proud grounding in one's own heritage. It is crucial to find the vital balance or golden mean between an internal locus of control and listening with the third ear (Reik, 1948), tuned to the sometimes melodic, sometimes discordant, rhythms and lyrics pulsating from the external world of those one is privileged to treat.

## References

Jung, C. *Modern Man in Search of a Soul*. New York: Harcourt, Brace & World, 1933.

Reik, T. *Listening with the Third Ear*. New York: Grove Press, 1948.

Richan, W. Training of lay helpers. In F. Kaslow (Ed.), *Supervision, Consultation and Staff Training in the Helping Professions*. San Francisco: Jossey-Bass, 1977.

**FLORENCE W. KASLOW, Ph.D.**
*Private Practice,*
*West Palm Beach, FL*

# 53. Family Therapy with Black, Disadvantaged Families

**Question:**

I am a therapist working in a social agency in Brooklyn, New York. I am white and the vast majority of my clients are black. Most of my referrals are adolescents who come with a parent, usually the mother. There is much hostility, usually seen in a nonverbal, silent manner on the part of the identified client. I feel part of the anger is due not only to the fact that the youth is a reluctant client, but also to the fact of color. I do not feel effective and then become frustrated in such cases. I have some training in family therapy and wonder if this modality would be of help.

**Discussion:**

The problem presented in the case given is a most common one and rarely discussed in the literature. It is also one that will be with us for many years to come because of the scarcity of black therapists.

There are two areas of importance in dealing with black families. One is transference and the other is the question of a value system. Transference is present in any therapeutic encounter and must be addressed. In addition, the race, religion, or national origin of the client will make his/her value system compatible or not with that of the therapist. It is an issue of great importance but one that can be dealt with as long as the therapist is aware of the difference between him/herself and the client. Spiegel (1956) suggested that such differences can be overcome but only if the therapist is most sensitive.

A black client meeting a white therapist will react to the color of the therapist and vice versa. If the experiences of the black person have been negative, the chances are that his or her feelings toward the therapist will also be negative. This can be alleviated by the use of multiple family therapy (MFT), originally used by the late Peter Laqueur et al. (1971) with the families of hospitalized schizophrenics. In this approach several families—I recommend three—are brought together for structured sessions in which the therapist introduces themes such as the need for adolescents to separate themselves from their family, the need for parents to let go, and the role of the identified patient in dysfunctional families.

MFT has two advantages. First, the medium of change is not primarily through interaction with the therapist and so transference is lessened. Second, the discussion brings out the value system of the clients and so the therapist learns how his/her clients feel about the issues of freedom for the adolescent, the need for parents to let go, etc. The problem, then, of a white, middle-class therapist imposing his or her standards on the client is greatly diminished. He or she is not telling clients how to behave but asking what they want to accomplish.

MFT uses identification as the medium of change. A member of family A begins to see similar problems occurring in family B as in his/her own and so the isolation that is often experienced is lessened. The "problem" is seen in the context of relationships and not as the private property of one person. Laqueur (1973) said of MFT, "The motto of the entire transaction is to teach families to help each other" (p. 85). Health as well as pathology is conceptualized in terms of the system.

What occurs in MFT is indirect learning whereby a member of one family sees how a member of another reacts to a given situation. Ideas, feelings, and behaviors that were not thought of before become possibilities when seen as effective in the lives of others. The contemplated change can be worked out in the group since the use of MFT has some of the advantages of a group, notably the use of role-playing. This means that members from family A can play those from family B and thus give them a new insight into how others see them.

A system functions by reason of feedback, and one of the main problems encountered by families is that the feedback that can help them make adjustments is not available. In MFT, however, there is the advantage of having feedback built into the therapeutic process. In addition, the suggestions that are given come from the members of the group and are not the ideas of the therapist, thus reducing the effects of negative transference.

MFT sessions follow the same phases as conjoint family therapy as I have suggested elsewhere (Foley, 1979): 1) observation; 2) intervention; and 3) consolidation. In phase one the members of the family are asked to talk about issues in their lives. It is an attempt at encouraging them to discuss the ongoing problems of their life by having them elaborate on themes. This helps the various family members see that there are similar problems in all families, such as freedom, drinking, and in-laws. Phase two is the stage at which interventions are made.

The emphasis is on problem-solving rather than dynamics. A refrain raised by the therapist is, "How does your behavior influence the behavior of others in the family?" This gets members thinking in terms of system rather than individual pathology. A corollary question is, "How do others here handle this issue?" This again utilizes the collective strength and wisdom of the group. Phase three is the one in which new behaviors and patterns are tried out, based on suggestions by group members. Sometimes these behaviors are tested out in the group and sometimes outside, but in each case an opportunity is given for change. The goal is problem-solving and mutual support.

MFT offers an effective way of helping a white therapist deal with problems presented by black clients. Since change takes place by reason of identification with other group members and not by the development of transference, the problem of negative feelings is mitigated. Change is the result of indirect learning by observation of others and by imitating the effective behavior of others. MFT has the advantage of group therapy in that it allows various members to experience different personalities; it has the advantage of conjoint family therapy in that a caring atmosphere is established which gives family members a secure place in which to experiment with new ways of acting.

## References

Foley, V. Family therapy. In R. Corsini (Ed.), *Current Psychotherapies*. 2nd edition. Itasca, IL: Peacock, 1979.

Laqueur, P., Laburt, H. and Morong, E. Multiple family therapy: Further developments. In J. Haley (Ed.), *Changing Families*. New York: Grune & Stratton, 1971.

Laqueur, P. Multiple family therapy: Questions and answers. In D. Bloch (Ed.), *Techniques of Family Psychotherapy*. New York: Grune & Stratton, 1973.

Spiegel, J. Some cultural aspects of transference and counter-transference. In J. Masserman (Ed.), *Science and Psychoanalysis*, Vol. II. New York: Grune & Stratton, 1956.

**VINCENT D. FOLEY, Ph.D.**
*Visiting Professor*
*Long Island University—*
*C. W. Post Center*
*Greenvale, NY;*
*Private Practice*
*Jamaica, NY*

# PART D

# *Family Therapy in Various Settings*

# 54. Family Therapy and Family Medicine

**Question:**

I am a family physician in general medical practice, and, like other physicians, am constantly dealing with patients who are obviously involved in serious marital or family conflict. Quite often, I try to do some "family counseling" with these families or couples, but am sometimes not sure whether I'm getting in over my head where I don't belong. In general, what kinds of family problems is it appropriate for the general physician to try to treat, and when should a referral to a trained family therapist definitely be the right decision?

**Discussion:**

Family physicians are in an ideal position to monitor, identify, and treat significant marital and family problems. However, family physicians often find it difficult to decide which problems to handle themselves and which to refer.

The decision as to which family problems to deal with himself/herself depends upon a number of variables, including the nature of the problem, type of family, physician characteristics, and the nature of his/her clinical practice. The family physician is often best able to handle situational disturbances of short duration and those associated with the crises of everyday life (e.g. illness, loss of job) or of development (e.g., emergence of adolescent, adjustments, or the last child leaving home). He/she has a clear knowledge of the health issues and often a long-standing historical knowledge and interaction with the family members, and thus starts ahead of the game. In addition, he/she is in an ideal position to monitor progress as family members visit for health reasons. The family physician can also deal with minor behavior and psychiatric problems, such as school refusal, grief and anxiety reactions, and reactive depressions. Marital and parent-child problems as well as adjustments to marital separation, if of short duration, are also reasonable problems to tackle.

Long-standing problems and those that occur in the context of a long history of significant family disruption can be addressed only if the family physician has sufficient skill and available time. Problems associated with major psychiatric disorders (e.g., psychosis) and those associated with complex medical/psychosocial interactions are difficult to deal with and require a family therapist with highly developed skills and the ability to incorporate and make use of concepts from a wide range of conceptual models. Complex and multiproblem families may require an assessment on the part of the family physician, but often are too demanding of time, energy, and skill to treat unless the treatment is directed toward limited goals which are clearly set and adhered to. In the more complex situations the family physician still has an important role. These cases may be seen by someone else for the family or other treatments, but the family physician can reinforce the treatment. In these circumstances, it is important to clarify who is responsible for the overall coordination.

Decisions about the type of problems to be addressed depend upon the physician's skill level. Beginners should start with simple and clearly delineated problems and obtain considerable training before they embark on work with more difficult and complex issues. Often individual family physicians find they are most effective with particular problems and certain types of families, and this should be considered in deciding whether or not to treat.

The nature and operation of a physician's practice may determine the family problems he or she should try to handle. Several of my family physician colleagues set aside one or two half-days or evenings and do their family treatment during that time. They find this separates their medical and family treatment roles, and increases their effectiveness and efficiency. They all report that the allocated time soon becomes booked and this forces them to make clear decisions about whom they should see, to be more active, to set clearer goals, and to establish time limits for treatment. It is also consistent with our own approach (Bishop, Epstein and Baldwin, 1980; Epstein and Bishop, 1981).

In addressing the question of what kinds of family problems are most appropriate for a family physician to try to treat, I have obviously suggested some situations in which referral to a trained family therapist would be the right decision. It is most important that all of those working in the health delivery system recognize those situations where either referral or consultation is most appropriate. I raise the question of consultation, as not all cases will necessarily have to be referred, and consultation leads to better referral decisions. It is always appropriate to seek outside advice, and physicians should never hesitate to do so. Those of us responsible for training in the various psychotherapy modalities in the Department of Psychiatry at McMaster University in Hamilton, Ontario, Canada, constructed a list of indications for referral and consultation. The general indicators apply equally well to other forms of therapy.

The family indications are as follows:

1) The existence of a potential for child abuse of an overt nature as well as in cases with a history of frequent visits to hospital emergencies.
2) When the psychopathology of one family member is obstructive to therapy, and when the therapist feels unable to understand the psychopathological dynamics and/or to use the knowledge within the context of a family systems approach.
3) When divorce, separation, or removal of a child from the home is being considered.
4) Significant and sudden change of any sort, which is a warning and should call for consultation to aid in assessing either the reasons for sudden deterioration or sudden positive changes which can be real or represent a covering-over of problems.

The general indications are as follows:

1) When there is suicidal ideation or the threat of violence to others.
2) When there is behavioral change potentially destructive to the person or to others.
3) When there is psychotic symptomatology (delusions, hallucinations), psychotic thinking disturbance or other behavioral changes where there was none before, or sudden increase in psychotic symptomatology.
4) When there is significant deterioration in mood (depression, anxiety, etc. with concomitant behavior).
5) When there is suspicion of organicity that was not recognized previously.
6) When there is stagnation (i.e., failure to progress in treatment during a series of two or three sessions).
7) When the physician feels uncomfortable with the situation for no reason that he can clearly understand.
8) When there is probability of some medical-legal encounter, or conflict with a political, medical, or social agency outside the practice.

It should be emphasized that the above guidelines all point to the need for the family physician to have adequate skills in individual and family assessment and treatment techniques. Previously at McMaster University, and now at Brown University, our clinical and research group has been attempting to address this area and we have conducted several projects focusing on these questions.

*References*

Bishop, D. S., Epstein, N. B. and Baldwin, L. M. Structuring a family assessment interview. *Can. Fam. Physician*, November, 1980, *26*, 1534-1537.
Epstein, N. B. and Bishop, D. S. Problem-centered systems therapy of the family. In Gurman, A. and Kniskern, D. (Eds.) *Handbook of Family Therapy*, New York: Brunner-Mazel, 1981.

**DUANE S. BISHOP, M.D.**
*Associate Professor*
*Section of Psychiatry and Human Behavior*
*Brown University Medical School*
*Providence, RI*

# 55. Crisis Intervention vs. Family Therapy

**Question:**

As a family therapist at a family crisis unit in a large urban area, lately I have become increasingly aware of the various paradoxes and double binds that our teams struggle with in dealing with patients and families both on a day-to-day basis and over time.

Specifically, the dilemma has to do with the contradictory, often mutually exclusive, mandates that our crisis teams have of: 1) prompt, empathic availability and concern, wherein we join with patients to support them in their transient emotional crises; this mandate being impossible to combine with 2) systems (usually family systems) oriented therapy aimed at differentiation, wherein therapists resist the family's pull to join in one way or another. These chronically dysfunctional, crisis-prone families require therapists to remain unentangled emotionally. Therapists must negotiate their availability meticulously and strategically in order to invite members of the family to differentiate. Is there any way to achieve the best of both worlds?

**Discussion:**

The history of crisis intervention implies active helping, reassurance, relief of anxiety, logical, nonparadoxical communication and instruction, and, most of all, availability when possible according to the patient's own perceived needs. Family systems intervention requires a different, sometimes opposite, approach, Selvini Palazzoli et al. (1978) for instance described their treatment of families with an anorectic or a schizophrenic individual. They believe that treatment is more effective when families are seen once per month rather than more frequently; paradoxical interventions are given at the end of sessions with prompt leave-taking by the therapist and without discussion of the intervention; and, most particularly, requests for unscheduled more frequent sessions are usually denied. Interaction and discussion dilute the power of the intervention to change the family. The Wizard of Oz, in other words, must keep the curtain closed. There is an accent *off* empathy. Unavailability is power.

The most important aspect of making this distinction concerns therapeutic efficacy. What is therapeutic in one situation may be quite anti-therapeutic in another. A strategic therapist focusing on avoiding connectedness to a depressed suicidal individual is as useless and anti-therapeutic as a caring, enveloping rescuer promising therapeutic change to a double-binding, psychotogenic family with two or three schizophrenic members.

The final consideration has to do with the fact that in many crisis units around the country, crisis teams themselves are, in Lynn Hoffman's (1975) terms, a "too richly joined system" made up of members from different disciplines, with different ideologies and purposes. Often, team members attempt to differentiate themselves by adhering solely to one paradigm, e.g., the physician's "fixing" individuals through medicine, advice or other "magic"; the social worker's caring"; or the family therapist's being enigmatic and maintaining disengaged understanding.

In many cases, the needs of the patient's system are clear and treatment can be adjusted to fit the bill. In some situations, however, overworked individual intake therapists (I.T. or index therapists) are confronted by an individual in distress from a family system which is dysfunctional and full of potential patients, some of whose crises might be more dangerous than that of the identified patient at hand. In such situations, these I.T. therapists can be overwhelmed by the decisions required. Should they heal, hold, and support family members actively, or should they maintain their own individuality and differentiation in the face of the family's effort to envelop the therapist and avoid change? When should we change from one approach to the other? Beneath the usual question of, "Who is the patient?", there are others; "Should we in this case help the family change or help the patient change back to his old, less symptomatic self?"; "What changes may occur in the family if we restore the patient?"; and "What may happen to all the family members as we help the family change?" It is seldom a question of one approach "versus" the other. To go towards homeostasis is to go away from therapeutic change although it is simultaneously a test of the family's adaptability and capacity for therapeutic change at some other point.

I believe it is necessary that we address these problems by using a team approach that emphasizes flexibility of roles among members of the team. Two physicians or two social workers will sometimes constitute a therapeutic team with only indirect or consultative coverage or brief contact with a member of the absent discipline actually being supplied. Knowledgability about each other's disciplines is encouraged. Each team member must be thoroughly aware of the limitations *and* the unique skills of his/her team members trained in a different professional discipline. Our main effort as a therapeutic team must be to remain aware of automatic, "textbook," mindless, "therapeutic" responses which undercut the power and specificity of other interventions designed to promote the desired movement toward homeostasis or change. We also shift our teams or use multiple teams for the different therapeutic purposes: for instance, one, differentiated (avoiding entanglement), and the other, supportive (avoiding alienating family and patients). We try to focus on the precise moment when the family's needs shift.

I view family crisis intervention as a specific subspeciality that requires a *long* view of family systems over time even if therapy consists of just a few sessions, and a *broad* view of the range of professional resources that need to be considered for effective therapeutic planning.

*References*

Hoffman, L. "Enmeshment" and the too richly cross-joined system. *Family Process*, 1975, *14*, 457-468.
Selvini Palazzoli, M., Cecchin, G., Prata, F. and Boscolo, L. *Paradox and Counterparadox.* New York: Aronson, 1978.

**HARVEY L. WHITE, M.D.**
*Senior Psychiatrist, Family Crisis Unit*
*Department of Community Psychiatry*
*St. Luke's—Roosevelt Hospital Center*
*St. Luke's Division*
*New York, NY*

# 56. Family Therapy in a Public School System

**Question:**

My colleagues and I are mental health professionals in a public school system. Our job titles include school counselor, school psychologist, and school social worker; however, our common job descriptions all include "working with families." Several of us have received some family therapy training, and we are excited about the possibilities of integrating family therapy into the public school setting. We are also concerned about potential drawbacks. Can you spell out the advantages and disadvantages of providing family therapy services in a public school? What are the ingredients necessary to make family therapy in a public school an experience which would enhance both family and school functioning?

**Discussion:**

Families and public schools can be seen as two subsystems with a common member, the child. Under optimum conditions, family and school form a positive alliance whose interest is the developing child. In situations involving troubled youngsters, however, family and school often interact in a cycle of mutual blame and recrimination, and contribute inadvertently to a dysfunctional triad in which a child cannot be loyal to home without being disloyal to school and vice versa. A family therapy project within a public school can begin to address this systems dilemma.

*Potential Advantages*

A school is a natural setting for the recognition of child-focused issues that may be indicative of family interaction problems or family-school

The author thanks the school psychologists and school adjustment counselors of the Pittsfield Public Schools, Pittsfield, MA. Their efforts to implement family therapy in a public school system contributed to the issues addressed in this discussion.

conflicts. Traditionally, schools have viewed troubled youngsters from a linear, individualistic perspective. The usual treatment to follow from this view has been individual counseling. Such services have tended to isolate parents, rather than enhancing their role with children. At worst, such services, especially with adolescents, have stressed the child's "independence," ignoring family interdependence and interactional processes, and relegating parents to the role of "intruder." The first major advantage of family therapy in the public school setting is that it provides a radically different way of conceptualizing problems and symptoms in school-age children. Issues previously seen from a unidirectional and blameful perspective (e.g., "It's the parent's fault," or, "He's a bad child") can begin to be seen from a contextual, non-blaming point of view.

Second, many families view going to a mental health center as stigmatizing. Such families resent referrals from a school, and often resist attending sessions at a clinic. Often, these families are open to coming to the school to work on problems involving their child.

Third, schools, for their part, have usually attempted many solutions with symptomatic youngsters. "Bad" children may be suspended over and over again. Psychosomatically ill children may spend hours each day in the nurse's office. Family therapy within the school, whose purview can be family *and* school interactional processes, can eliminate "more of the same wrong solution" strategies (Watzlawick et al., 1974), and devise interventions to transform family and school functioning for the benefit of all concerned.

Finally, provided within a public school, family therapy can work to eliminate conflicts between the two most significant subsystems in a child's life, home and school. Rigid or conflictual boundaries between family and school can be altered. Escalating feedback loops of mutual condemnation and mistrust can be interdicted. Problems can be reframed as requiring the cooperation of home and school for their solution.

## Potential Disadvantages

Family therapy in a public school setting runs some potential risks that also need to be addressed. First, problems expressed by children are not always indicative of family dysfunction. Rather, such difficulties may relate to the classroom, peer group, or overall school system dysfunction. Family therapy that is encouraged by and given by the school may, in some instances, place the locus of problems in the family that rightly belongs within the school itself. Rather than creating a family-school partnership, such an error may be experienced by the family as blaming. Rather than alleviating stress, the school, by its suggestion that the family needs family therapy, may inadvertently become a source of stress to the family.

Second, schools providing family therapy services may unintentionally violate a family's confidentiality. Families entering a school building for family therapy can be seen by various school personnel who are not trained in the ethics of the therapy professions. In addition, family issues may become part of a child's record within a school system, thereby compromising the integrity of family-school boundaries.

Third, in situations in which family-school relations are characterized by complementarity, with the school in the one-up position, the family may experience the school's suggestion and provision of family therapy as perpetuating the status quo, rather than as promising change.

Finally, the school may become overinvolved in the life of the family, entering a widening circle of concerns and handicapping the family's appropriate independent problem-solving abilities.

## Requirements for Successful Family Therapy in the Public Schools

In order to potentiate the advantages and obviate the disadvantages, family therapy in public schools must attend to several dimensions. Family therapy projects within schools are best done *quietly* by a small group of colleagues who are trained in and committed to a systems view of human problem formation and resolution. Such a group requires the affirmation by administration for in-service training, videotape equipment and consultation, the development of an appropriate site for sessions that will protect families from undue gossip, and flexible working hours that enable their availability at times amenable to family needs. The providers of family therapy must be skilled in inviting parents and school personnel to sessions in ways that are nonblaming, must be able to join disparate, often conflictual subsystems in ways that avoid inadvertent coalitions which support, rather than alleviate dysfunction, and must be able to maintain leadership in sessions in order to frame issues as joint problems of home and school requiring joint exploration and resolution.

The family therapist in a public school must carefully assess the function of a child's symptom, both for the family system and for the school system, in order to assure that interventions are tailored to and implemented in the pertinent subsystem. He or she must deal with the issue of being an employee of a system that a family may experience as the source of its stress. To be effective, the family therapist in the school setting needs to work from a position of neutrality (Selvini Palazzoli et al., 1980). When the achievement or maintenance of such neutrality is not possible, the school family therapist should be responsible for an appropriate referral.

It is the responsibility of those providing family therapy in schools to develop criteria for defining the sorts of problems and issues that are germane for such treatment, and to prevent family therapy from being seen first as a panacea and ultimately as a disappointment for promising more than it could deliver. (Family therapy may be capable of blocking dysfunctional sequences that interfere with a child's learning; family therapy will not, however, teach children to read.) The school family therapist needs to create and maintain a clear problem focus and a treatment contract, the aims of which are circumscribed and can be evaluated.

## Conclusion

Family therapy in public schools, when implemented with care and caution for potential pitfalls, can facilitate the natural alliance of home and school, benefiting both subsystems and contributing to the development of their member in common, the child.

## References

Selvini Palazzoli, M., Boscolo, L., Cecchin, G., and Prata, G. Hypothesizing, circularity, neutrality: Three guidelines for the conductor of the session. *Family Process*, 1980, *19*, 3-12.

Watzlawick, P., Weakland, J. and Fisch, R. *Change: Principles of Problem Formation and Problem Resolution*. New York: W. W. Norton, 1974.

**EVAN IMBER COPPERSMITH, Ph.D.**
*Associate Professor and Training Coordinator*
*Family Therapy Program*
*Department of Psychiatry*
*University of Calgary Medical School*
*Calgary, Alberta, Canada*

# 57. Family Therapy at a College Counseling Center

**Question:**

> During the past few years, family therapy as a treatment approach has been practiced in diverse settings ranging from the family's home to the public school which their child attends. As a clinician in a college counseling center treating students with symptoms such as depression, eating disorders, attempted suicide, psychotic episodes, loneliness, and a plethora of problematic and bizarre behaviors, my questions are: Can the theory and practice of family therapy be incorporated into mental health services of any college or university and if so, are there any special considerations?

**Discussion:**

The college counseling center where I have been the director since 1970 has changed dramatically during the past four years:

1) There has been an epistemological shift from a linear to a systems view of problem formation (Minuchin et al., 1978).
2) Insight and support-oriented therapy have been replaced by the problem-solving approaches offered by structural (Minuchin, 1974) and strategic therapies (Haley, 1980; Madanes, 1981).
3) The nature of prevention and education programs has reflected these changes.

Let me briefly comment on these three areas of change and conclude with some thoughts for other counseling center staff members who might consider following suit.

*Theoretical Orientation*

Clearly, the theoretical shift in our therapeutic work has progressed from a linear, intrapsychic model to a systems, family developmental perspective. Our work has been influenced greatly by Haley (1980), as student symptomatology and problematic behavior are conceptualized as functional and indicative of the family's need to stabilize and not change at a time when family interactional change is necessary. Even though hundreds of miles from home, families can continue to remain very organized in response to their college-age children through frequent distressing letters and phone calls. At the same time, it can be difficult to maintain a family contextual view with college students, since they hear from both their parents and college officials that they are now responsible young adults and accountable to themselves.

Traditionally, professionals in the college mental health field have avoided the parents of college students, since this period has been seen as being critically important to individual development and independence. It has been assumed generally that it was likely that the parents created and caused the problem which motivated the student to seek help in the first place. It becomes a very profound inferential leap to view problematic behavior of college students as a sacrificial, stabilizing phenomenon which simultaneously maintains, and is maintained by, the family's organization. Obviously, this perspective of human problem development has influenced the treatment of many problems which the college students present at the center.

## Methods of Practice

It should be made clear from the outset that the family members of every college student who seeks counseling do not attend conjoint family therapy sessions. The nature of the presenting problem and physical distance between the college and the student's hometown are the greatest determining factors regarding regular family meetings. Ongoing treatment with families who attend scheduled sessions have been primarily with those families who reside in the New England states and whose son or daughter has come to the center because of a suicide attempt, schizophrenic-like behavior, psychosomatic concerns (i.e., anorexia, bulimarexia, chronic asthmatic and diabetic problems), and those students who, for "no apparent reason," continue to have marginal academic and social success. It has been my experience during the past four years that this therapeutic approach, which involves a joint alliance of concern between the college and the family, has enabled students to remain in college. Parents have demonstrated a willingness to attend sessions and usually, after a lot of hard work, begin to more positively influence the life of their son or daughter. In the years past, these "more disturbed students" were medically withdrawn from college, returned home and were often hospitalized.

With students whose presenting problems are not as severe or life threatening, the strategic approaches developed at the Mental Research Institute have been incorporated (Watzlawick et al., 1974). Interventions, which often include strategic letters to home, are designed to break the cycle of "more of the same wrong solutions." On some occasions, we have also worked directly with on- and off-campus roommates as they become organized around and consumed by the bizarre behavior of one of their peers.

## Education and Prevention

Much of the education has taken the form of providing in-service training with the health center nurses and physicians as well as other professionals on the student personnel staff. It has been helpful for these support service professionals to be knowledgeable about the center's "new" orientation as they often make referrals to the center.

Within the residence halls, members of the counseling center staff have met with students, freshmen in particular, leading discussions on their experiences leaving home to attend college. Often, these discussions have led to students talking openly about such issues as their parents' impending divorce, a recent death of a family member, and handling becoming a part of a blended family. Students have commented that before the discussions, they had felt they were alone dealing with these issues, in addition to attempting to progress with their own lives. The discussions have created opportunities for students to expand their own support systems.

In terms of communicating family therapy services to the parents of students, a letter, which described leaving home to attend college as a developmental change for the entire family, was mailed to the parents of all freshmen. Parents were advised that if they received a crisis phone call or letter from their son or daughter indicating a desire to quit school or that he or she was being overwhelmed by homesickness, they could contact the center to arrange a family meeting. In 1981, 30 parents from a freshmen class of 500 called the center looking for advice or desiring to schedule a meeting. Also, a parents' association newsletter which is mailed quarterly to the parents of all students included a feature article describing the family therapy services at the college.

In conclusion, it is clearly possible to incorporate the theory and practice of family therapy into a college counseling center. What began hesitantly and cautiously four years ago when I invited the parents of a student to travel 300 miles to meet with me regarding their daughter's suicide attempt has clearly expanded and changed my theoretical and treatment assumptions. For those who wish to add family therapy to the multiple approaches available at college and university mental health services, it cannot be overemphasized that staff members need to be competently trained and to have strong institutional support. Our efforts have been supported philosophically and financially by the dean of students, the college president, and the parents' association. Such support has enabled me to purchase a one-way mirror and videotape equipment, which has improved the training and supervision of graduate interns in the college's masters program in marriage and family therapy, as well as enabled the staff to work with families using a live supervision model. Finally, to work with college students' families, who often travel great distances to attend sessions, the staff commitment to this model of therapy needs to be great, since appointments are often during the evenings or on weekends. It is also not uncommon for sessions to be lengthy, since the parents are often highly stressed when they arrive on campus, and it takes time to reach an agreement that the student's problem can be best resolved by having the parents return home, the student remain in college, and all of us meet again.

## References

Haley, J. *Leaving Home*. New York: McGraw-Hill, 1980.

Madanes, C. *Strategic Family Therapy*. San Francisco: Jossey-Bass, 1981.

Minuchin, S. *Families and Family Therapy*. Cambridge, MA: Harvard University Press, 1974.

Minuchin, S., Rosman, B. and Baker, L. *Psychosomatic Families*. Cambridge, MA: Harvard University Press, 1978.

Watzlawick, P., Weakland, J. and Fisch, R. *Change*. New York: W. W. Norton, 1974.

**RICHARD A. WHITING, Ed.D.**
*Director*
*Counseling Center*
*Springfield College*
*Springfield, MA*

# SECTION V

# The Growth of
# the Family Therapist

## 58. Facing the Hidden Effects
## of Doing Therapy

**Question:**

> With the accumulation of experience in doing therapy and su-
> pervising others, and through commiserating with colleagues
> about therapy's vicissitudes, I am discovering that therapy may
> not be as benign a process as it appears to be on the surface. What
> are your impressions of the hidden effects on the therapist of doing
> therapy?

**Discussion:**

With respect to the malignity of doing this work, therapists fall roughly
into two groups. One group reports that they are bored and angry with
clients or that they feel ineffectual too much of the time. Another group
reports that they are continually excited and turned on by therapy and
that they experience more of a sense of power and efficacy in therapy
than in their private lives. Both of these views may constitute different
forms of professional burnout. For when one follows a considerable
number of therapists into their private lives, as I have, one finds that
both groups suffer from some of the hidden effects of doing therapy.
Members of *either* group may report that, in the privacy of their home
and in their family and intimate relationships, they feel emotionally
bankrupt or detached; they drink too much as a vehicle for reentry;
they have a hard time reading or playing; or their personal relationships are problematic. I would suggest that there are two key sources
of therapy's negative effects on therapists—the *kinds of contracts* we
have with clients and the way we exercise our *options as professional
bystanders*.

We therapists exist during working hours under extremely skewed
terms in the primary contracts we have with our clients. In these
contracts, or *rules of communicative control*, we are paid and otherwise
rewarded for buying into two assumptions: 1) that we, the therapists,
know more than they, the clients, about what is "right" and "wrong"
about them and their situation; and 2) that their feelings are more
relevant than ours in what goes on in therapy.

Both of these primary contracts or rules of control have hidden consequences for therapists. The assumption of knowledge is a seductive arrangement—it gives us power we have not earned in face-to-face negotiations. The irrelevancy of emotion is a repressive arrangement—it asks us to work in circumstances in which we suppress and deny our real feelings much of the time, and then monetarily rewards us for this denial of freedom. But the most damaging consequences occur when we carry these asymmetrical rules of control over into our private lives, which we might tend to do from sheer momentum alone (to say nothing of the peculiar appeal that "elitist" deals hold for our worst selves).

A key factor in the extensiveness of the damage done by these asymmetrical rules of control is whether our family and friends challenge or support the arrangements. For example, when the grown son of one therapist, whose family I was seeing in therapy, said to him at dinner, "Please don't talk to me in that pontifical tone of voice—I want us to talk as equals in an open-ended way, and I surely don't wish to be taught, manipulated, or talked down to by you . . . ," he was doing his father a favor. Likewise, when the therapist's wife, after early morning sex, said, "Remind me only to make love on Sundays when you are one day and two full nights away from your 'therapist self'—I can't tell whether you are regarding me as a partner, a specimen, or a 'bit' of systems information . . . ," she was also doing her therapist/husband a favor. But the therapist did not at once rush to collect his good fortune. Moreover, even after his family's challenge took hold, this therapist confessed, "Look, I like my work and enjoy the power I feel in therapy. At home I have to work hard for that power and still the outcome is uncertain. As for my emotional distance, I simply forget I have feelings of my own."

In the final analysis, responsibility for counteracting these effects rests not with our families and intimate communities but with ourselves and professional communities. It matters to each of us individually, for example, from which method or school of systems therapy we draw upon in completing our repertoire of therapeutic techniques. The affectual involvements of Satir's communications approach, the power involvements of Haley's strategic therapy approach, and the unique use of inner process modeled by Whitaker offer quite different options. It also matters whether we work in isolation or in a community, and if the associations with our colleagues and peer groups are designed to offset and balance the rules of communicative control we agree to with clients. It matters most, however, how we play out the various therapist orientations available to us and how we distribute these from moment to moment in therapy.

Basically, there are three participant-observer options available to therapists in their interactions with families. I call them professional, informed, and disengaged bystander.

The *professional bystander* primarily observes and manages the rules and affects of the family's social reality and the effects these have on family members. The essence of this orientation is professional distance. Distance is recommended lest our vision blur and we contaminate the field with our own issues and realities. Objectivity is one form of distance. Another is empathy, i.e., experiencing the *other's* feelings, social realities, and world views rather than our own.

Valuable as it is assumed to be for clients, the distance of the professional bystander takes its toll on the therapist, for professional burnout has two major sources—too much objectivity and too much empathy. Both are heavily demanded of the professional bystander. Each denies the real self and reinforces the skewed rules of contract that tend to carry over into our private lives.

Two alternative orientations are available to therapists, one convincingly efficient (yet more personally risky than we dare suppose), the other personally quite rewarding, yet more difficult and not without its own vicissitudes. I start with the latter, the *informed bystander*.

I use the designation "informed bystander" in two senses: formed from *within the self*; and formed from being *inside the family context*. In other words, where the professional bystander is distant, the informed bystander closely approaches or even crosses the family's interior boundaries, interweaving his/her own and the family's realities, but as a separate entity that both influences and is influenced by those realities. Becoming informed about the family from such phenomenological proximity requires a high degree of self-knowledge, and a capacity for self-observation and self-management under conditions that, momentarily at least, establish the therapist as a virtual member of the system he is treating. It also requires a high degree of psychological mobility—the flexibility to remove the self to a more distant stance from which to therapeutically manage the family's social realities.

Difficult as it is to perform at this level of awareness (Carl Whitaker is the best known exemplar), all family systems therapists do maintain this level some of the time. (An obvious risk of this therapeutic option is the license it may give to unformed or undeveloped therapists who may irresponsibly project their own inner realities into the social realities of families they treat. The best way to reduce such risk is in proper selection at the outset of training and through helping in the appropriate application of the informed bystander orientation throughout training.) I am beginning to view the activities of the informed bystander as a separate form of therapy that achieves its effects rather differently from other systems therapeutic modalities—from the structural or strategic family therapy, for example. Besides being an effective way to bring about change in families, it is, for me, the best *in-process* means available for counteracting some of the personally damaging effects of the skewed rules of control that govern therapy. Indeed, the orientation of the informed bystander highlights a form of therapeutic activity that might be called "in-process therapy."

The *disengaged bystander* is primarily in the business of managing the rules and effects of the family's social reality, from which he or she assiduously stands apart. A therapist exercising this option evidences some of the distant observer but little of the empathy of the *professional bystander* and none of the personal involvement or awareness of the *informed bystander*. One feature of this orientation is the tendency to carry out a technique of therapeutic program irrespective of *who* or *what* happens to be on the other end. At its best it represents a highly efficient form of therapy. At its worst, it snares both therapist and family in a net of rigid premises, which, regardless of their proof or falsity, become partially self-validating. Examples of this are the therapist who, himself a casualty of unfinished mourning, sees loss and separation ubiquitously in all families and ends up treating "depressed families"; or the therapist who, himself despairing about the possibilities for successful intimacy, overuses the technique of trial separation and thus "helps" too many couples to divorce. Additionally, this stance is unlikely to protect the therapist from the seductive effects of therapy's asymmetrical rules of control.

In all of the above, I am obviously espousing a preference for an *in-process* view of family therapy, one where the therapist alternates between the orientations of the professional and informed bystander and limits the use of the disengaged bystander option. In this view, therapy is seen as a formative process where all participants take equal responsibility for shaping the structures that need changing and for the change process itself.

**DAVID KANTOR, Ph.D.**
*Director*
*Kantor Family Institute*
*Cambridge, MA*

# 59. The Female Therapist as Symbolic Father in Family Therapy

**Question:**

I have found references in family therapists' work on ways male therapists may expand their role as the "symbolic mother," but somewhat less suggestion of ways for female therapists to increase their role as "symbolic father" in family therapy. This seems to be an increasingly important issue as my practice involves a greater proportion of middle-class enmeshed families who themselves are relatively rigid in sex-role relationships. I would like to see some discussion of this, especially with respect to specific stages or issues in family therapy.

**Discussion:**

Your question may be addressed in part by the literature on techniques of structuring and forming therapeutic alliances. The skilled use of such techniques is an important way in which the therapist establishes influence in the family while retaining the flexibility to be outside it, and at the same time clearly conveys the expectation that the family will not be permitted to be passive recipients of the therapist's care-taking. In this sense, the conditions necessary for the female therapist to establish herself as a symbolic father are those required for any effective therapy.

It would be misleading, however, to imply that the use of such techniques alone would be sufficient for creating the symbolic father quality in interaction with a family. Rather, the use of such techniques may elicit reactions from the family that the therapist may in turn use to assess which components of the interventions may have held symbolic as well as concrete value for the family. Simply put, it is not power, toughness, risk-taking, the ability to set limits on the therapist's caring, directiveness, experience, wisdom, or even any combination of such qualities that constitutes a symbolic father. Keying in on what any particular family experiences as paternal, in the widest sense, is thus at base a matter of assessment, both of the family itself and the transferences of family members to the therapist. Projections and experiences of "father" are highly likely to vary by family, by members within a family, and over the course of therapy.

It is thus critical that the therapist have the capacity to be aware of and responsive to such varying potential father-symbolic qualities. Enactment of the symbolic father requires more than transference interpretation, partly because the skills of a family therapist require one to be more than a "blank screen." Such enactment requires the therapist to 1) gain some sense of the family members' conflicts over their experiences of "father"; 2) test hypotheses about these experiences through interactions which in part embody aspects of that "experienced" father; and 3) interpret these interactions to the family. In essence, there are two tacks the female therapist can take in developing such a capacity. The first is to increase her own access to her direct or indirect experiences of "father." The therapist's exploration of her expectations, dreams, disappointments, and especially any unresolved issues in her family of origin is likely to be a useful beginning. Although this may take many forms, a family genogram is one particularly useful alternative, paying attention to family rules, myths, and stories about fathers (and to family views of any men who, for one reason or another, have not become fathers). Thoughtful reflection on images of men generally and fathers in particular as portrayed in the popular press may prove illuminating, especially vis-à-vis the juxtaposition of such images as: ambitious and productive—bumbling and lackadaisical; cold and aloof—kindhearted and warm; self-controlled and "upright"—self-destructive and potentially dangerous; cutthroat—compassionate; and wife's "man,"—wife's "little boy." Parallels, if not direct similarities, in the therapist's own self-perceptions, fantasies, and feedback about androgynous aspects of her interpersonal impact from trusted others may also be incorporated to expand her sense of the range of potentially symbolic "father" qualities.

Access to such experiences and fantasies alone, or even in combination with careful assessment, does not automatically enable the female therapist to capture and express the kinds of symbolic father qualities in ways that may be important in the therapy of any family. The second means available, collaboration with a co-therapist, is in this stage a way to experiment with the task of translating increased awareness into therapeutic action. The (usually opposite sex) co-therapist functions both as a co-role model of flexible sex-role relationships and as a source of feedback about the impact of the female therapist's interventions on the family. The co-therapy relationship also permits increased freedom for each therapist to engage with the family in a variety of ways, i.e., listening and accepting, setting limits, directing, expanding family fantasies, interacting with the children, and interacting with the parents. Emotional distance is thus available to assess the impact of the therapist's interventions and if necessary to review and change her hypotheses about the type of symbolic father sought or responded to by the family.

The ability to attend to, interpret, and therapeutically reflect the family symbolic father(s) is likely to be an especially important task with families who are in crisis, whether in an initial session or at some other point in therapy. At such times it is not only leadership and direction but also the kind of leadership and direction that the family experiences as powerful that is therapeutically essential. Attention to the therapist's impact as a symbolic father may also be useful when separation issues emerge. While most family therapists are familiar with the concept of the "good-enough mother," somewhat less attention has been given to ways in which processes of leaving and checking back with the father are important in separation and individuation in a family therapy context. A third situation in which the therapist's activity as a symbolic father may be important is when the wife seeks more independence either psychologically, in developing more ties and concrete activities outside the home, or, as is usually the case, both. Activity as a symbolic father may both provide the woman with an awareness of the possibility of introjecting aspects of her own father that were previously in one way or another inhibited, as well as modeling to the family acceptance of her need or wish to do so.

The above does not constitute an exhaustive set of either ways in which the female therapist may expand her capacity to behave as a symbolic father or of the range of situations in which this skill may be therapeutically useful. What have been suggested are some ways that therapists may begin to develop this skill and some of the ways in which it may prove useful in family therapy. As a final word, it should be emphasized that developing one's capacity as a symbolic father is not mutually exclusive with increasing one's capacity as a symbolic mother. Furthermore, this is true for therapists of *both* sexes. Rigid adherence to any sex-role stereotype, real or symbolic, is likely not only to restrict therapeutic effectiveness, but also to elicit a complementary role rigidity on the part of family members. The abilities to care, to demand, accept and set limits, as well as to respond to what is elicited from family members as symbolic of their experiences of "mother" or "father," are marks of a skilled family therapist, regardless of sex.

**SHARON W. FOSTER, M.A.**
*Project Coordinator*
*Wisconsin Psychiatric Institute*
*University of Wisconsin Medical School*
*Madison, WI*

# 60. The Dilemma of Personal Authority for the Female Family Therapist

**Question:**

Do you feel that the female family therapist has more difficulty in the exercise of personal and delegated authority as a family therapist than the male family therapist? What factors do you see influence and contribute to the difficulties of the exercise of personal authority for the female? Does this de-skillment evidence itself in certain therapeutic situations more than others? Finally, what are some practical suggestions for the female family therapist in how to deal with these dilemmas?

**Discussion:**

In general, the beginning family therapist is confronted with a highly anxiety-producing situation, one which is more anxiety-producing than that facing the beginning individual therapist. To have the emotionality and the human drama residing and happening in one's office is quite different than hearing about it from an individual's reconstruction of these events. Persons in training continually report the anxiety that they feel in seeing whole families and readily admit to a preference at times to see individual representatives of that system. This anxiety for trainees, regardless of gender, could influence the exercise of personal and delegated authority. By "personal authority," I am referring to the sense of authority that a person brings to the role of family therapist. The authority becomes delegated when a family agrees to see the therapist and authorizes him/her on their behalf to act in the role of family therapist.

Because of her gender, the female family therapist faces issues that can produce difficulties in the formation of the therapeutic system that the male family therapist does not have to face. Specifically, how she is perceived by others and, in turn, how she perceives herself in the exercise of the authority inherent in the role of therapist are worthy of examination. The psychosocial factors involved are numerous. For example, the psychosocial influences of the society at large, and the traditional American family specifically, regarding the exercise of authority as related to gender are marked. These, in turn, influence the institutions in which people work and the individual's experience brought to that context.

Let me briefly highlight these influences, giving some brief examples. First, the influence of the structure and division of labor in the traditional American family is marked. The male in the husband-father role is the primary manager of the external boundary. He is seen as the primary wage earner, the one who deals with the external world on behalf of the family. The female in the wife-mother role has been ascribed the task of internal management of boundaries concerned with the internal workings of the family. An emphasis is on nurturance and supportive functions. Let me hasten to say while some might object that this is an antiquated model, that life-styles have changed, it is hypothesized that it will remain at least an "ideal" for decades to come. The women's movement has sensitized us to the inequities toward women in a significant manner; however, the results of this sensitization in terms of the normative family structure will not be seen for many years. This model of male and female family roles does impact the manner in which men and women exercise their personal and delegated authority in the work setting.

Although the notion of going to see a therapist who happens to be female should not be so foreign to us since we have all had a similar experience when we scraped our knees as children, the idea is both quite familiar and also, because of these early associations, rather frightening. Bayes and Newton (1976), in their paper on women in authority, make reference to the primitive images that we all have in terms of working with women. They review anthropological evidence in which women are portrayed through history in three distinct fashions: the Good Mother who is seen as nurturing and supportive; the Terrible Mother who is ensnaring, aggressive, and devouring; and the Great Mother who combines all of these characteristics. They conjecture that these primitive fears or ghosts are kept in check by all of us through the process of devaluation of women and the regulation of women to positions of less delegated and/or personal authority.

Thus, the female family therapist brings with her, by virtue of these processes, factors that influence her use of personal authority. These factors in turn influence the manner in which women are perceived in their role in the work setting: for example, the institutions in which the female is practicing family therapy. This also affects the manner in which she perceives herself in her role, how she perceives others perceiving her, how she perceives others perceiving her perceiving them and so forth, as influenced by her experience in her family of origin.

Three examples will illustrate the difficulties for the female in her role as family therapist. The examples highlight the management of the external boundary of the institution, which protects the primary task, i.e., the function of providing family therapy.

At the time that the family initially calls the agency to set up an appointment, there can be signposts of future difficulties for the family therapist who is a woman. How the secretary views women in authority will influence how they communicate across the institutional boundary with the client. Whether the secretary sees the female family therapist as friendly and more available, or less competent and experienced, the female family therapist is more likely to be referred to without her title and by her first name. For example, one supervisee reported that when the secretarial staff set up an appointment for her they deleted her title as "Doctor" and referred to her by her first name. Her male colleagues were referred to by their title and last name. When a family learned that they were being scheduled to see a female, they protested with such rationalizations as, "I would prefer to see a male. My son will relate to him better"; or, "My husband would prefer to see a male"; or, "I don't think he will come in if you schedule him with a woman." (I purposely select these examples to remind us all that women are as much participants in the de-skillment and devaluation of other women as men.) Also worthy of note, when asking female supervisees how they handled this situation with the secretarial staff, quite frequently they choose to do nothing to avoid being thought too aggressive.

Another example of difficulty occurs after the family proceeds into the institution across the external boundary and has its first appointment. It is this time that the de-skillment of the female family therapist is most evident in what Whitaker and Keith (1981) call the "battle for structure." As they have noted, the therapist runs the therapy, the family runs the lives of its members. Due to her experiences growing up in families where men received cultural and family support for external boundary management, the woman in authority experiences more difficulty in managing the external boundaries of her work, i.e., the boundaries with the outside world. Generally, she comes with more comfort and ease in using her skills in providing nurturance, and supportive and educative types of activities in the family, having had less practice in managing external boundaries. Thus, the female family therapist experiences more ambivalence than the male.

In exercising leadership regarding these external boundaries, the female family therapist evidences difficulties with the following important tasks: session-time boundaries, membership requirements, and the establishment of fees and the primary task. She reports being indecisive about who should come to the session. One female family therapist reported repeatedly having difficulties with domineering males who did not wish to bring the siblings of the identified patient into the session. Another female family therapist had repeated difficulties setting appointment times in accordance with her schedule requirements and gave in too often in favor of the family's preferences. Another female family therapist took a strong stand on not meeting without the whole family and gave in when the family arrived without the father and siblings. While males also have difficulties in exercising their personal and delegated authority as family therapists, they evidence these difficulties in different ways and for different reasons.

In addition to the first two sets of examples that highlight the institutional influences and the problems in the formation of the therapeutic systems, there is a third example worthy of consideration. This deals more with the individual's internal experience that the female family therapist brings to the family system. Circularity is operating throughout this analysis. It is a matter of punctuation, i.e., where we break into the circle for study. At this point, I am talking about the individual system interacting or interfacing in the context of the family, institution, and the society at large. Specifically, this refers to the hesitance, the ambivalence, and the questioning of her own authority that the female might evidence in the management of the boundaries outlined above. "Shouldn't I have a male co-therapist so that the family might feel more comfortable?" is not an unusual question from the female family therapist. It is important that she examine the influences of her own family of origin on her development of attitudes in the exercise of personal authority as related to gender.

Spending much time in blaming the state of affairs on history or the present context is not particularly helpful. What I see as the most effective way of dealing with these dilemmas is to draw from the theories of structural and strategic therapy, and family of origin work. First, in order of procedure, the female therapist must be aware of the problem. She must be especially sensitive to those brief or long moments when she feels discounted, disconfirmed, or stripped of her authorization to work by the institution in which she works. She should pay close attention to the disquieting feelings of de-skillment when a client confronts her with how he or she wants the therapy run and she feels pulled to go along with it. She needs to note the anxiety she feels when she is requesting the session to be videotaped because that is how she likes to work, and the family refuses. She must not ignore the moments in which she feels her authority disconfirmed and her own collusion in the process. Or, to punctuate the circular process in a helpful way in terms of mastery, the female family therapist must attend to the way she colludes in turning over her authority, the way she holds up cue cards saying she is uncertain about the use of her authority in this role.

Second, after clearly focusing on the problem it is crucial to analyze the solutions she is using, by establishing the repetitive dysfunctional situations that are used over and over again. Third, she must develop strategies to enable her to apply new solutions, to learn how to take 180°-degree turns. The female family therapist must learn how to use techniques for dealing with perceived resistance with precision, learn how to ride the horse in the direction it is going, not to argue. She must apply her structural family therapy knowledge in creative ways. For example, if she is on the phone locked into a struggle with family members regarding the membership issues, she should leave the field by getting off the phone and call them back after she has analyzed carefully what is happening to the use of her authority. She can leave the therapy sessions when she feels out of charge of the sessions. There are no rules that say a therapist cannot leave the room and hypothesize about the family session.

Fourth, a review of the therapist's participation in her family of origin with reference to issues of gender and sexuality as related to the exercise of authority is particularly valuable. She can learn about how women were perceived in her family, what legacy she is carrying in her role as a woman in authority that is enhancing or determining the exercise of her authority.

In summary, the person whom the therapist has the most chance of changing is herself. To understand the context in which she feels de-skilled as related to gender is highly important. To understand the psychosocial factors is indispensable in bringing about change. But that fluctuation in the system moving towards the process of change is most likely to start with the female family therapist's own initiative. If the rest of the system changes in response to this initiative or changes "spontaneously" in response to some unidentifiable perturbation, consider it a blessing. The responsibility for changing and influencing the context is primarily with the female family therapist.

*References*

Bayes, M. and Newton, P. *Women in authority: A sociopsychological analysis.* Paper presented at the National Scientific Meeting of the A. K. Rice Institute, Minneapolis, MN, April, 1976.

Whitaker, C. and Keith, D. Symbolic-experiential family therapy. In A. Gurman & D. Kniskern (Eds.), *Handbook of Family Therapy.* New York: Brunner/Mazel, 1981.

**MARGARET D. SHEELY, M.S.W.**
*Houston-Galveston Family Institute*
*Houston, TX*

# 61. Therapists' Feelings of Partiality

**Question:**

> Each time I teach a course in family therapy, one or more of the
> therapists will say, for example, "I would like to do more couple
> and family work but I don't know how to handle my feelings of
> partiality to one member of the family. I want to be impartial and
> I know that I should be. Many times, however, I am not and this
> makes me avoid doing work with couples and families." What
> suggestions do you have for a therapist to deal with such feelings
> of partiality in family and couples work?

**Discussion:**

In my work with couples and families, the issue of partiality toward
one member of the group is part of the larger issue of my authenticity
as a whole person. From the results of most of my work I believe that
the essence of my effectiveness is my willingness to face my limitations
as well as my talents. One aspect of this humanness is that I sometimes
like one client in the same family more than another. There are various
reasons for this partiality but the reasons are only interesting, not
crucial to our process of therapy. What is crucial is that I become
increasingly conscious of this feeling when it arises and that I am
perfectly willing to hear about my partiality and how disturbing it is
to the less favored one. Only as I risk this imperfection and error and
entitle myself to both of these do I model for my clients what I want
for them; namely, the courage to be fully what they are, to risk exposing
their deep fears about their worth, to make mistakes, and to be entitled
to and responsible for these mistakes. When I can acknowledge the
insensitivity of my partiality, this issue does not remain a stumbling
block to our process. This last fact is especially vital when I consider
the alternative, which involves denial and pretense.

What I have described so far is possible for me when I am feeling
good within. When I am feeling defensive and self-critical, I often need
to hide my imperfections and mistakes from others, my clients in-

cluded. At those times I am likely to deny my client's reality—his or her feelings of hurt and resentment at being unfairly dealt with by me. Or, even worse, I will hide from myself my feelings and try harder and harder to become impartial, once again a denial of reality, this time my own. When I make this latter choice, I model for my clients deception, fear of exposure, lack of entitlement to err, and unwillingness to take responsibility for behavior. It becomes increasingly clear to me that all of us, each family member and I, are far better off when I can risk feeling partial and can hear about it with all of the feelings aroused in each of us than when I either try to become what I am not—perfectly impartial—or actively to deny my partiality.

Now, once I have entitled myself to feelings of partiality as a therapist, I can pay attention to some of the conditions under which I behave partially or, in some cases, seem to be behaving so. The most frequent occasions arise when I work very actively with one member of a couple, paying very little attention to the other. I do this for my comfort, out of a need to be effective as well as out of my limitations, since the person who is most available and willing to engage with me seems to provide the best opportunity for my energy. The person who hangs back takes more work and is, at least on the surface, not responsive to me. At these times, interestingly, I seem to favor neither or both, as the one I engage sometimes feels picked on and the other feels neglected. Each one can experience that the other is being favored.

There are, of course, the rewarding times when I pay close attention to the issue of non-engagement and that becomes the focus of our work together, including the feelings of each of us around the non-engagement. This focus arouses another partiality in me. Lately, I am especially appreciative of persons who are careful in their responses, who take time to find what they want to say, and then who say it simply and honestly from the depth of their search. This appreciation is rooted in my development and growth, and can appear in a session as a bias or partiality. Words have always come easily to me and I have often used them carelessly in order to make a point. Although this made me a spontaneous and facile conversationalist, it made unavailable to me the option of thoughtful, deep, and accurate expression. In other words, I am often partial to the person who is grossly unlike me, yet symbolizes a quality which I have begun to value in myself. At other times, paradoxically, I appear to be partial to the person who is much like me in that I can truly understand him or her from the inside.

On a more unconscious level, occasions of my partiality can arise from deeply personal issues such as the peacefulness or struggle of my current self-image as a wife, mother, daughter, professional, or friend.

While struggling with my husband, will I be more understanding of the wife in a client couple and harsher to the husband? I might favor a son or a daughter in a family, depending upon my relationship with my own son or daughter or brother or sister. From the other side of the therapeutic relationship, the client might project his or her parents' partiality onto me, in which case that unfinished hurt and resentment could become our focus. I, however, can only treat this as a projection after I have willingly searched myself for evidence of my partiality. When the issue is my partiality and everyone's feelings about that, then this confrontation between us becomes potentially therapeutic.

I am aware that many of my colleagues could view my method of dealing with therapist partiality in couples and families as irresponsible. They might choose to "work out" their "hang-up" within their own therapy. I might choose this path, too, if I found that I consistently favored one category of client (woman, man, or child) and that my behavior impaired my effectiveness. Since this does not seem to fit my experience of my work, I choose to remain flawed in this respect, to be conscious of this flaw, and willing to appreciate its impact on my clients. So long as my clients experience therapeutic benefit and I experience freedom and well-being in myself from acknowledging my partialities (as well as other limitations), I will continue to choose the path offered in this discussion.

**FLORENCE HALPERN, M.S.W., L.C.S.W.**
*Private Practice*
*Studio City, CA*

# 62. The Use of Teams in Family Therapy

## Question:

Beginning in the 1970s, the "systemic school(s)" of family therapy have used a team approach more and more frequently in their work with families. Is this just "a fad," or is there some therapeutic advantage in the use of teams?

## Discussion:

Like any other human endeavor, the field of family therapy is subject to fads and fashions, and the development of the team approach is certainly not exempt from at least some faddishness. One only has to glance at flyers and brochures for the multitude of workshops and conferences to see the popularity of "systemic approaches" and to begin to suspect some faddishness. Or, one need only talk with some people who use a team approach to discover their slavish devotion to the rituals of one of the pioneer teams; what is more, they use these rituals in such a manner that they seem to have become a liturgy of the "correct way to do family therapy."

For the most part, however, therapeutic teams have developed their own approaches for working with difficult families. Frequently, the members of these teams have varying theoretical backgrounds and by working together over a period of time they develop a new way of working which is not quite structural, not quite strategic, not quite à la Milan, and not quite à la MRI. Thus, the multiplicity of points of view blend together in such a way that a bonus develops: a new method of working with families that integrates the methods of the various schools.

Since therapy is part art (with aesthetic elements) and part science (with pragmatic elements), the question of faddishness readily arises when it becomes evident that similar techniques and procedures are being used by various teams in various places. However, it is a truism that techniques are usually developed before theory, while an epistemology is yet implicit. As Milton Erickson, an innovator of many techniques aptly stated, "I know what I do, but to explain how I do it is much too difficult for me" (Bandler and Grinder, 1975, p. viii). Haley, too, found Erickson's "therapeutic approach difficult to encapsulate in some general theory of therapy" (Haley, 1967, p. 534). Of course, this does not mean that a theory cannot be constructed to explain Erickson's work, nor does it mean that Erickson did not have an epistemology (although it was not explicit).

Consequently, the rapid development of teams may appear faddish rather than a harbinger of theory. For many therapists the use of a team approach began intuitively as a useful way of working with difficult families; then, pragmatically, they discovered that it "worked."

The foundation for the team approaches seems to lie in the way systems *know*, which Maruyama (1977) described as a poly-ocular or cross-subjective way of knowing. This way of knowing is similar to the way in which the two eyes work together in developing depth perception. The right eye sees an object from a particular point of view, while the left eye sees the same object from a slightly different point of view, and the bonus of depth perception develops because of the angle developed between the two points of view. Binocular vision allows us to see three-dimensionally because of the difference between the two images. This difference enables us to compute a dimension that is invisible to either eye separately. This is similar to Bateson's (1979) idea that it is the *difference which makes a difference.* Further, Bateson describes an "idea" as a bonus that develops from having two descriptions of the same process or sequence which are differently coded or collected—a bonus similar to the bonus of depth perception.

Thus, a team as a system can be seen to use poly-ocular ways to develop its knowledge about families. Each team member sees the family and its situation from a different point of view because of his or her individual training; thus, each member subjectively knows something different about the family. When the multiple views are taken together, the resulting cross-subjective analysis enables the team to compute otherwise invisible dimensions of the family and its problems. That is, a bonus develops because of the relationship or angle between the various points of view. Ideas develop which increase the amount of information available to the team for understanding the family and for designing interventions. The therapist working alone can, therefore, be seen as being as handicapped as a one-eyed man, not only because he is deprived of the bonus which results from the multiplicity of points of view, but also because he is in greater danger of getting "sucked into" the family system because of its absence.

The team approaches to family therapy may not appear to be "scientific" at first because they depend on cross-subjective analysis and differences between points of view rather than on the "objective" facts of the therapy situation upon which all observers may agree. However, as Capra (1977) points out, there are striking similarities between contemporary science and Eastern thought. Maruyama describes the "objective" parts as the most "insignificant parts of our thinking. The Japanese do not even bother to find out about 'objectivity' because they can go much further with cross-subjectivity" (Maruyama, 1977, p. 84). In fact, the objective parts of descriptions can be seen as an impoverishment of our vision, or of the system's way of knowing, since it is similar to the vision of one eye alone.

Thus, what at first may appear to be a fad (and in some cases may, indeed, be one) can be explained by the fact that technique precedes theory and explicit epistemology (de Shazer, 1982). As soon as the epistemology is expressed more clearly, the distinct therapeutic advantages of the team approaches become evident: namely, that it provides the necessary set of circumstances in which can evolve a new way of working which is based on the differences between various models of family therapy, yet adds up to something different and greater than the sum of all of them. Therefore, integration rather than eclecticism develops.

## References

Bandler, R. and Grinder, J. *Patterns of the Hypnotic Techniques of Milton H. Erickson, M.D.* Cupertino, CA: Meta, 1975.
Bateson, G. *Mind and Nature: A Necessary Unity.* New York: Dutton, 1979.
Capra, F. *The Tao of Physics.* New York: Bantam, 1977.
de Shazer, S. Some conceptual distinctions are more useful than others. *Family Process,* 1982, 71-84.
Haley, J. (Ed.) *Advanced Techniques of Hypnosis and Therapy: Selected Papers of Milton H. Erickson, M.D.* New York: Grune & Stratton, 1967.
Maruyama, M. Heterogenistics: An epistemological restructuring of biological and social sciences. *Cybernetica,* 1977, *20,* 69-86.

**STEVE DE SHAZER, M.S.W.**
*Director*
*Brief Family Therapy Center*
*Milwaukee, WI*

# 63. Using Mental Imagery to Create Therapeutic and Supervisory Realities

**Question:**

Therapists often think of therapeutic technique in abstract ways. It is sometimes difficult to prepare oneself for a session thinking in this manner. How can therapeutic methods be translated into a personally relevant, experiential frame in a way which can help organize a therapist's conceptual processes before, during, and after a session?

**Discussion:**

The process of training family therapists involves a substantial challenge to the realities of trainees. First, they are confronted with and then struggle to understand and use a new epistemological lens—one emphasizing interactional rather than monadic, intrapersonal processes. If adopted, this ecosystemic epistemology (Keeney, 1979) brings with it an attendant shift in techniques which are consistent with this new view. Thus, trainees are additionally challenged in their conception of useful therapeutic methods. It is not uncommon for trainees to evidence considerable difficulty in translating this interdependent body of knowledge and technique into practice (Liddle, 1982b; Liddle and Saba, 1982a). Therapists often understand a technique only in a narrow digital (definitional) sense, thereby becoming handicapped in the experiential translation process. In this regard, a supervisor often faces a formidable task in preparing a therapist for a session. The trainee may have a general sense of the session's objectives but be unable to connect the unfamiliar, abstract techniques to the therapeutic goals in a personally meaningful manner. Live supervision/consultation, videotape supervision, and simulations of therapy sessions are all crucial elements of the training enterprise (Liddle and Saba, 1982b). It is not the intent here to suggest withdrawal of these supervisory methods. Rather, a technique is offered which can serve as a useful, adjunctive tool for trainers and therapists to help alter and expand the range of available therapeutic skills (Liddle, 1982a).

Family therapy was founded upon the belief that transactional patterns hold the key to understanding and treating human problems. In this sense, to use Rabkin's (1970) dichotomy, "outer" rather than "inner" space has been construed as crucial to the therapeutic endeavor. As family therapy's core theoretic construct—systemic theory—has evolved, the role of individuals within contexts has been an increasingly discussed topic. Rather than excluding the concept of the individual, systemic theory in its currently developing form allows for the singular unit to be considered important. Individuals can thus be seen as subsystems, influencing and being influenced by their social contexts (Minuchin and Fishman, 1981). This appreciation of the "self-in-context" can allow frameworks previously untapped by systems purists to emerge and be pragmatically useful. Mental imagery (MI) is one such framework.

Imagery is far from a new phenomenon. It has been used over the centuries as an essential adjunct to both creative thought and everyday living. Einstein, Nietzsche and Jung are among those whose productivity and novel work have relied upon MI for inspiration. Koestler (1964) summarizes by saying that in the work of scientists, "thinking in pictures" dominates creative effort. Thus, many of our visionaries are so in figurative and literal ways. For Arnheim (1979), however, the issue goes beyond the genius of a few. He sees visual thinking as an inevitability—a given in human consciousness.

MI, especially during the last two decades, has achieved widespread experimental attention and usefulness in a variety of fields. The self-help movement, sports psychology, computer technology, acting, hypnosis, and art are among those areas drawing concepts and methods from MI. The therapy profession has similarly made ample use of MI. Although utilized mainly in the clinical practice domain, MI can be accessed and developed as a training device. This can be effectively accomplished if we utilize the principle of the parallel nature of therapy and training. Briefly, this position holds that training and therapy can be considered isomorphic to the other since each attempts to influence and change human behavior in a goal-directed, planned, stage-specific, or sequential way. This principle helps trainers to not only understand the parallels between training and therapy but also make practical use of these dimensions of connection in the training process.

For example, in therapy previous realities are challenged and new ones are created which offer behavioral alternatives to family members

(Minuchin and Fishman, 1981). In training, an identical process occurs. Supervisors challenge *epistemological* (lineal thinking—the identified patient is the problem) and *personal* (these techniques are foreign and too difficult for me) realities of their trainees. MI can assist in the construction of these supervisory realities for trainees. It allows for an internal self-manipulation which prepares and organizes a therapist for the work of therapy.

The premise here is that therapists already engage in pre-, within- and between-session internal dialogues. More generally, research has demonstrated that human beings are constantly playing out and re-playing past events and preparing for new ones as they go about their everyday business. The mind, then, is not a passive entity, but an organ of activity—of ongoing work.

In live supervision a supervisor intervenes to redirect and guide a therapist in the conduct of a session. MI similarly redirects and guides a therapist—this time in a preparatory and organizing way. It is, in essence, a rehearsal technique for the novel and difficult experience to follow. MI allows therapists to transcend digital descriptions of technique, translating the concept of intervention to an active, process-focused, experiential frame. Techniques can no longer be sterile or impersonal. They must be individualized since in using MI the trainee actually imagines him/herself carrying out the interventions.

In *Concave and Convex*, one of M. C. Escher's typically paradoxical prints, the viewer is struck with the impossibility of holding the discontinuous realities in his/her consciousness simultaneously. We become focused at one of the perspectives (seeing the print as concave or convex) and then our perceptions transport us to the complementary but different reality. The use of MI can lead to a similar "transportation." The therapist can travel back and forth between the theoretic (techniques as things) and the experiential (techniques as operations *I* perform). This journey can, especially at the earlier stages of training, be guided by supervisory input which elicits and develops useful images for trainees.

*Method*

For Haley (1976), therapy's goals include building an appropriate degree of complexity into people's lives; for Minuchin (1974; Minuchin and Fishman, 1981), they involve providing new experiences of relational reality *during sessions* which increase the behavioral repertoires of family members. Again, recalling the principle of the parallels between training and therapy, the present discussion suggests that MI can help achieve both clusters of goals.

Consider the following use of MI in training. A supervisor and trainee meet in a pre-session and generate the goals of the session—both for the therapist (stylistic objectives) and for the family (therapy objectives). With the technique of MI they can together generate the visual and auditory images which would be helpful in preparing the therapist for the session. These images can then be accessed during sessions to redirect, guide, and prompt effective therapist behavior. First, however, the session's intended destination must be clear. Along these lines, the therapist must have a minimal cognitive (definitional) comprehension of the spectrum of techniques/interventions available.

Further, the supervisor must be cognizant of the therapist's developing ability to generate useful, vivid visual and auditory *process images*. Process is emphasized since "snapshot" or "still photo" metaphors are more static and therefore less useful. Interventions are defined as multi-staged activities, involving, for example, a sequence of formulation, implementation, and assessing feedback. Therapists can be instructed to imagine what a videotape of the entire session would be like, then to quickly scan it for nodal events. In this sense, the entire session can be reviewed and prepared for simultaneously, and before it ever begins, with MI techniques. This allows therapists to quickly organize themselves at both macro (form) and micro (implementation of interventions) levels. Madanes' (1981) masterful pretend techniques of strategic therapy are clearly related and can similarly be applied to a kind of strategic supervision. The therapist can replay crucial parts of moves in a session over in the imagined or pretend state, embedding visual images (e.g., which dyads should be put in proximity, who should be blocked from intruding) and auditory cues (e.g., "what will I say to prompt such enactments?") which will help him/her "remember" the keys of implementation. Therapists are thus assisted in creating a priori, through imagery rehearsal, intended outcomes to important interactional sequences in sessions.

Induction can be construed as a morphostatic or morphogenic process. The intentional induction occurring with a supervisor in relation to the trainee through imagery rehearsal uses induction in the latter sense. Stanislavski, one of the world's greatest acting teachers, utilized the concept of "if" in producing his own kind of induction with actors-in-training. He felt that "the word had the ability to arouse an inner and real activity by natural means" (Gabbard, 1979, p. 357). In Stanislavski's words, "*If* acts as a lever to lift us out of the world of actuality into the world of imagination" (Stanislaviski, 1936, p. 43). Our translation of this concept might be known as the *acting-as-if technique*. As such it can aid therapists in preparing for the implementation of specific interventions, in preparing for sessions, and, more broadly, in the professional preparation or socialization of therapists.

Therapists can be helped to expand the use of planned imagery in attempting to make their therapeutic plans self-fulfilling. They can be guided to replay video- and audiotapes (past images) in their mind's eye and ear. As tapes of master family therapists become more available, many more therapists have firsthand opportunity to observe and model high-level clinical skill. Specific scenes (visual images plus dialogue) of a variety of therapeutic situations should be available to the therapist's imagination—available for immediate recall and use. The therapist can have an imaginary Rolodex file on which are videodiscs of the techniques of therapy as demonstrated by the great clinicians, as well as his/her own previous catalog of sessions. The therapist can activate the mind's computer by specifying key words or situations which relate to certain stimuli presented in a session. From this would emerge the needed "segment(s) of tape." The therapist could then replay as many times as necessary the desired behaviors, recapturing the kinesthetic feel and cognitive structure of the intervention. Thus, we could all have available a kind of "Greatest Hits" record, our own MI version of a "Most Effective Interventions" tape. Sports psychology's muscle memory thus becomes *intervention memory,* where mechanisms are devised to help therapists intellectually and experientially remember the variety of therapeutic interventions.

In summary, several points can be underscored about the usefulness of MI as a training device. Broadly speaking, MI works at the interface of the intra- and interpersonal domains. In this capacity its use might assist in further clarification of the interconnected nature of these territories. Viewed as a skill, MI allows therapists to develop confidence, mastery, and ultimate independence from a supervisory context. Effective MI permits therapists to bring supervisory realities to contexts where no supervision exists. MI expands the alternatives available to trainees in a way which reduces the personal threat of experimenting with the unfamiliar. MI provides a means of improving the concentration and focusing capacities of trainees. Finally, to paraphrase another classic acting teacher, continual rehearsal allows one to create, to expand oneself within the part or role (Boleslavsky, 1933). Thus, the structured imagery rehearsals can paradoxically move the therapist beyond the stage of a parrot therapist. This is the position where trainees will no longer only mimic the techniques of others but find creative ways of placing their own personal signature on a school of therapy's particular methods.

*References*

Arnheim, R. Visual thinking in education. In A. Sheikh and J. Shaffer (Eds.) *The Potential of Fantasy and Imagination.* New York: Random House, 1979.

Boleslavsky, R. *Acting: The First Six Lessons.* New York: Theater Art Books, 1933.

Gabbard, G. The creative process of the actor. *Bulletin of the Menninger Clinic,* 1979, *43,* 354-364.

Haley, J. *Problem-solving Therapy.* San Francisco: Jossey-Bass, 1976.

Haley, J. *Leaving Home: The Therapy of Disturbed Young People.* New York: McGraw Hill, 1980.

Keeney, B. Ecosystemic epistemology: An alternate paradigm for diagnosis. *Family Process,* 1979, *18,* 117-130.

Koestler, A. *The Act of Creation.* New York: Macmillan, 1964.

Liddle, H. On the problems of eclecticism: A call for epistemologic clarification and human scale theories. *Family Process,* 1982(a), *21,* 243-250.

Liddle, H. Family therapy training: Current issues, future trends. *International Journal of Family Therapy,* 1982(b), in press.

Liddle, H. and Saba, G. On teaching family therapy at the introductory level: A conceptual model emphasizing a pattern which connects training and therapy. *Journal of Marital and Family Therapy,* 1982(a), *8,* 63-72.

Liddle, H. & Saba, G. *Live supervision/consultation I: The isomorphic nature of training and therapy.* In J. Schwartzman (Ed.), *Macrocontexts in Family Therapy.* New York: Guilford, in press.

Madanes, C. *Strategic Family Therapy.* San Francisco: Jossey-Bass, 1981.

Minuchin, S. *Families and Family Therapy.* Cambridge, MA: Harvard University Press, 1974.

Minuchin, S. and Fishman, C. *Family Therapy Techniques.* Cambridge, MA: Harvard University Press, 1981.

Rabkin, R. *Inner and Outer Space.* New York: Norton, 1970.

Stanislavski, C. *An Actor Prepares.* (E. R. Hapgood, tr.). New York: Theatre Arts Books, 1936.

**HOWARD ARTHUR LIDDLE, Ed.D.**
*Director*
*Family Systems Program*
*Institute for Juvenile Research*
*Chicago, IL*

# 64. The Conceptual Development of Family Therapy Trainees

**Question:**

As a trainer of family therapists, I am interested in encouraging my trainees to plan and conceptualize between their sessions with families. Can you suggest a way to evaluate the amount and quality of the between-session work they are doing?

**Discussion:**

Before planning a specific format for encouraging your trainees in this way, I think it important that you know how much conceptualizing and what kind of planning you want them to do. Some schools of family therapy do not encourage any between-session planning for fear that the trainee will be distracted from his/her experience of the family in each session. Other schools expect that a great deal of thought go into specific strategies and goals for the next session and for the general "game plan" for the case.

I train students from a combined structural-strategic model of family therapy. Successful implementation of this model requires careful preparation and thought before each session to define general goals and strategies for the family. To both stimulate and evaluate this kind of thinking in trainees, I designed a simple worksheet system which has come to serve several purposes for our training program.

This system consists of a one-page worksheet which is to be filled out by the trainee during the interval between sessions and given to the supervisor before the succeeding session. The worksheet helps trainees focus on five different areas of practice: 1) diagnosis and hypotheses (or changes in these) of the case based upon the *previous* session; 2) assessment of the *previous* session's goals, strategies, and interventions; 3) goals (or changes in goals) for the case and for yourself based upon the *previous* session; 4) specific objectives (therapist's) for the *next* session; and 5) strategies for attaining the therapist's objectives for the *next* session. Thus, the trainee's attention must include both global goals for the family and specific strategies and goals for each session.

This simple system serves a wide variety of functions in training. First, it forces the trainee to plan specific strategies while keeping the overall goals for the case in mind. Beginning trainees are often not aware of or lose sight of their general objectives for the family while worrying about what to do in the next session, so that their interventions seem disconnected and without theme. Also, this system continually reminds trainees that their diagnosis is not static, that it may change with each session as new information emerges.

Second, this system provides the trainer with continual data to evaluate the trainee's ability to conceptualize. I have used these data in two different ways. I first used the system as a teaching tool by going over each worksheet with the trainee to help shape his/her conceptualizing. Now I use it as an evaluative measure by giving no feedback on the worksheets and watching the changes in conceptualizing that take place through the course of the training program. We plan to develop a coding system which would allow us to use these worksheets as part of our program evaluation as well as part of each trainee's individual evaluation.

Third, live supervision is a large component of our training program and there is often too little time for a pre-session conference where the plans for the session can be formulated. If the trainer gets the worksheet before the session, he/she has, behind the mirror, a statement of what the trainee plans to do and why. From this statement he/she can assess the trainee's strategies, as well as his/her performance of these strategies during the session. This will also serve as a base for supervision during the post-session conference.

Fourth, depending on the requirements of your agency, the worksheet serves as progress notes for the case record.

In conclusion, this type of between-session worksheet may be used to stimulate, teach, and evaluate trainees, as well as to provide trainers with useful data on the conceptual progress of trainees and on their use of strategies. The headings you choose for a worksheet will probably differ depending on your training model. In general, however, I have tried to find a balance in these headings between requesting highly specialized types of information, which limits the trainee's range of thought, and requesting very general impressions, which become too vague to be of use.

**DICK SCHWARTZ, Ph.D.**
*Family Systems Program*
*Institute for Juvenile Research*
*Chicago, IL*

# INDEX